THE HOO PENINSULA

The story of

THE HOO
PENINSULA

Philip MacDougall

John Hallewell Publications

John Hallewell Publications,
172 High Street,
Rochester,
Kent.

ISBN 0 905540 19 0

Printed in Great Britain by A. Wheaton & Co. Ltd., Exeter

CONTENTS

ACKNOWLEDGEMENTS

I would like to express my gratitude and thanks to the following people who generously gave up some of their time and allowed me to conduct interviews with them: Mr. Len Batchelor; Commander C. H. Drage R.N. (retd.); Mr. G. H. Emory; Mr. J. Foster; Mr. R. Hutchings; Rev. W. J. Hirst; Lt.-Col. Kitchener C.R.E.; Mrs. Florrie Miskin; Mr. Arthur Plewis; Mr. Eric Smith and Mr. and Mrs. Allan Vidgen.

In addition I would also like to express my thanks to Mr. S. J. Alcock, Mr. R. A. Baldwin, Ms. Carol Batchelor, Mr. C. Billingham and Mr. Dave Collyer (of the Kent Air Historical Research Society) who helped in a number of ways and answered an endless stream of questions.

Thanks are also due to the staff of Rochester and Chatham libraries who must have spent a great deal of their time searching for some rather obscure books.

Finally, I must reserve special thanks for my wife who carefully read the manuscript on a number of occasions and removed many errors and offered a number of good ideas.

The publisher would like to acknowledge all the undermentioned names, whose subscriptions have made this book possible.

A. F. Allen, Shorne
J. F. Ashbee, Grain
G. Andrews, Hoo
Mrs. B. Beck, Hoo
D. Baker, High Halstow
Bromley Library, Bromley
B.P. Oil Refinery Ltd., Grain
N. Blandrage, Hoo
Mrs. J. E. Bucknell, Hoo
James Bucknall, Ontario, Canada
Mrs. S. Brodie, Hoo
A. V. Basson, Hoo
Mrs. E. Belsey, Allhallows
A. Bradley, Strood
Mrs. H. Burden, Strood
C. H. Billingham, Grain
Mrs. A. Collins, Hoo
Mrs. J. Cooke, Allhallows
W. A. Craig, London
J. W. Castle, Frindsbury
Chatham Book Centre (50 copies)
J. Chubb, Dartford
Mrs. J. Cowley, Hoo
Miss H. Constance, Battle, Sussex
PRI. 12. RSME Regiment, Chattenden
Central Electricity Generating Board,
  Grain Power Station
Mrs. J. Cooper, Grain
Dr. B. R. Currell, High Halstow
T. H. & Mrs. Dray, Frindsbury
T. S. Delieu, Strood
Dr. Peter Draper, Dartford
East Sussex County Library, Lewes
B. F. J. Ellen, High Halstow
E. C. W. & Mrs. Fairbrother, Gravesend
L. R. Field, Hoo
G. C. Foord, Frindsbury
G. Ford, Southampton
H. & Mrs. Fry, Cliffe
J. M. Fright, High Halstow
Goblins Bookshop, Staplehurst
E. R. Green, Gravesend
Juanita Blacker, California, U.S.A.
Greenhead Books, Huddersfield
J. A. Grims, Walton on Thames, Surrey
S. E. Grice, Bungay, Suffolk

K. A. Gough, Hoo
Hamdens Bookshop, Gillingham
  (6 copies)
R. Hiscock, Gravesend
R. Howarth, Allhallows
R. F. Hutchings, Cliffe
C. A. Hoffman, Cliffe
Hoo St. Werburgh Middle School, Hoo
Mrs. B. G. Hargrave, Hoo
High Halstow C.P. School, High
  Halstow
Humberside Library, Hull
J. Hill, Strood
W. E. Hall, Northfleet
C. S. M. Hamilton, Hoo
Mrs. P. Hodge, Milton Keynes, Bucks
Hundred of Hoo School Library, Hoo
  (3 copies)
Hundred of Hoo School (Miss Gardner),
  Hoo (3 copies)
D. N. & Mrs. Jack, High Halstow
Malcolm John, Rochester
D. Jones, Lower Stoke
F. Keeler, Herne Bay
P. Keene, High Halstow
Kent Book Company, Maidstone
  (6 copies)
Kent County Library, Maidstone
  (63 copies)
V. T. Lane, Hoo
University of Leicester Library,
  Leicester
Tower Hamlets (London) Library,
  London
M. Luxton, Grain
London Library, London
J. Luck, Allhallows
R. Lazell, Hoo
Mason Hall Books, Gravesend
  (12 copies)
D. L. & Mrs. Martin, Hoo
M & E Meredith, Grain
Radio Medway (BBC), Chatham
Mr. & Mrs. MacDougall, Epsom,
  Surrey
C. Martin, Sidcup

INTRODUCTION

As the title suggests, this book is about the Hoo Peninsula. So far, so good. But what exactly are the confines of the Hoo Peninsula? It is not an area which is readily defined. Should the parishes of Higham, Upnor, Cliffe and Frindsbury rightly be included in a book about the Hoo Peninsula? Looking at the maps didn't help in the slightest. For, every time I looked at one or other map, the Peninsula seemed to grow and diminish in size, with alarming regularity.

One definition of the Peninsula I have come across states that it is that area of land north-east of the old Thames and Medway canal. As the route of this canal runs right through the parishes of Frindsbury and Higham, this would still leave the problem of whether or not to include these two parishes.

Reading the local papers soon indicates that my problem is not, by any means, unique. Reporters themselves seem most uncertain as to the correct name for the area. They are quite happy, it would appear, to give it any one of four names; these being Hoo, the Isle of Grain, Frindsbury Peninsula or, even, the Cliffe Peninsula!

Mention of the Isle of Grain immediately introduces a new dimension to the problem. Should the Isle of Grain really be included in a book which is about a peninsula. At one time in its history Grain was very definitely an island and, of course, was not part of the Peninsula. Indeed, at that time, it had closer affinities to Chatham and Gillingham rather than Hoo.

In the end, the problem was quite simply resolved. I decided just to include those villages and parishes about which I wished to write. They are a group of eight villages which, I feel, have a natural affinity to one another, and are all, certainly, within the bounds of what most people would regard as the Hoo Peninsula. This book, then, is an historical account of that area of Kent which encompasses the villages of Allhallows, Cliffe, Cooling, High Halstow, Hoo St. Werburgh, St. James on the Isle of Grain, St. Mary's Hoo and Stoke.

Geographically, the Hoo Peninsula is the most northerly area of Kent and lies a few miles to the north of a straight line drawn between Rochester and Gravesend. Further, it is bounded by two

great rivers: the Thames and Medway. These, of course, have had
a great influence on Peninsula life. Sometimes they have brought
prosperity by providing easy access to the Peninsula. At other
times, by frequently overflowing their banks, they have instead
created both poverty and destruction. Residents of the Peninsula
have had a constant love–hate relationship with these rivers.

Previous to this book, there has only been one account
published, which dealt specifically with the entire Peninsula. Now
long out of print, and difficult to obtain, this is Ralph Arnold's *The
Hundred of Hoo*. Written in 1949, it is somewhat dated and rather
patchy in places. His format was to take the area village by village,
with a rather over-zealous one-third of the book devoted to the tiny
village of Cooling.

Other books, of course, have featured the Peninsula. The most
recent was Brian Matthews' *History of Strood Rural District*.
Published by the then, Strood Rural District Council, this is quite
a reasonable little book though, by nature of its small size, it can
only treat such a large area in a most superficial fashion.

In addition to the more general accounts of the area published
during this century, there have also been published two books
confining themselves to specific villages on the Peninsula. One of
these, *The Story of an Outpost Parish* written by the Rev. F. J.
Hammond, must easily rate as a first-class piece of local history
writing. Published in 1928, the Rev. Hammond took well over
twenty years in researching the book and discovered a great deal of
original source material. The second book, relating to a specific
village, is *A History of the Isle of Grain* by C. B. Burnett. At the
time of its publication, in 1906, Burnett was stationed at Grain in
his capacity of sergeant-major in the Royal Engineers. Considerably dated it is, nevertheless, quite a useful little book.
Unfortunately, apart from a few copies held in various reference
libraries (such as Rochester and Chatham) it is now absolutely
impossible to get hold of a copy.

In this present book I have tried not to lean too heavily upon
previously published material. I have tried to introduce as much
original research as possible. This in particular, will be found in the
chapters dealing with indigenous malaria, smuggling, the growth of
industry and the two world wars. Further, I have interviewed a
number of residents on the Peninsula who have supplied me with

valuable information regarding the changes that have taken place over the last sixty or seventy years.

Generally, the book is not intended as a piece of sophisticated local history. It is written for those who are either visiting the Peninsula or live there. It is aimed at those who may be intrigued at discovering the wealth of history that the Peninsula offers. My aim is to make the book readable, therefore, I hope, the academics of the area will excuse the lack of footnotes. The information they require, however, is in the book but has simply been completely relegated to the final pages.

Finally, I hope that you, the reader, will enjoy this book and, if this is the case, the book will more than have served its purpose.

PHILIP MACDOUGALL
Isle of Grain, 1980

CHAPTER ONE

IMPRESSIONS

'Ours was the marsh country, down by the river, within,
as the river wound, twenty miles of the sea.'

Great Expectations

One of the more remarkable things about the Hoo Peninsula is the very small number of people who have either visited the area or recorded their impressions of it. Moreover, those who have handed down to us a glimpse of the Peninsula in some dim and distant age, rarely have anything favourable to say.

Perhaps, in many ways, this is not surprising. Much of the Peninsula is made up of marshlands, giving it a bleakness which once deterred the visitor, and still attracts only a small number of people fed up with the stuffiness of the towns. So, for many centuries, the major part of the population was made up of sheep and a few sheep farmers.

In addition, these marshes, particularly around the Isle of Grain, have given rise to another deterring factor – 'ague'. This ague, sometimes known as marsh fever, is now more commonly termed malaria.

Malaria was not uncommon in England at one time. It was indigenous to many east coast marshland areas, but on the Peninsula with its particularly temperate weather, it was second to none in the virulence of the fever. Although the area is now completely disease free, modern day residents receive frequent reminders, following the bite of the very agile local breed of mosquito. One often-told local story recounts how ambitious gentlemen (if that is the correct term in the circumstances) would marry into rich families and bring their spouses to Grain for a honeymoon. During this period of matrimonial bliss they would be called away unexpectedly for a week or two. On their return, they would often have acquired a fortune with no strings attached.

Holinshed is one of the earliest writers to leave an impression of the area. Born in Kent, he was the sixteenth-century historian upon whom Shakespeare drew. Amongst his works are included: *A Short Tour of England*, and in this he gives the following view of the Peninsula:

'He that rides into the hundred of Hoo,
Besides pilfering seamen, will find dirt enow.'

Another person not greatly endeared with the area, was a certain
Dr. Johnson, who visited the Isle of Grain on July 13th, 1629. The
following is his account of the visit:

'Having left our small boat we walked five or six miles, but
discovered nothing that could afford us any pleasure. It was in
the middle of a very hot day, and, like Tantalus, we were
tormented by an intolerable thirst in the midst of water which
was all salt. Nor were we less oppressed with hunger in this
barbarous country where there was not a village near, nor the
smoke of a chimney in site, or even the barking of a dog within
hearing, those usual signs of inhabitants, to raise our languid
minds to any kind of hope.'

Fairly dismal reading! Turning to Edward Hasted's *History and
Topographical Study of the County of Kent* we find no relief.
Hasted is the most well known of all the county's historians,
carrying out a very thorough survey of Kent during the middle part
of the eighteenth century. The thoroughness of his survey can
readily be appreciated, when it is remembered that his *History and
Topographical Study* has since been published in twelve particularly heavy volumes. The Hoo Peninsula is split between volumes
three and four. Hasted writes of the Hundred of Hoo:

'Formerly it used to be noted for the wealth of the yeomen
who inhabited it, but there are now few but bailiffs and lookers*
who live in it, the farmers and occupiers of the lands dwelling at
Rochester and Stroud, and elsewhere; nor is there a gentleman's
house, or a clergyman residing, in it, owing to the depth of the
soil, the dirtiness of the roads and the unwholesome air from the
neighbouring marshes.'

Of Cooling, Hasted is even less flattering:

'Cowling is an unfrequented place, the roads of which are deep
and miry, and it is unhealthy as it is unpleasant.'

Writing about Cliffe he adds:

'The situation of it is pleasant, but exceedingly unhealthy,
* Shepherds.

owing to its nearness and exposure to a great quantity of marshland.'

It is, however, for the Isle of Grain that Hasted reserves his greatest hostility:

'The greatest part of it consists of pastures and marshes, the vast tracts of the latter, in the neighbourhood of it, and the badness of the water, makes it as unwholesome as it is unpleasant; so that the inhabitants mostly consist of a few lookers and bailiffs, and of those ... who have not the wherewithal to seek a residence elsewhere.'

In contrast to all this, was Hogarth's visit of 1732. In the early summer of that year William Hogarth, the artist, together with four friends, decided on a five-day tour of Kent. It was agreed that Hogarth should furnish the sketches whilst another of the party, Ebenezer Forrest, should write an account of the journeyings. Unlike the modern-day traveller, Hogarth's party decided that the best approach to the Isle of Sheppey would be to cross the southern part of the Hoo Peninsula, as far as Grain. From Grain they hope to get passage across the Medway, as a regular ferry service was then operated.

This was no serious adventure intent upon scientific discovery. It was a joyous holiday of five carefree individuals. A humorous vein runs throughout the whole of Forrest's account and clearly distinguishes it from any previous witness. Perhaps, even more striking, is that the visitors find the area pleasant! For instance:

'At four we left Hoo, and an agreeable widow landlady who had buried four husbands. As we travelled along this charming country, the weather was exceedingly pleasant ...'

After visiting Rochester and Chatham the party arrived at Upnor. At this point it should be remembered that humour is never far from the surface with these travellers:

'We made a hurry scurry dinner at the "Smack" at the ten gun battery, and had a battle royal with sticks, pebbles and hog's dung. In this fight Tothall was the greatest sufferer and his cloaths carried the marks of his disgrace.'

From Upnor the party journeyed to Hoo, following a pathway close to the banks of the River Medway. On arrival at Hoo a few drinks were partaken of at a local hostelry before continuing on to Stoke:

> 'At five we took a view of Stoke church and passed through the country, but saw nothing worth observation till we came to a farmhouse not far distant, where, on an elm tree at the door, was placed a high pole, with a board that moved with the wind, painted in the form of a cock, over which was a fair weather cock, and above that a shuttle cock. This variety of cocks afforded much speculation.'

Passing on to North Street, the party eventually reached Stoke, where they took some rooms at the Nag's Head. Here another battle, this time with soft cow dung, took place.

> 'Night coming on, we drew cuts who should be single, there being but three beds, and no night caps. The lot fell to Tothill and he had satisfaction of lying alone.'

It is, perhaps, at this juncture that the party might have felt that their earlier praise of the area was misplaced:

> 'Monday at 3, awakened and cursed our day; our eyes, lips and hands, being tormented and swelled by the biting of gnats.'

Nevertheless, with a great deal of effort, some sleep was gained and the party set out the following morning for the Isle of Grain. Once more the group had a small adventure when they managed to take the wrong road and added some two miles to their journey before eventually reaching the village of St. James on the Isle of Grain.

> '... passing the church there, we stopped at the Chequer Ale House, kept by Gooddy Hubbard, who entertained us with salt pork, bread, butter and buns, and good malt liquor.'

The object of coming to Grain was to catch a ferry to Sheerness, but because of high winds none of the boatmen were prepared to cross the Medway. Instead, Gooddy Hubbard suggested that they ought to go along to a beach, now called Cockleshell Beach, and try to hail a passing boat.

> 'We accordingly went down to the shore which was covered with a variety of shells and accidentally espied a little boat coming on our side of the water below us, which Thornhill and

Tothall went down to meet and brought up to us, and with some difficulty took us in and we set sail for Sheerness.'

It is from this account, usually referred to as *Hogarth's Peregrination*, that we get an excellent view of the Peninsula during the seventeenth century. Admittedly it is rather short, for Hogarth's company only spent a day and a night in the area, but it is one of the few 'human' accounts written about the locality. To us, it might seem amusing that the company had such great trouble sleeping because of the gnats. These were, of course, the notorious mosquitoes. Amongst them, undoubtedly, was the Anopheles variety – a malaria carrier.

To digress, it might be useful to say a little, at this point, on the subject of indigenous malaria. Ague, or marsh fever, as already mentioned, was not uncommon along the East Coast. Large tracts of East Anglia and other Kent marshes suffered from this affliction. However, a survey carried out in the 1930s concluded that it was on the Hoo Peninsula that malaria was most common. The First World War proved particularly troublesome for the Isle of Grain as the constant movement of people in and out of an important military area, often brought one time malaria sufferers. If such a person then underwent a relapse and was bitten by an *Anopheles* mosquito, the mosquito would then be in a position to transmit the disease to others.

Following a serious outbreak of the disease in 1917, attempts were made to completely eliminate the disease from the Peninsula. Regular spraying of the marshes was undertaken whilst householders were later issued with small spray guns. By the fifties, malaria was unknown and a recent survey concluded that the marshes no longer contained the dangerous *Anopheles* mosquito.

Returning to *Hogarth's Peregrination* it is interesting to note that many of the places mentioned still remain. Stoke church has changed only slightly since Hogarth's visit, but there is little chance that the party would recognize Grain church as it is now. At Upnor only the ruined site of the ten-gun battery can now be seen. In Stoke, a 'Nag's Head' exists, but it is a newer building. The least changed of all the buildings mentioned is the 'Chequer' at Grain. This is the oldest building in the village, apart from the church. It is a Tudor building which started life as an inn. Much later it became a post office, then a general store, and now it has

reverted to its original use. Renamed the 'Hogarth', in memory of
the artist's visit, it is once again providing drinks for parched
throats.

Lest those living in the north-east part of the Peninsula feel
themselves neglected, one other, and equally famous visitor has yet
to be mentioned. This is Charles Dickens, the novelist. Living at
Gads Hill, just outside our area, many of his favourite walks were
on the Peninsula. One of his most popular books, *Great
Expectations*, was partly set around the area opf Cliffe, Higham
and Cooling. Through the book's characters Dickens has much to
say about the Peninsula. Of these characters, the convicts from a
prison hulk stationed in Egypt Bay, have least reason for liking the
Peninsula. One such convict, on being asked his opinion of the
area, replies:

' "A most beastly place. Mudbank, mist, swamp, and work:
work, swamp, mist and mudbank." '

This, though, was certainly not Dickens' viewpoint. He is known to
have liked the area: one of his favourite walks ended at the
churchyard in Cooling, and it is here that Dickens gained
inspiration for at least one scene in *Great Expectations*. He
discovered the originals of the 'five little stone lozenges' which
were sacred to the memory of Pip's brothers – Pip Pirrip being the
main character in the book. Actually, thirteen such stones are to be
found in the churchyard, marking the graves of the various
children of the Comport family.

In the book Pip comments on the area a number of times:

'Ours was the marsh country, down by the river, within, as the
river wound, twenty miles of the sea.'

Near the village of Cliffe once stood the remains of an old gun
battery and here Pip often used to retire:

'It was pleasant and quiet out there with the sails on the river
passing beyond the earthwork, and sometimes, when the tide was
low, looking as if they belonged to sunken ships that were still
sailing on at the bottom of the water.'

Dickens wrote about the Peninsula in the early nineteenth
century. At that time it was on the verge of change. Changes which
had already occurred elsewhere were about to appear on the

Peninsula. Previously mentioned writers visiting the Peninsula a century later would find the area totally unrecognizable. Today, it is a marshland infiltrated by industry and the numerous compact houses of the villages.

Of these villages easily the largest is Hoo St. Werburgh. In many ways, it is a small town with a flourishing shopping centre, several schools and a population in excess of 7,000. Unfortunately, this increased size has brought with it a considerable loss of community spirit.

Most of the other villages on the Peninsula are also fairly sizeable and in most cases, this is due to two post-war building phases. The first came immediately after the war when the, then, Strood Rural District Council undertook the construction of a series of housing estates. The second phase came in the late sixties and early seventies when private developers took advantage of cheap land and rising house prices to add a number of estates of a simple and rather uniform design. Only two villages have so far avoided both the post-war building booms and these are, naturally enough, the Peninsula's two smallest villages – Cooling and St. Mary's Hoo. Having escaped the developers both villages consequently, maintain a much more 'olde worlde' and 'villagey' atmosphere.

As well as the villages there are a number of farm houses dotted about. Some, due to the rapid growth of the Peninsula, have actually been engulfed by the villages from which they were once so remote. The oldest farmhouse on the Peninsula is that of Manor Farm, Cliffe. Dating from the reign of the first Elizabeth, it is typical of this period, having a wooden framework and a fine brick chimney stack. Other farmhouses, such as Brick House and Newlands, date from the eighteenth century.

The village of Cliffe can boast one of the finer collections of buildings on the Peninsula. One particularly ancient building is the medieval rectory. Originally built by the monks of Christchurch Priory, Canterbury, it started life as a manor house but later came into the hands of the rectors at Cliffe. Other interesting buildings in, or near, the village are Quickrills, a house of the late seventeenth century, and Courtsole, again of this period. Cliffe also boasts one of the areas few haunted buildings. This is the former 'Black Bull' inn which, according to one story, states the building is haunted due to it being built on the site of an old graveyard. An

alternative account puts the haunting down to the return of a sailor
drowned at sea and who is in search of his 'true love'. Either way,
it is said that footsteps are heard and locked doors mysteriously
open.

Although Cooling is one of the smallest of the Peninsula villages
it makes up for it with its great wealth of interest. It has a
medieval castle, a church with smuggling connections, associations
with Charles Dickens and one of the most beautifully sited houses
in the whole area. This is Cooling Court, which dates, according to
a plaque set in the wall, from the year 1700. It is built of blue and
red brick placed in a chequered pattern and lies off a farm lane
from which it is partially obscured by a willow tree hanging above
a garden pond.

Allhallows is another Peninsula village with smuggling connections. The eighteenth-century smugglers, here, mostly occupied
the foreshore area of the parish – then called Bell's Hard. In fact,
at that time Allhallows consisted of two completely separate
communities. There was the fishing village of Bell's Hard which
has been mentioned and then there was the village proper, which
consisted of a few houses clustered around the church. Nowadays,
of course, the fishing community has long since disappeared and
the village of Allhallows, far from consisting of a few houses
clustered around the church, has expanded right down to the
foreshore.

Smuggling connections can also be found in the parish of High
Halstow. Smugglers, it is believed, landed goods in Egypt Bay and
later concealed them at Shade House. For such purposes Shade
House could not be bettered as it lies right out on the marshes and
far from any other inhabited site. High Halstow is a Saxon name
and, as the name indicates, it lies on one of the highest points of
the Peninsula. Despite its Saxon name, though, the village is
mostly modern. The only exceptions to this are its medieval church
and the 'Red Dog' which is partly Tudor.

Stoke is divided into three separate communities. There is
Upper Stoke, which consists of a number of houses grouped around
the church; Middle Stoke a small community situated around the
sharp bend of the A228 and the main village of Lower Stoke. It is
this part of the village that houses the school and shops. Midway
between Middle and Lower Stoke lies MacKay's Court Farm with

its interesting red brick farmhouse dating from the eighteenth century.

Strictly speaking the Isle of Grain should not be included as part of the Peninsula: it is an island – or at least it was. During the early Middle Ages the Yantlet, which once divided the island from the mainland, was used by the majority of ships attempting to avoid the more open waters of the Thames. Later, a bridge was built connecting the island with the mainland. This bridge is marked on a number of early maps including Symonson's map of Kent which is dated 1596.

The Peninsula has three major topographical features. These are the marshes, the saltings and the uplands. About half the Peninsula consists of marshes and saltings; marshes being the reclaimed land inside the sea walls; whilst the saltings exist outside the walls. In places, the marshes form a narrow band between the uplands and the rivers whilst, in others, there is a much more extensive belt of marshland, such as that at Cooling and Grain. The marshes are drained by a system of fleets – these are natural and are the original tidal creeks prior to reclamation – and man-made dykes. The marshes have always been used extensively for sheep grazing, though some farmers in the Cooling/High Halstow area have drained the marshes far more extensively than usual and are using the land for wheat.

Seventeenth-century maps of the Peninsula show the saltings to have been much more extensive than they are today. Symonson's map shows the Medway, as it flows past the Peninsula, to have been very narrow and bordered by extensive saltings. The change is partly explained by the extensive clay digging once carried out by the cement industry.

The marshlands and saltings between them provide the area with an interesting variety of bird life. Amongst the most common marshland birds are skylarks and common partridge, though the heron is a familiar sight in many parts. During the winter, the marshlands are the home for Brent geese, white fronted geese, wigeons, pintails, shovelers, knots and curlews. During the summer, the marshes are frequented by shelducks, common terns and wagtails. During the migratory periods, the bird population of the marshes is considerably expanded by amongst others, whimbrels, redshanks and ringed plovers on their way to summer or winter grounds. The best places for viewing these birds include the Stoke

Saltings, the pools at Cliffe and Egypt Bay. At High Halstow the Royal Society for the Protection of Birds has a reserve. It is open daily and has a marked-out nature trail. Apart from the ornithological interest of the marshes there is a great variety of insect and plant life.

The upland area is a chalk belt which gently forms itself into a ridge running like a spine, through much of the central area of the Peninsula. This is the part farmland and part woodland of Lodge Hill. It is the upland area, of course, which contains the Peninsula's eight villages and numerous farms. The predominant crops grown in this area are wheat, vegetables and fruit.

At the present time the Peninsula is in the midst of considerable change. Better drainage of the marshes has been responsible for attracting industry to the area. The earliest changes came in the late nineteenth century with the arrival of the railway. In turn this was followed by a few small factories. World War One brought an air station and an airship factory. Other industry followed during the inter-war period and this included two small oil refineries. After the war one of these refineries grew into the massive Kent Oil Refinery at the Isle of Grain.

The Peninsula is now blessed with two electricity power stations, whose power cables criss-cross the many once bleak stetches of land. It is these ugly refinements of civilization which really destroy the undoubted desolate beauties of the area. It is only in such out of the way places as Egypt Bay and parts of the Cliffe and Cooling marshes that one is completely free of such visual intrusions; and so it is only in these places that one is able to imagine the Peninsula as it must have been in former days.

CHAPTER TWO

EARLY DAYS

'In view of various obstacles, however, it was unanimously agreed that we should meet once a year on the first of August at the place called Cloveshoo.'

Bede: *A History of the English Church and People*

Although the Hoo Peninsula has probably been inhabited by man from the earliest of times, signs of his occupation are not very forthcoming. This is partly because of the great climatic changes which have occurred over the last two million years. Four ice ages, with interglacial periods, have considerably affected the lie of the land. At times the Medway was so broad as to flow over much of the Peninsula and the entire Isle of Grain. At others, the river was a mere trickle.

About a million years ago, the Peninsula was part of a much broader land mass connected to Essex. This was at a time when the Thames was much further north and a mere tributary of the Rhine.*

During the ice ages, the Hoo Peninsula would have been part of a tundra region with a permanently frozen sub-soil. The much reduced Medway would have been frozen solid for nine months of the year. During the inter-glacial periods improvements in climate would have brought small hunting and fishing communities to the area. Proof of the frequent comings and goings of these primitive peoples, whose normal mode of transport were small dugout canoes, has been verified by finds of their small stone spearheads on the beach at Allhallows.

As man's rise to civilization continued, so hunter became farmer and stone worker became metal worker. The first of the metals to be worked was bronze and there have been a number of bronze age finds on the Peninsula.

One find, discovered at Stoke, was a hoard consisting of fifty-two objects, most notably bronze axe heads, palstaves and swords. In addition, an amount of raw, unworked, bronze was also found. A further two hoards have been found in the parish of Allhallows close to the border with St. Mary's Hoo. One, of

* See in particular *The Face of the Earth*, G. H. Dury (1959).

thirty-seven objects, was found at Little Coombe Farm in 1875 by workmen engaged in trenching a field. The other, of twenty-seven objects, was found at Home Wood Farm in 1873. Both contained axe and spearheads of various sizes, whilst the former had a number of copper cakes stored in pots and the latter a very rare hog's back knife.

All the above finds were made in the nineteenth century and are held in the British Museum. Much more recently a large bronze age hoard was discovered near Hoo during pipe laying work. Containing similar material to that already described, it can be viewed in a special display cabinet at Rochester Museum. Expertly cleaned and preserved it not only looks very impressive in the museum, but it is one of the very few archaeological finds made on the Peninsula that is readily available for local public viewing.

The four hoards described probably belonged to travelling traders who sold their goods and also collected bronze material prior to returning to a workshop. No satisfactory explanation has ever been given for the burial of such hoards though the most obvious explanation is that during a time of strife the owner felt it wiser to bury them and collect them later.

About 700 B.C., a new wave of settlers arrived from the Continent bringing with them the art of iron smelting. They also brought distinctive pottery designs which help archaeologists distinguish iron age sites. Of this period dates pottery fragments found at Wallend, on the Isle of Grain. Imported iron age pottery has also been discovered near Cliffe.

During pre-historic times Hoo St. Werburgh was probably a fairly important settlement. The discovery of a Phoenician coin at a point just south of the present village also suggests that Hoo may also have been a small trading centre. The coin was discovered in 1903 and is said to be a drachma dating from the reign of Philip of Macedon. This particular king will probably be better recalled if one remembers that he was the father of Alexander the Great.

The importance of the coin demonstrates that Kent had trading links with the Phoenicians, traders who ranged far and wide bringing with them such saleable commodities as silver, high quality pottery and wines. Perhaps, indeed, it was the Phoenician traders who brought the imported pots found near Cliffe. It should be pointed out that these pottery fragments do not come from so far east but would have been collected by the Phoenicians on their journeyings.

Hoo is not the only place in North Kent where Phoenician coins have been found. Not very long ago a number of such coins were unearthed at Higham. They were all contained inside a hollow flint purse.

Another aspect of iron age Peninsula life is the existence of salt extraction works along the banks of the Medway. This is an industry of which we will hear a lot more of later, and it is interesting to note that it has roots going back to before the Romans.

With the successful invasion and colonization of British shores by the Romans, Kent was catapulted into the main stream of civilization. Within a few years, a large number of towns had grown up and not the least of these was Rochester with its impressive city walls. Already important as an iron age community, the expansion of Rochester by the Romans was obviously to have an important influence on the Peninsula.

During the period of Roman occupation the area became fairly heavily populated with settlements being established at Cliffe and Hoo. To the Romans, the region must have been of some economic importance for, apart from the establishment of a number of small industries that will be discussed later, the whole area was of considerable importance for stock rearing and cereal farming.

It would appear that Cliffe was particularly well populated during most of the Roman period. Some twenty-one separate Roman sites have been uncovered here, and they include six farming settlements. The Black Shore region was the most heavily populated with its inhabitants engaged in such diverse industries as weaving, salt extraction, metal working and fish caging. The latter consisted of scoops being dug into the river clay and topped with wicker work baskets, in order to trap the fish.

A considerable amount of Roman pottery has been found in the marshes, so much so, that it has been suggested that Cliffe probably had a small pier and was the importation point for pottery from Gaul. Gaul was an important centre for pottery production during the Roman occupation period and many of the pottery fragments found around Cliffe have been identified as coming from Central and Eastern Gaul.

Cliffe is also at the centre of quite a heated archaeological debate. This concerns the existence (or not!) of an extensive complex of allotments. It is stated by one school that such allotments did exist at Cliffe and were used either by the soldiers or citizens of Rochester. Their evidence for the existence of such a site is the road system in the Cliffe area, which, they say, much resembles the traditional grid pattern. Not everyone would agree with this view and the singular lack of archaeological finds in the supposed grid pattern area woould seem to undermine this argument.

At this point a little more explanation is probably required. The method of establishing allotments is peculiarly Roman. The field and road pattern followed the traditional chessboard style. Each road was an exact distance apart, and formed a right angle to any other road it crossed. The squares, so created by the road system, became the fields. All this preliminary work was done by a body of professional surveyors – known as 'agimensores' – who maintained that there was no other proper way of setting out a field system. The Romans, of course, were noted for their tidy mindedness and exactitude in laying out road patterns in town and country.

If such a site existed at Cliffe the first thing the Roman surveyor would do, would be to ascertain the exact angle of Watling Street – the road running between Dover and London. Although at its nearest point to the settlement at Cliffe it is over a mile away, the Roman 'agrimensores' regarded it as essential that the new allotments should be aligned on its axis. Once this was done, the two main roads would be established, again at right angles to one another, and then the remainder of the small roads, until the grid was completed.

The lack of archaeological evidence of this system has not necessarily worried the supporters of the theory. They would argue that it was not necessary for the allotment holders to live on site, but that they would return to Rochester each night. To my mind, though, the distance does seem too great to be practical. Also, one would expect to have found more coins, broken farming implements and bits of pottery in the particular area than is actually the case.

At Hoo there was another fairly important Roman settlement. Once again considerable pottery finds have been made, a Roman cemetery has been located, and there are signs of permanent buildings. The buildings, which lie to the south of the present village, could be either part of a villa or, more likely, a small village. It has been suggested that Hoo's strategically important position on the Medway might well have led to the building of a small fort for the protection of Rochester from sea raiders.

For the Romans, salt was a particularly important commodity and fetched a fairly high price. The Roman soldier even had a special salt allowance. It is, therefore, not surprising to learn that the Peninsula's very first industry greatly expanded during the Roman period with salterns being established at Cliffe, Cooling, Hoo and Stoke. In the case of Cliffe evidence has been discovered relating to two separate salterns. The discovery of one of these was made in 1964 by an Ordnance Survey team. This particular site lies close to Cliffe Creek. The site at Cooling lies on Broomy Farm, and that at Hoo and Stoke on the adjacent saltings.

The method of salt extraction used on these sites was similar in each case and was to remain unchanged for many centuries. Sea water was collected in large clay-lined pans and placed over a hearth with a fire blazing. Once the sea water had evaporated, the salt was simply collected from the sides of the pan.

Another common feature on the Peninsula during this time was the pottery kiln. The Romans, themselves, were greatly noted for their fine pottery ware. No Roman site is without its highly polished red Samian ware, but the potters of the Peninsula were not up to this standard. They were individuals selling to the local community and what they produced were the more essential needs of that community – coarse kitchen ware. Once again Roman period kilns have been located at Cliffe, Cooling and on the Isle of Grain.

Something that should be borne in mind is that, although the Romans occupied British shores for only a few years short of four centuries, these sites were not in continuous occupation for this entire period. Archaeologists have gone to a great deal of trouble to estimate when each site was occupied and for just how long. With salt works, in particular, it is very difficult to estimate the period of occupation. Partly, this is because of the very short period of usage before the owner moved on.

The most universal method of dating a Roman period site is through its pottery. Fragments, even very tiny, can often convey sufficient information as to style and where it was produced. This information can then be used to construct an approximate date that the area in question was occupied.

Another possible method of dating occupation is the method by which the dead were disposed. In the earlier part of the Romano-British period, bodies were cremated, whilst in the later years, probably as the result of an increasing influence of Christianity, they were buried. The Roman cemeteries at Hoo and Cliffe both contain cinerary urns which would suggest an early occupation with possible abandonment at a later date. Signs of cremation have also been found at Stoke and Allhallows.

A fit and proper disposal of the dead was extremely important to the Romano-Briton. Death was not the end merely a passing over to another life in which a good person would be well rewarded. A full and ritualistic burial would ease the passage into the new life, whilst cremation left the soul purified and free of its earthly ties.

The body would first be laid on a funeral pyre and then the ashes would be carefully washed with wine before being placed in a large urn. The urn, together with a number of other articles the deceased might find useful in his after life, were placed in a pit and then covered over. A nine-day period of mourning then followed.

The type of articles deposited in the pit varied greatly but were usually of a simple kind. One good example exists on the Peninsula. At Damhead Creek, near Stoke, two cinerary urns were discovered both containing the remains of human ashes. Together with these there were four Samian dishes, a black ware dish and a vase with two handles.

Before concluding this survey of the Peninsula during the years of Roman occupation it should be stated that although the Romans did bring wealth and prosperity to these islands it was not by any means equitably distributed. The majority of the population, and this applies to most of those living on the Peninsula, were extremely poor and farming, for the most part, at a self-sufficiency level. These, the original native stock, would have noticed little change with the coming of the Romans. A few may have had an intermediate wealth which allowed them to sell cattle and sheep at Rochester but they would have been few in number.

The years of peace created by the Romans had ceased to exist even before the final departure of the legions. Those living in coastal areas had already been subject to Saxon pirate raids, but with the exit of Roman troops, the floodgates were opened.

Kent, once more, became a kingdom, under Vortigern. It is he who was responsible for the use of Saxon mercenaries to defend Kent. He gave them, as payment, the right to settle on the Isle of Thanet. Not content with the conditions of their employment, these mercenaries soon deposed Vortigern and, under their leaders Hengist and Horsa, took over the whole of Kent.

One can only speculate what was happening on the Peninsula at this time. Most likely the area was constantly raided during the period immediately following the departure of the Romans. During this time the most prosperous would have taken the opportunity to leave. Eventually, with the Saxons taking over Kent, many of the original landholders would have lost their property, some even becoming slaves. It would not have been long before the area once more reverted to its traditional role of stock rearing.

It is to the Saxon era that the peculiar name of Hoo originates. In Old English 'Hoh' is a piece of land jutting out (i.e. Peninsula) and during the middle ages this was changed to 'Ho' and eventually 'Hoo'.

Kent, itself, prospered considerably during these early years of Saxon rule. It became, for a time, the most powerful kingdom in the land. One Kentish king, Æthelbert, ruled all of England south of the Humber, for a period of thirty years.

We have no hard and fast evidence relating to the Hoo Peninsula until the year 664. Dating from that year, a document exists granting land at Hoo to the monastery of Peterborough. The wording of this particular document is rather interesting and has been variously interpreted. Written in Latin it refers to the land granted as being at: 'Hoghe close upon Hebureahge Island'. Some have taken this to mean that the whole of the Peninsula was then an island, whilst others suggest that Hebureahge was the old name for the Isle of Grain. It does seem rather unlikely that the Peninsula was then an island and, a far more probable suggestion is that the name refers to the large island which once existed to the south of the village of Hoo and appears on a number of early maps.

The land granted to the monastery at Peterborough was later used for the founding of a nunnery. The founder was St. Werburgh, and it is she who has also given her name to the village of Hoo, and its church.

Werburgh was the daughter of the powerful Mercian king named Wulfhere. Sometime during the middle of the seventh century he chose to marry Erminhilda, the sister of King Egbert of Kent. Egbert's kingdom was very much on the decline, whilst Mercia was constantly gaining strength. The marriage alliance was useful to both sides. For Egbert, it helped to prop up his ailing kingdom, and for Wulfhere it offered great possibilities of further extending Mercian power.

The young Werburgh did not choose to become a further pawn in this game of power politics. Instead, she entered the church and seems to have had considerable connections with her mother's former homeland. For one thing, she became Abbess of the nunnery at Minster-in-Sheppey, and for another she founded the nunnery at Hoo sometime towards the end of the seventh century.

Werburgh died in the year 700 and was canonized as a result of miracles attributed to her. It seems that she died near Repton and following upon instructions given prior to her death her body was removed to a place named Heanbirig. There is a great deal of evidence which suggests that Heanbirig is another spelling of the location upon which was sited Werburgh's nunnery at Hoo.

We do not have to wait very long before another Mercian enters into the early history of Hoo. About the year 741, King Ethelbald felt the time was right to mount a full-scale invasion of Kent, in order to annex the kingdom. Little is known of the planning and complexities of the operation but one thing is certain, it was a very successful campaign.

King Ethelbald was a cousin of St. Werburgh and much revered her name. So much so, that upon entering his newly acquired kingdom he chose to found a church at Hoo dedicated to the name of his saintly relative. Ethelbald also seems to have turned Hoo into some kind of cantonal capital. Apart from the church he also established a large country estate which he named Werburgh Wic. This became his royal residence with Hoo rapidly becoming a fashionable town.

For the next few years Ethelbald seems to have based himself upon his town of Hoo St. Werburgh. In the year following his successful invasion, his presence is recorded at a great church council held at Cloveshoo.

With so many Saxon events the exact locations are often hard to pinpoint. So it is with the church council at Cloveshoo. All that we know about Cloveshoo was that it must have been somewhere in the south and not far from London. A number of places have been suggested but none more consistently than Cliffe, or Cliffe-at-Hoo to give the village its full name.

As far back as 673 church dignitaries decided that it was necessary to hold regular meetings to iron out all ecclesiastical problems and the site chosen was Cloveshoo. It is not known just how regularly the meetings were held, but the earliest we know of is the one held in the year 742. A further six of these meetings, stretching over an eighty-year period, are known to have been held.

The eighth century was the time of Mercian pre-eminence, and having conquered Kent, together with most of southern England, they brought a further period of peace to the Peninsula – a peace that was to be shattered in the middle of the ninth century by the appearance of Viking raiders.

The Peninsula suffered particularly badly. It was constantly plundered by raiding parties passing up the Thames and Medway. In 857 and 1017 Viking armies wintered on Sheppey, and scavenging parties must have been a constant menance to life and limb. It is these Viking raiders which brought a sudden end to the, then, prospering area around Hoo. The country estate of Werburgh Wic would have been plundered and then destroyed, whilst the chroniclers tell us that the body of St. Werburgh was removed to Chester Cathedral at this time, as it was feared that the grave would be desecrated. Nor can it be coincidence that the last church council held at Cloveshoo was in 825.

The eleventh century, though, saw a few decades of peace, prior to the arrival of the Normans. In the early part of that century, the Danish raiders had won a mighty victory and their own king, Canute, had come to the English throne.

The Saxons, as well as establishing the name of Hoo also christened – or re-christened – most of the villages on the Peninsula. Many of these names are very informative. Thus, High Halstow started life off with the Saxon name of 'Haligstowe' which means Holy Place. This could well be indicative of either a very early church, of which we know nothing, or of an early Christian event.

Sharnal Street is, on the other hand, a little insulting to the people living in the vicinity. It is derived from the Old English

'Scean Welle' which quite simply means 'the spring running near the rubbish heap'!

It is also of interest to see exactly how the original Saxon name arrived at its present-day derivation. Take, for example, Cooling. The Saxons, in an eighth-century document, refer to it as 'Culingas' (meaning the place of Cula's people). In the Domesday Book survey it becomes 'Colinge' and in a map of 1596 'Cowlinge'. The normal nineteenth-century spelling was 'Cowling'.

Modern-day historians have taken an interest in the dating of the original Saxon community of Cooling. The dominant school of thought on the matter states that because the original Saxon name – Culingas – ends in 'ingas' that Cooling must be amongst the earliest Saxon communities in Kent.

As I have already said, some of the original Saxon names are very informative. This is very much the case with Stoke which is referred to as 'Andscohesham'. Meaning the homestead of Hondscioh, this was obviously a main settlement, but at a later point, a smaller settlement – namely Stokes, or alternatively Estoches – began to grow close by Andscohesham, and eventually overtook it in size. Once again we have no idea where the original settlement was, but ending in 'ham', as it does, it would indicate a fairly early settlement.

The origin of Grain, as a name, particularly interests me. The Old English derivation was 'Greon', meaning a gravelly, or sandy shore. Nowadays, visitors to Grain can easily be forgiven for expressing surprise at this. The shore at Grain is pebbly, perhaps. Covered in shells, definitely. But sand most certainly is not a major feature of the beach front.

What we learn from the Saxon name is that Grain once had a very prominent sandy shore. It must have done, for otherwise it would not have received such a name. We know from other evidence that the Peninsula has lost much land to sea erosion. In Grain, the loss was probably greater than anywhere else. One early statement about Grain indicates that the church of St. James was once situated in the centre of the village. A modern-day map would dispute this. Over the centuries the tides claimed a large area of beach and the original extent of the island – say at the time of the Saxons – was probably as far as the present low water mark. Thus came the name Isle of Grain.

CHAPTER THREE

LIFE IN THE MIDDLE AGES

Thine father was a bond man
Thine mother curtsy non can
Every beast that lyeth now
Is of more freedom than thou
Peasant song of the fifteenth century.

To those living on the Peninsula the Norman Conquest meant very little. Life after the Conquest went on very much as it had done before – the main features during this period being poverty and malnutrition. If a child reached adulthood without contracting one of the many prevalent diseases, then life expectancy was still little beyond the age of thirty.

Only for the rich and powerful did the conquest have any significance, as many Saxon lords subsequently had their lands confiscated. Such was the case on the Peninsula, where the major landholder was the defeated King Harold. Amongst Harold's possessions was the Great Manor of Hoo together with the Manor of Stoke, whilst the former king's brother, Earl Leofwyne, owned the Manor of Cooling. All of these manors were taken over by the Normans.

Having two such noble landholders did not, during those closing years of the Saxon era, confer any spectacular importance upon the area. Although the Godwin's (Harold's family name) were the country's greatest landholders, they would rarely have visited the major portion of their estates. The only advantage to the area may have been an occasional grant for the improvement of a parish church or two.

Manors, to which we have already made reference, were the usual method of land ownership. Throughout the whole kingdom, the countryside was divided into manors and each had in common the following characteristics: a demesne (land retained by the lord of the manor but tended by tenants of the manor as payment of rent); land farmed by the tenants for their own needs and a number of unfree tenants.

High ranking nobles, in particular, had estates consisting of numerous manors often dotted around the country. In these cases, the actual administration of each manor was carried out by a bailiff who was directly responsible to the lord.

For administrative purposes, these manors were grouped into Hundreds, and these, in turn, were grouped together in units which, according to county, were given a variety of names. In Kent the grouping of Hundreds was known as lathes – of which there were five. It is suggested that the origin of the hundred as an administrative unit may have resulted from a hundred hides, or a hundred heads of families. Its main use was for purposes of collecting taxes.

The Hoo Peninsula was part of the Lathe of Aylesford, and at the time of the Conquest, the Peninsula was divided into several different manors. Each of these manors varied greatly in size, with the Manor of Hoo as the largest. This encompassed not only the village of Hoo but also Allhallows, High Halstow and St. Mary Hoo. Cliffe, Cooling, Grain and Stoke were all separate manors.

Although the whole Peninsula is nowadays often referred to as the 'Hundred of Hoo', not all these manors were part of that original Hundred. Cliffe, Cooling and part of Stoke were in the Hundred of Shamel, whilst the Isle of Grain was in the Hundred of Chatham and Gillingham. This is not surprising when it is remembered that water transport provided the easiest means of access to many places during the Middle Ages.

The inhabitants of the manor could be divided into several distinct classes. To start with there was the basic division of serfs and freemen: of every ten peasants in Kent, four were usually free. They were not necessarily richer than the serf, but, after payment of rent to the lord of the manor, they were quite unhindered by any other manorial claim. Most important of all, they were free to leave at any time that they wished.

The majority of peasants, those not free, were known as serfs. Amongst these there was yet a further sub-division: the relatively wealthy villein, who may have held as much as thirty acres of land, and the cottar, who often held a mere pittance of only two or three acres. A number of historians have suggested that, because of the inefficiencies of medieval farming methods, ten acres was the normal area of land necessary to produce enough food for a small family to survive on. Thus, many cottars were often employed by the richer villeins in order that they might purchase additional produce with the money so earned.

Whatever the serf's relative prosperity, he was still tied to the land. When property changed hands, he went with it. If he tried to escape, he could be forcibly returned to the land. In return for the land the serfs held, they had to work on the lord's demesne at least twice a week and at additional times during harvesting. If the serf's daughter wished to marry, a fine had to be paid in order to acquire the lord's permission. At numerous other times additional payments and services were rendered. A tenth of his produce (known as a tithe) went to the parish priest; at Easter time eggs might have to be rendered to the lord (in order to gain permission to keep hens), whilst in times of war he was liable for military service.

To get a closer insight of life on the Peninsula during the Middle Ages, we must now turn to the many documents that have survived, and relate in some way, to the area. Clearly ranking as one of the most important of these, is the 'Domesday Book'. Completed a few years after the Norman Conquest it was intended, as the title suggests, to be the all-time definitive account of land ownership.

Some idea of the detail that went into the compilation of the 'Domesday Book' can be gleaned from the writer of the *Anglo-Saxon Chronicle*:

> 'Also he (King William) had a record made of how much land his archbishops had, and his bishops and abbots and his earls – and though I relate it at too great a length – what or how much everybody had who was occuping land in England, in land or cattle, and how much money it was worth. So very narrowly did he have it investigated, that there was no single hide nor a yard of land, nor indeed – it is a shame to relate but it seemed no shame to him to do – one ox nor one cow nor one pig left out, and not put down in his record: and all these records were brought to him afterwards.'

And so, about the year 1087, the King's commissioners arrived on the Peninsula. Asking various questions of the many property holders, they carefully put together the situation of land ownership and property values. As a result of their careful work, we can learn much of the Peninsula at this time. For the Great Manor of Hoo they recorded the following information:

'The Bishop of Bayeux himself holds Hov in demesne. It was taxd at fifty sulings, and now at thirty-three. The arable land is 50 carucates. In demesne there are 4 and 100 villeins, less three, with 61 cottars, having 43 carucates. There are six churches, and 12 slaves, and 32 acres of meadow. Wood for the pannage of 30 hogs. The whole manor in the time of King Edward the Confessor, was worth 60 pounds, when the archibishop received it the like, and now as much, and yet he who holds it pays 100 pounds. To this manor there belonged nine houses in the city of Rochester, and they paid six shillings, now they are taken away. This manor earl Godwin held. Of this manor Richard de Tonbridge held half a suling, and wood for the pannage of 20 hogs. In the time of King Edward and afterwards it was, and now is worth 40 shillings. Adam, son of Hubert, holds of the same manor one suling, and one yoke of the bishop, and one of his tenants has there in demesne half a carucate, and four villeins with half a carucate and one cottar. It is and was worth thirty shillings. Anschitil de Ros held the same manor three sulings, and he was there in demesne one carucate and five villeins, with twelve cottars, having one carucate and a half. There are five slaves and one mill of ten shillings, and 12 acres of meadow, and two fisheries of five shillings. In the time of King Edward and afterwards, it was worth six pounds, now six pounds and five shillings.'

Hoo was one of the largest manors in Kent. As previously mentioned, it had once been in the possession of King Harold himself. However, the 'Domesday Book' only ever refers to Harold as Earl of Kent, for King William never recognized Harold's title of king. After the Conquest, the Manor of Hoo, together with a large portion of Kent, was given to William's half brother, Odo, Bishop of Bayeux. Odo was also given Harold's title of Earl of Kent.

In size, the Manor of Hoo was between 7,000 and 10,000 acres of farmland (for a suling is, in measurement, over 200 acres) and of this area some 5,000 acres was ploughed (a curucate equalled about 100 acres of ploughland).

Apart from its size, Hoo had little that was not typical of many other manors of this time. Its population was put at something over one hundred villeins. As this probably refers to households, the actual number of people, including women and children, would have been just over five hundred. The total population for the entire Peninsula at this time, was almost certainly something between eight hundred and a thousand persons.

The mention of six churches within the Manor of Hoo has created many problems for historians. Only four of these churches can definitely be located; these being the village churches of Allhallows, High Halstow, Hoo St. Werburgh and St. Mary Hoo. The village churches of Cooling, Grain and Stoke have been alternatively put forward as candidates for the remaining places.

Stoke, however, mut be eliminated at once. The church, here, is given a separate mention in the Domesday Book whilst there are no separate references to Grain or Cooling churches – although both are known to date from the Saxon period.

Cooling, of course, is not usually associated with the Manor of Hoo but, during the eleventh century, the rather worldly Bishop Odo had a great knack for acquiring land not belonging to him. One such piece of land – according to the evidence of a twelfth-century document* – was the three sulings (approximately 700 acres) held by Anschitil de Ros. This land was in Cooling, and according to the above extract of the 'Domesday Book', Odo added it to the Manor of Hoo. This he had no authority to do, for the land rightfully belonged to the Archbishop of Canterbury. Eventually, the land was returned to the Archbishop but it seems most likely that this land contained the church of Cooling. If this was the case, the Cooling church can be included in those six churches of Hoo Manor.

The final church is much more of a mystery. Certainly it could have been the church at Grain or, equally, it could have been a small chapel within the confines of the manor. A chapel, of whose existence, we now know absolutely nothing.

The reference, in the quotation, to slaves is most interesting. It is not cleār how extensive slavery was in Medieval England or how such a condition came about. The most probable source of slaves may well have been the result of lost battles.

The meadowland mentioned would have been situated, in portions, adjacent to each village community. Held in common by all the villagers, it would have been used in the winter months for grazing animals, whilst in summer it would have been cropped. Another term used in the extract is pannage. This was a payment

* See Appendix 4 with its discussion on sources.

made by tenants in order to gain the right to graze certain animals in the woods.

In addition to the meadows and woods, animals would also have been grazed on any areas of wasteland surrounding each settlement. During the winter months, however, villagers would be hard put to find sufficient food for all their animals. Thus, at the onset of winter it was common practice to slaughter all but a few animals. those that were slaughtered were salted and eaten during those winter months.

The two fisheries existing on the manor would have been used in order to help supplement the meat. The method used in these fisheries is debateable, but the creation of an artificial waterway was, by far, the most common. Once built, it would have been staked out with a series of nets. We know, from other sources, that stake nets were used in Yantlet Creek during the thirteenth century and, it is possible, that one of these 'Domesday Book' references refers to the Yantlet.

The mill would have been powered by water and was probably the centre of a number of grievances. Every manor had its mill and it was compulsory to take corn to be ground there. Grinding corn at home was deemed illegal. With this monopoly the miller could not only take his time but also charge exorbitant rates.

Elsewhere in the 'Domesday Book', we learn who owned other parts of the Peninsula at this time. Odo was in possession of Cooling Manor (in addition to that land held by Anschitil de Ros) and the manors of Stoke and Cliffe. A second manor at Cliffe was in the hands of Christchurch Priory and the *Domesday Monarchum* (a survey of ecclesiastical land made at the same time as the 'Domesday Book') states of this manor:

'Cliva is a manor of the monks and belongs to their clothing; and at the time of King Edward the Confesor it was assessed at 2½ sulings, and it is valued at sixteen pounds.'

In other words, profits made from the sale of produce on this manor went towards the purchase of clothing for the monks. The Priory of Christchurch also owned Oyserlands at Stoke.

Towards the end of the eleventh century, a dispute arose between Odo and the Archbishop of Canterbury concerning land ownership. Lanfranc, the newly appointed archbishop, was concerned over the loss of valuable churchlands to Odo. Most of these lands were in Kent and included the Manor of Stoke.

Lanfranc and Odo were long time bitter rivals. So different were they, that it is hard to believe that they were both high ranking dignitaries of the same church. Odo was ill-adapted to religious orders and had only reached such an exalted position as a result of his half brother, William. Odo was much happier in the temporal world.

For the conquest of England, it is said that Odo brought together one hundred of the 782 ships used by William. At the Battle of Hastings, Odo played an outstanding part. Master Mace, a chronicler of those times, described the Bishop's role in the battle:

'He had put a hauberk on over a white alb; wide in the body with the sleeve tight, and sat on a white horse, so that all might recognize him. In his hand he held a mace and, whereever he saw the most need, he led up and stationed the knights, and often urged them on to assault and strike the enemy.'

As a reward for his help during the conquest Odo was given a great deal of land. According to Orderic Vitalis (an eleventh-century monk who wrote a history of England and Normandy):

'all that Kent he committed to his brother Odo, Bishop of Bayeux, a prelate distinguished by great liberality and worldy activity.'

It was shortly after the Conquest that William appointed Lanfranc to the Archbishopric. This, certainly, could not have pleased Odo who must have had designs on such a high ecclesiastical office.

In 1072 matters became worse when Lanfranc started legal proceedings against Odo, regarding the lands which he was accused of holding illegally. In the case of Stoke, the root cause of the problem went back to the days of the Danish invasions. During that period the owner of Stoke, the Bishop of Rochester, lost his lands here as a result of those troubles. It was never returned to him, and was later granted to Odo by King William. Odo, of course, had no intentions of parting with this or any other lands in dispute, and the upshot was a fairly long legal wrangle.

Proceedings started at a special assembly held on Penenden

Heath, near Maidstone. Judgement went against the Bishop of Bayeux and, at a later hearing, he was deemed to forfeit the lands in question. The Manor of Stoke was thus returned to the Bishop of Rochester.

After this loss of land, Odo appears to have turned his attentions to rivalling the king. News of these activities soon came to William's attention and a confrontation occurred between the two. According to Vitalis, Odo declared that he, a bishop of the church, could not be arrested by anyone outside the church. William is supposed to have replied:

'I do not condemn a clerk or a Bishop, but I arrest an Earl whom I myself created.'

Odo's arrest and imprisonment took place in 1085 and he remained in prison until King William's death in 1087. Odo was then released and had his lands restored. However, before very long Odo was plotting against the new king and this time became involved in an insurrection. On this occasion Odo was arrested after an attempt to hold Rochester castle against the Royal forces. This time he was exiled to Normandy and his lands in England were confiscated once and for all.

On the Peninsula this meant that all of the lands once owned by Odo fell into the hands of the king and, in most cases, remained there until the late twelfth century. From that time onwards, Odo's lands were given out in much smaller blocks. As a result of this, Manors appeared at Beluncle, Abbots Court (Little Hoo) and Windhill amongst others.

All these grand affairs of state, though, did not greatly affect the ordinary peasant on the land. They carried out their daily routine more or less oblivious of changes occurring. Theirs was a totally different life from that of the nobles about which we hear so much.

At the core of each manor would have been the various cottages – or, more appropriately, hovels – belonging to the peasants. Usually these were one roomed affairs made primarily of wood. In the middle of this room, there would have been a fireplace, the smoke from which was suposed to disappear out of a hole cut in the roof. Needless to say, it rarely did and at the height of winter a blazing wood fire would be barely visible through thick clouds of smoke.

To make matters worse, there would have been no windows. Glass was far too expensive for any peasant to possess. Instead, the cottages would have had holes cut into the walls which, in winter, would have been firmly shuttered. Furnishings inside the cottage would have been sparse, usually no more than a wooden table, a few rough chairs and some straw set aside for sleeping upon.

Also, somewhere around the centre of the manor there would have been a much larger house – the property of the lord or bailiff. Often of stone, these houses were palatial in comparison to the dwellings just described. The main feature of these houses would have been the great hall. This was used for meals, when a great long trestle table would have been set up for the servants, whilst the head of the house would have had a separate table at one end. At night the servants also slept in the hall. Other features of the manor house would have been a courtyard, kitchen, cellars, larders and a solar (or private living room for the lord and lady of the house).

An example of just such a medieval building still exists on the Peninsula. This is the rectory at Cliffe which was so much altered in the nineteenth century that it is hardly recognizable for what it once was. Nevertheless, a writer of that century did note it as having a large hall and solar. Originally built during the thirteenth century, at the request of Archbishop Langton, as a manor house, it became the rectory shortly after the Archbishop's death.

The foundations of another medieval manor house were excavated in 1963. This was an emergency 'dig' conducted by the local archaeological society. This occurred when the site of what was thought to be the Manor House of Little Hoo (more recently known as Abbot's Court) was threatened by gravel diggings. The excavations indicated a wooden building which was dated to the fifteenth century.

In many villages of medieval England, manors were farmed on the strip system. This was a highly inefficient farming method, where each of two or three fields were partitioned off into numerous strips. These strips were then divided out amongst the various tenants. Strips were not kept together but were shared out haphazardly, so that a man with thirty strips would find them equally shared over the three fields in an otherwise random pattern. Such a system was supposed to avoid any one villager getting more than his fair share of poor land.

It seems likely that at one time this was the system practised on the Peninsula but, soon after the period of the Conquest, a number of peasants began to acquire blocks of land in whole fields.

In some cases, tenants, finding there was not enough land to go round, moved completely out of the village and on to areas of hitherto wasteland. Here, they could set up a new dwelling and cultivate fresh lands. If they did this, they could disregard the practice of having strips. On the Peninsula this would have been comparatively easy as the population was fairly small (it was estimated at fifteen families per square mile during the fourteenth century – this estimate being arrived at on poll tax returns, and giving a population total in excess of 1,500). Subsequently, modern-day historians have concluded that the present-day field pattern on the Peninsula may date back some six or seven hundred years.

Certainly, there would have been a land problem in the various Peninsula villages, as the normal method of inheritance was 'gavelkind'. This meant that on the death of the father all land was equally divided between surviving sons. As a result, a piece of land, barely adequate to maintain self-sufficiency, would be useless once divided between, say, six sons. This, of course, would continue from one generation to another, forcing families to seek land elsewhere – usually in the wastes outside the village. This sort of situation seems to have occurred on the lands of John de Cobham in 1276, when lands held by his tenants were declared to be below subsistence level. The Cobhams, as will be seen in the following chapter, were fairly extensive landholders on the Peninsula.

Under the manorial system, the normal method of land transference was by payment of a fine to the lord of the manor. Sometimes, of course, the right of succession was disputed and the matter had to be taken to court. Usually, such disputes were dealt with in the manor court, but sometimes they were taken to much higher courts. The two examples quoted below both come from the courts of Westminster during the reign of Edward II.

The first example was tried in 1313 and regards land in Hoo:

'Stephen le Noble, plaintiff: John le Mounsh, senior, and

Agnes, his wife, defendants: 1 messuage* 6 acres of land in Hoo
St. Werbura.
    Right of Stephen admitted.
    10 marks paid for admission.'

The second case was tried in 1311 and relates to land at Cliffe:

'Between John, son of Adam Simon, of Cliue, plaintiff, and
Edmund, son of John le Clerk, of Clyue, and Alianora his wife,
defendant, of one messuage with appurtances, in Clyue. Edmund
and Alianora admit it to be the right of John; and for themselves
and the heirs of Alianora, grant to him and to his heirs, and
receive 40 shillings for the concession.'

The foregoing, then, has been a brief description of life on the
Peninsula during the early part of the Middle Ages. It was a life
governed by two major factors: the passing seasons and the
demands of the lord. If, at the height of the harvest, the lord
demanded two extra days' work on his demesne, then two extra
days' work he received. No serf was in a position to refuse – his
work was only of secondary importance. And of the non-serf
tenant, what freedom did he really have? Could he just up and
leave when things got worse? Perhaps, if he was young and had no
family commitments; but could an older man afford such risks?

Sometimes the oppressive nature of the manorial system
provoked confrontations. Such was the case in 1298 when a tithe
collector, at Cliffe, was attacked by a number of peasants. Tithes,
in fact, seemed to be a particularly troublesome problem at Cliffe,
as a later rector, John Bishopston, was actually besieged by
peasants in his own church.

Doubtless, there were peasants from the Peninsula who were
involved in the great rising of 1381. Under Wat Tyler the Kentish
peasantry laid siege to Rochester castle before marching on to
London. However, it is to the year 1450 that we have the clearest
indication that peasants from the Hoo Peninsula felt themselves
sufficiently oppressed to join a serious uprising.

The middle of the fifteenth century was a period of declining
wages, poor government and unjust taxes. The time was ripe for
rebellion and only a leader was missing. In 1450 a leader emerged.
This was Jack Cade, an experienced soldier, and a very proficient

* Messuage – a dwelling house with land attached to it.

agitator. The actual rising seems to have started in mid-Kent but
quickly spread, so that the chroniclers were able to record the
entire county as being up in arms.

On the Peninsula the rising had the sympathy of some of the
richer families. Among them was Richard King of Cooling and
John Turner of High Halstow. These two were both local
landholders and government officials for the area, and they used
their powers to call upon the local peasantry to join the rising. In
addition, they were backed by John Clerk, the priest at High
Halstow church, and Henry Spencer, chaplain to Cooling church.
One presumes that these two, with perhaps other local priests, used
the pulpit to enourage local involement in the rising. We also know
that John Pardour and Roger Smyth, both of Cooling, together
with Stephen Newlyn of High Halstow, also joined the rising. We
know all this because their names appear in official documents of
the time and we also know that their names would not have
appeared in these documents unless they had been fairly substantial local landholders. Doubtless, there were many others who
joined the rising but as they were mostly drawn from amongst the
ranks of the poor in classes their names do not appear in any
documents.

The rising, itself, was a failure. Cade's rebels occupied London
for three days. They were tricked into accepting pardons and
Cade's army dispersed. Cade was later killed and only a few of the
Kentish grievances were ever, really, remedied. Interestingly
enough, though, it was as a result of Cade's rebellion that attempts
were made to deal with at least some small complaints that had
arisen on the Peninsula in the years immediately prior to 1450.

Afraid that a similar uprising might again occur, King Henry
VI had a number of commissioners appointed whose task was
basically to investigate complaints made against corrupt officials.
In August 1450 one case was heard before the King's Bench which
concerned John Ram of High Halstow. Ram had been the steward
for Richard Islington, a local landholder, and was accused of a
number of crimes which all concerned abuse of his position as
steward.

One of the crimes for which he was indicted concerned a
labourer who possessed two horses worth thirty shillings. Ram
must have accused the labourer of stealing the animals for the man

fled the area and Ram took over the horses for himself. As the indictment stated:

'... the said John Ram, who continues to profit from them and ought to answer for them to the king.'

On this same occasion Ram was also accused of extorting sums of money from a number of local residents.

Ram's name also appears at an inquest held in September 1450, at Maidstone. Here he is again accused of extortion for it is stated that he threatened Stephen Devyll, of St. Mary's Hoo, with imprisonment unless Devyll paid him six shillings and fourpence. The inquest at Maidstone also saw an indictment made against Robert Clerk, parson of Ridley church, accusing him of taking three shillings from the church at Stoke. John Ram's employer, Richard Bruyn, also had an indictment brought against him. This was heard in August 1450 and accused him of illegally enclosing land which included a royal footpath.

Unfortunately, the outcome of these trials is unknown. As with so much of the material which dates from the Middle Ages the story is incomplete. We can only hope that John Ram, Richard Bruyn and Robert Clerk got their just deserts. However, this may not have been the case. In setting up the investigatory commission, Henry VI was not really trying to satisfy rightful demands, but simply to do the least necessary to prevent further risings. As such, John Ram and Richard Bruyn may both have received extremely lenient punishments.

Despite their activities in the Cade rebellion the peasants of the Peninsula were very pasive. Like peasants everywhere they just could not afford to rebel. The repression maintained by the lord of the manor was as nothing when compared with the repression of the passing seasons. If the peasant was away fighting, who was there to tend his crops and prevent him, and his family, from starving during the long winter months? As yet, the manorial system had a long time to run, and only met its match with increased industrialization and the growth of towns.

CHAPTER FOUR

THE MEDIEVAL CHURCH

'And let a tenth of every newly born animal be paid by
Whitsun; and of the fruits of the earth by the
equinox ...'

A reference to tithes.
Laws of King Edgar (956–975) taken from *Ancient
Laws and Institutes of England*, I. B. Thorpe (1840)

In this day and age it is almost impossible to fully understand the
importance accorded to the medieval church. It is no coincidence
that in most medieval communities – including those on the
Peninsula – the church was to be found in the centre of the village.
This was, after all, its properly accorded position in medieval
society.

Between the medieval church and its modern day successor
there can really be no comparison. The medieval church building
was rarely empty. On Sundays, and certain holy days, the nave
would be packed, with virtually every villager in attendance for at
least one service. A fair proportion also attended a second service.
Moreover, during the week, the church was not ignored. Apart
from well attended morning services, the church building served
other functions. It was the village meeting place, civic centre and
on occasions, the local market. The church, then, was totally
involved with the daily life of the community.

Even the idea of a parish church grew out of the manorial
system. During the early part of the Middle Ages, the ecclesiastical
authorities determined that every village should have its own
church, and the task of building these churches, if one did not
already exist, was entrusted to the local lord. As such, manorial
lords grew accustomed to thinking of the local church as their own
personal property, as such, they frequently claimed it as their right
to also appoint the parish priest. Such was the case at Cooling
where, during the fourteenth century, the church of St. James was
completely rebuilt by the Cobhams and the family appointed,
during the reign of King Edward III, Reginald de Cobham as
rector.

To the ordinary villager the church was something very special.
It was a building of immense beauty that contrasted sharply with

the small hovels set around. Open to their continual comings and goings, it was not the distant place tht so many of today's churches have become.

For the peasant with ambitions for his children, it provided the easiest means of climbing the social hierachy, and so escaping the drudgery of a daily hand to mouth existence. With the lord's permission, a son could enter the church. As a monk, or a priest, there was nothing, in theory, stopping this same peasant's son reaching the very top of society.

Inside the church building there would rarely be any stalls or other kind of seating for the ordinary villager. This was not the case when it came to the lord of the manor and his family. If they attended the village church then there would be special stalls. Such stalls can today be seen in the churches of Cooling and Cliffe. Usually, though, the nave would be one vast open space, with its floor strewn with rushes. Although palatial when compared with other village buildings – excluding the manor house – most medieval churches would have been dark and particularly cold during the winter months. The early Norman churches had only the very smallest of openings for the purpose of admitting light, and in many cases, glass was too expensive to glaze even these. Artificial light, in the richer churces, would have been provided by a multitude of candles but the smaller, and poorer ones, often went without. Heating, of course, was unknown.

Apart from the points already noted, the greatest difference between a church of the medieval period and a present-day church would have been the walls. The majority of modern-day churches are whitewashed. The medieval church wall was a riot of colour in comparison. Not only the walls, but the arcading as well, were painted in varying shades of reds, blues, greens and so on. The walls abounded in biblical scenes – for this was the poor man's bible. And, if one requires proof of this, there is no need to search further than the colourful wall displays to be found on the north and south transepts of St. Helen's church at Cliffe. These were discovered during the last century, when restoration work required removal of whitewashing and in its place was revealed some splendid murals.

It is now probably quite easy to imagine any one of the Peninsula churches as it was during earlier times. On Sundays, there would have been four or five different services with matins probably the best attended. Made up of both serfs and freemen, the congregation would question nothing of the service – what was good enough for their forefathers was good enough for them. They bestowed upon the church a great wisdom, whilst they themselves had a simple but touching belief in God and the rewards of Heaven.

The church service was in Latin – a language they did not even pretend to understand. Few in the congregation actually joined in, and instead, they were left to their own devices. Some would plan out future crops for the coming year, others would whisper amongst themselves, whilst the more devout would study the wall paintings.

On the Hoo Peninsula there are eight parish churches and in each case the original foundations can be dated to before the Norman conquest. The pre-Norman churches, however, were most probably of wood and the new Norman landholders were fairly quick in dismantling these and replacing them with much larger and sturdier stone structures.

However, the exact material of the Anglo-Saxon churches on the Peninsula must really be conjectural. The Reverend Hammond, vicar of Allhallows during the early part of this century, has suggested in his book *The Story of an Outpost Parish* that the original Saxon church at Allhallows was of stone. His evidence is mainly based on a piece of stonework discoverd in the south-west respond of Allhallows church. Hammond feels that the patterning on this is Saxon in design and was re-used from an earlier church. From this, Hammond goes a little further to suggest that the original Saxon church at Allhallows:

> 'would be quite small; perhaps a simple oblong, with or without an apse at the east end, such as could be accommodated with the present church, omitting the chancel and side aisles. There would be an entrance in the west wall, of which the arch, though a later one, shows the position; a small narrow window in the west wall also, and other small windows in the north and south walls.'
> (*Story of an Outpost Parish*, Hammond, 1928)

Whilst not disputing that a stone church did exist at Allhallows, I feel that the evidence that we have at the moment is far too restricted to draw any firm conclusions. However, if Allhallows did

PLATE 1   St. Helen's Church, Cliffe. One of Kent's largest churches, this
is an outstanding example of medieval church architecture.

PLATE 2   The interior of St. Helen's. From a drawing made during the
late nineteenth century. (*Archaeologia Cantiana* Vol. IX.)

PLATE 3   Allsaints Parish Church with its grand mixture of architectural styles. The south aisle dates to about 1190, the nave is earlier, but the windows are of the fifteenth century. The porch and bell tower are Victorian.

PLATE 4   St. Mary's Hoo. One of the Peninsula's deserted churches, an attempt is currently being made to turn this building into a house.

PLATE 5 An old print of Cooling Castle Gatehouse.

PLATE 6 The Gatehouse today. Towards the top of the right-hand tower can be seen the copper plate with its interesting inscription (see Chapter 5).

PLATE 7 The strange stone face of Grain Church. Some say it originates from an ancient pagan temple.

PLATE 8   Victims of marsh fever? The lozenged-shaped gravestones of
Cooling churchyard made so very famous by the novelist Charles Dickens.

PLATE 9 The tiny village school of St. Mary's Hoo. For the purpose of education this building finally closed its doors in 1947.

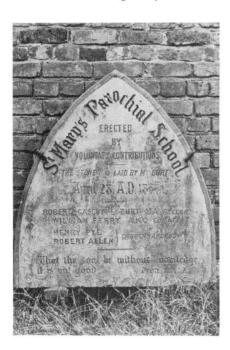

PLATE 10 The stone which commemorates the opening of St. Mary's Hoo school.

PLATES 11 and 12 Nonconformist chapels. (*Above*) Stoke Methodist Chapel from an early postcard. (*Below*) the Chapel at Grain.

PLATES 13 and 14 Two old postcard pictures of Stoke. In the bottom picture can be seen the old windmill which was demolished during the 1920s.

PLATES 15, 16 and 17 Further views of Stoke taken during the early part of this century.

PLATE 15

PLATE 16

PLATE 17

PLATES 18, 19, 20 and 21   Hoo during the period 1910–1920.

PLATE 18

PLATE 19

PLATE 20

PLATE 21

PLATE 22   A pre-1914 glimpse at life in Allhallows.

PLATE 23   Willow Place, Isle of Grain. This photograph was taken some-time prior to 1904. In the background can be seen the church before it was given a tower and the old village school.

PLATE 24   Grain Spit.

PLATE 25   Wall End. All these houses have now been removed.

PLATE 26   St. James's High St., close to junction with Green Lane.

PLATE 27   Home Farm, Isle of Grain.

PLATE 28   The days when the Hoo Peninsula had a passenger railway.
Taken before World War One, a train stands on the old Port Victoria
Pier. (Photo courtesy BP.)

PLATE 29   A further view of the pre-1914 Port Victoria Pier. This time the temporary structure of the Port Victoria Hotel can also be seen. (Photo courtesy BP.)

PLATE 30   The royal yacht is here seen tied up to the Port Victoria Pier whilst in the foreground the Corinthian Clubhouse can be seen. (Photo courtesy Chatham Public Library.)

have a stone church, then it might well have been as Hammond describes it. Moreover, if there were any other stone churches on the Peninsula during the Saxon period, then they too would not have been too dissimilar to Hammond's description.

The first church to be founded on the Peninsula was probably that of St. Werburgh, at Hoo. The early history of this church, together with its foundations by the Mercian King Ethelbald, has already been outlined and there is nothing we can usefully add here. It is also likely, however, that this same Mercian king also established the churches of St. Mary's Hoo and Allhallows. These would have been built as chapels to the church of St. Werburgh and would help explain the use of the word Hoo in St. Mary's Hoo and Hoo Allhallows (to give Allhallows its full name). However, as late as 1252, a document was produced referring to Allhallows as a chapel to the church of St. Werburgh. A further document of 1274 refers to St. Werburgh as 'the Mother Church' of the church at St. Mary's Hoo.

For the church at Cliffe we can actually give a date for its founding. According to an ancient Saxon charter, the church of St. Helen at Cliffe was founded by King Offa (of Mercia) in the year 774. This same Mercian king also chose the dedicatory saint.

Helen was a popular saint amongst the Mercians and a number of churches founded during Mercian domination of England were dedicted to her. Legend has it that she was the daughter of the British king named Coel – the 'old king Cole' of the nursery rhyme. Coel was supposed to have led a rising in this country during the period of Roman rule. The rising was put down by the Emperor Constantine who subsequently married Helen. The only part of the legend which is born in fact is the marriage of Helen to Constantine. In reality, Helen most probably came from Asia Minor. Her canonization is as a result of her supposed association with the discovery of the Holy Cross at Calvary.

So far then, we have accounted for the foundation of four churches on the Peninsula. The foundation of the remaining four probably did not come until the eleventh century and the period of peace between the end of the Viking raids and the arrival of the Normans. To this period probably belongs the emergence of churches on the Isle of Grain, Cooling, High Halstow and Stoke. Of one thing, we can be absolutely certain and that is these four churches, together with the original four, were all standing at the time of the Norman Conquest. For this we have two sources of evidence. First, the Domesday Book. Work on this started shortly after the Conquest and a long time before the Normans got round to building any churches themselves. Where the Domesday Book mentions a church it can only refer to a Saxon structure. Specifically, it mentions Stoke and Cliffe churches, whilst indirectly it mentions a further six as being within the Manor of Hoo. Without any doubt, four of these six can be firmly established as the village churches of Hoo, Allhallows, High Halstow and St. Mary's Hoo.

The second source of evidence is the surviving records relating to the payment of an annual fee to the See of Rochester during the period 1080–6. Amongst the churches mentioned as paying this fee, are those of Cooling, Grain, High Halstow, St. Mary's Hoo, Hoo and Stoke. This second source covers all the churches over which there is any doubt, and proves conclusively that the foundation of all eight churches on the Peninsula came prior to the Norman invasion of 1066.

It was some time before the Normans felt fully secure in their newly conquered territory, and so it was many years before the Norman lords felt able to build for the glory of God. In those early years they were too busy building castles and manor houses to worry about the after life. However, things began to settle down during the twelfth century, and during those years, a veritable building boom took place: a boom which saw the wholesale destruction of hundreds of small stone Saxon churches and their wooden counterparts.

Not only was this the pattern nationally, but it also describes what happened on the Peninsula. Although we know there were eight Saxon churches in the area, not a trace survived the Norman building boom (though the small piece of stonework at Allhallows may be the one exception). In most of the Peninsula villages a Norman church was built, and it is this structure which forms the core – be it much altered – of the majority of parish churches in the area.

Thus, the normal sequence of church building on the Peninsula was a Saxon church (of either wood or stone) followed by its replacement by a Norman styled church consisting of no more than a nave and chancel. Further, between the end of the twelfth century and the sixteenth century, each of the parish churches received numerous additions such as aisles, towers, new chancels and porches, but all appended in some way to the original structure.

There can be little doubt that it is St. Helen's, at Cliffe, which takes pride of place of the Peninsula churches. Not only is it the largest church in the area, but it ranks as one of the larger parish churches in the country, consisting, as it does, of a nave and chancel (totalling in length 149 feet) together with aisles, transepts and a tower.

A number of earlier writers have given the year 1260 as the date for commencement of the present church, but it would appear that an earlier date is much more probable. Architectural styles by the mid-thirteenth century had become slim and graceful, but the nave pillars in particular, are of the much more massive solidity of an earlier period. The alternative suggested date is somewhere around the year 1190.

During the thirteenth century, and here the year 1260 might usefully be considered, the church was more or less completely rebuilt around the late-Norman nave; specifically the building of the transepts and the lower part of the tower. Again, during the following century, the church had acquired suficient wealth for further extensive rebuilding work. It is to this period that we owe the present chancel (which was completely rebuilt at this time) together with the present-day aisles.

The last major alteration that took place in the Middle Ages was some work on the tower, when the upper stages were either rebuilt or completed. This, then, is more or less, the church as we have it today. Admittedly, there were some alterations made in the nineteenth century (a new east window and parapets to the tower together with the restoration of the transepts and nave) but these are remarkably restrained when compared with work that went on in other parish churches in the country, which virtually obliterated any medieval work.

It could be asked whether these thorough going rebuilding projects were continually necessary. The answer to this is fairly simple. Throughout the Middle Ages, architectural styles were developing. The solidity of the Norman period has already been mentioned. This, in turn, was followed by a much more graceful style – known as Early English – which emerged at the beginning of the thirteenth century. The following century saw a much greater elaboration of this style – hence it is given the name, the Decorated style. The final architectural style of the Middle Ages, which emerged from about 1450 onwards, was that known as Perpendicular.

Each style was an improvement on its predecessor. Thus, it became synonymous in the minds of men, that the old style was second best. Only the latest would do. If the whole structure could not be rebuilt then as much as possible should be remodelled. Here, then, we have the answer to why Cliffe church was so frequently altered. Nor, of course, would this have occurred if the money had not been there, as the result of numerous bequests of either the living, or from the wills of the dead.

A particularly interesting feature of the church at Cliffe are the medieval wall paintings. Located in the north and south transepts, they give a good clue to the splendour and colour of a medieval church. Concealed for many years by successive whitewashing of the walls, they were uncovered during the restoration work of 1864.

At one time the whole church must have been covered with such works, but now all that remain are those in the north and south transepts. The mural in the north transept shows the martyrdom of St. Edmund, whilst the south transept shows a figure of Christ. A further splash of colour can be found on the nave pillars with their red zigzagging. The origin of this may go back to the church's Norman builders.

The martyrdom of St. Edmund is by far the most interesting painting. It shows a series of scenes depicting the saint's death. Briefly, the story is that Edmund, king of the Angles, was defeated by the Vikings in battle. He refused to share his kingdom with these Viking non-believers, and so angered them, that they tied Edmund to a tree and shot him full of arrows. On being cut down from the tree his body was beheaded. Much of this story can be seen on the thirteenth-century wall painting. Edmund's body is tied to the three in one picture, with archers facing him; a further scene shows an axeman in the process of beheading the body.

Another treasure of the church at Cliffe, is the medieval stained glass. This is fourteenth century in origin, and can be seen in the two south windows of the chancel. Originally, it belonged to the east window of the chancel. When this was removed during restoration work, the glass was thrown away, but was later rediscovered and placed in its present position.

To my mind it is the church of St. Werburgh, in Hoo, that would look the most at home in any English village . With its soaring tower, rising sixty feet above the ground, it is the very epitome of English country life. Situated in the older part of the village, it has a number of earlier buildings clustered around, which gives this particular part of Hoo a certain timelessness. The rest of the village is out of character with its ribbon development of large housing estates and busy main road.

Work on the present stone church started during the thirteenth century, but it was greatly enlarged in the fourteenth and fifteenth centuries. So, what exists at Hoo is a chancel built in the Perpendicular style (c. 15th), together with the aisles. The fifteenth century work on the aisles took a rather curious form, for they were greatly widened, but the earlier fourteenth-century windows were kept intact.

The tower, originally, was Norman, but it has many fifteenth-century additions. It is likely that the spire also originated from this time as did the stair turret and battlemented top.

During the thirteenth century St. Werburgh church, with its lands and tithes, was appropriated by the Prior and Convent of Rochester. Although they were probably responsible for some of the rebuilding work that took place during this time, they left the encumbent without any support. So it was decreed in 1337, that the Priory should be responsible for supplying the priest at Hoo with his basic needs. These included wheat, barley, peas, porridge, straw and books for the church.

The most incongruous of the parish churches on the Peninsula is probably that of Cooling. Cooling is the second smallest of the area's villages and yet, it has, one of the largest churches – one not much smaller than St. Werburgh.

The reason is that although Cooling has always been a small village, it has had influential benefactors. Sometime in the thirteenth century, the powerful Cobham family acquired the manor and church of Cooling. For much of the middle ages, their family home was at Cooling castle, and as regular worshippers at the church, they would obviously wish for something grander than just a small village church. Money, therefore, came freely to Cooling church.

The church of St. James, at Cooling, consists of a lengthy nave and chancel with a particularly tall west tower. The original stone church appears to be Early English but it was more or less completely rebuilt during the fourteenth century and in the Decorated style. Later, a few Perpendicular style alterations were also made.

A particularly marked feature of this church are the twelve stone canopied stalls to be found in the chancel. They are considered by one authority to be the finest in Kent and they probably date from the reign of Edward I.

The three northern most churches of the Peninsula, Grain, Stoke and Allhallows, are remarkably similar. During certain periods of alterations it seems highly probable that the same master builder (architect) was employed in all three. In each case a Norman church was built, consisting originally of a small nave with a chancel; at about the turn of the twelfth century each church received side aisles. A study of the pillars in each of these churches (Grain church lost its side aisles in 1815 but the shape of the pillars can still be traced in the walls) show considerable similarities. Each has the same square piers whilst the arches show further similarities in the way they are pointed.

From the twelfth century onwards, however, the three churches take on very separate histories. In the fourteenth century the chancel at Allhallows was rebuilt and a clerestory added in the fifteenth century. The chancel at Grain was rebuilt during the thirteenth century.

The peculiar stump of a tower at Stoke was originally meant to be somewhat taller, and probably a steeple was to be set upon it. However, after completion of the second stage of the tower, during the fifteenth century, money for the final completion ran out, despite numerous bequests for the tower 'funds'. Some of these bequests make quite interesting reading:

'I will one cow to the making of the steeple of Stoke Church. John Peche, 1506.'

'My tenement in Stoke to be sold and the money to the reparacion of the steple of Stoke. Adam London of Greane, 1507.'

'To the edifying of the tower of Stoke church 3/4d. Sir James Barne, Vicar, All Hallows, 1512.'

'To the building of the stepill a kowe. Thomas Stephen, Snr.,
1522.'

There is an interesting tradition concerning the church of Grain.
This is, that it was originally built on the site of a heathen temple.
No proof exists, and the chances are that it has no basis of truth,
although it is further suggested that the strange figure, above the
inner south doorway of the church at Grain, came originally from
this same temple.

At one time Allhallows' church possessed a small chapel which
was dedicated to St. Mary Magdalene. The only visible indication
that this chapel once existed is the blocked arch at the east end of
the north aisle. The chapel, itself, stood to the north side of the
chancel and appears to have been built sometime during the
fifteenth century. For many years, the chapel was the burial place
for members of the two richest families resident in Allhallows: the
Copingers and the Pympes.

Sometimes referred to as a north chancel, the chapel of St.
Mary Magdalene is known to have fallen into decay during the
eighteenth century. Hasted, in his *History and Topographical
Study* (1760), refers to the structure as 'becoming ruinous, and the
communication to it from the church being stopped up'. Presumably, within a few years the chapel had fallen into such
extreme decay that its complete destruction was considered the
only viable course of action.

The church at St Mary's Hoo has been much restored. There is
some doubt as to whether there was an earlier stone-built Norman
church, for this one is a completely thirteenth-century affair
(though it could be built on Norman foundations). The chancel
was rebuilt in 1881, but the east window is part of the original
thirteenth-century church.

The church of St. Margaret, at High Halstow, appears to show
no material that would indicate a stone church existing earlier than
the twelfth century. The nave, in particular, shows signs of Early
English work. At this early stage in the church's career, it probably
consisted of little more than a nave and chancel. Aisles were added
about a century later.

During the fifteenth century a great deal of work was put into
the church, with much Perpendicular style additions. These include
remodelled aisles and chancel, and a new tower. When built, this

tower probably had a steeple, but this had been long lost. Proof
that the church had a steeple comes from a Dr. Harris writing in
1719. He describes the church in his *History of Kent* as:

'neat and good repair, with a spire steeple.'

A map of Kent prepared by Philip Symonson in 1596, also shows
the church as having a spire. Today the church is topped only by a
small pyramid. The fifteenth-century work on the aisles saw their
extension forward in order to form the two chapels. The south
chapel was dedicated to the Blessed Virgin Mary and the other to
St. James.

The churches of High Halstow and St. Mary's Hoo provide us
with an interesting piece of the Peninsula's history. Tithes have
already been mentioned as a cause of friction in Cliffe and,
between the encumbents of High Halstow and St. Mary's Hoo,
they were the cause of a legal wrangle. This occurred in 1476,
when John Mapulton, rector of High Halstow, brought a suit
against Richard Fletcher, rector of St. Mary, for the recovery of
certain tithes. A local ecclesiastical court granted the claim in
favour of John Mapulton.

The tithe system frequently put the medieval clergy in a difficult
position. As representatives of Christian virtues, they were
supposed to act in a benevolent fashion. Yet the system of tithes,
whereby they were entitled to a tenth of any man's produce, caused
innumerable difficulties. Frequently, disputes arose between priest
and peasant, or, as in the above, between different priests whose
parish boundaries were not clearly delineated. All this obviously
made it very awkward for the priest to carry out his job for,
however enlightened he might be, he relied heavily upon the tithe
system for it supplied his main income and source of survival.

The description of High Halstow church rounds off this short
tour of the Peninsula's eight medieval churches. It will be
remembered that the dominant style at High Halstow is the
Perpendicular, and this was the last of the medieval architectural
styles. Following this particular style, a new age was about to open
which not only heralded completely new architectural styles, but
also brought with it the end of feudalism, of which the church was
so much a feature.

CHAPTER FIVE

COOLING CASTLE

'Knouwyth that beth and schul be
That I am mad in help of the cuntre
In knowyng of whyche thyng
This is chartre and wytnessyng.'

Just outside the small village of Cooling lies the partly ruined remains of a castle. Nestling in wooded surrounds, and partially obscured by modern farm buildings, this relic of an age now passed must come as a surprise to any unsuspecting traveller.

The only part of the castle that now stands completely intact is the gatehouse. Lengthy stretches of the walls still remain, but these are badly cracked in places, and partially collapsed in others. Time has served the walls badly. That, and the siege cannons of one Sir Thomas Wyatt – but this part of the castle's history is best left until later.

The gatehouse, which at its very least is impressive, rises to a height of forty feet and is topped by battlements. All the innovations of medieval castle warfare are incorporated here.

The gatehouse has two flanking towers. Both are horseshoe shaped presenting rounded exteriors to any intending assailant equipped with siege engines. These oblique edges will simply deflect any missile aimed in their direction. In the waist of the tower small arrow slits have been cut, from which the defenders, together with others on the battlements, will be able to rain havoc on the enemy below. Moreover, both towers have what are known as machiolations. These are stone platforms projecting out from just below the battlements and which allow defenders to fire missiles, or drop quicklime, upon any attacker foolish enough to approach the base of the tower. Finally, the entrance itself had huge wooden doors and a long-since-removed drawbridge. The latter once spanning a moat which has now mostly dried out.

In a later age we would call this plethora of defences a good example of overkill; but it must be remembered that the weakest point of any castle was its entrance. If any enemy could approach

the wooden doorway with impunity he would very soon have gained
entry to that same castle. All these defences were to prevent just
this.

Incidentally, the small square holes to be seen rising up the sides
of the two flanking entrance towers are not some fiendishly clever
castle defence, but far less exciting putlock holes, these would have
been used by a medieval stonemason to carry wooden blocks upon
which rested his building platform.

The gatehouse also carries a most interesting and somewhat
novel inscription which explains the purpose of the castle. Sited
high up on the east tower it was placed there when the castle was
first built. Carefully cut onto copper plates, and subsequently
restored, it reads:

> 'Knouwyth that beth and schul be
> That I am mad in help of the cuntre
> In Knowing of whyche thyng
> This is chartre and wytnessyng.'

On passing through the main gateway one enters the outer
ward. This is completely enclosed by a curtain wall some of which
still stands to a height of twenty-seven feet. The main gateway is
situated on the south-west corner of this wall, and on each of the
other corners there are three further horseshoe-shaped towers.

The horseshoe tower design is a familiar feature of the
fourteenth century and a really fine example of it can be seen in
the two towers of Canterbury's West Gate. Interestingly enough,
Henry Yvele, the builder of Cooling castle was also involved in the
work on this same gate at Canterbury.

The outer ward of Cooling castle has a further gateway cut into
the curtain wall at a point midway on the west wall. This gives
access to the inner ward. Both wards are separated by an arm of
the moat which, at one time, would have been crossed by a
drawbridge. Nowadays, though, the moat at this point is non-
existent. Once again the inner ward is totally surrounded by a
curtain wall which has a tower at each of the four corners. The
gatehouse to the inner ward is not as impressive as the main
gateway, and in itself, only rises to a height of thirty feet.

In former times this ward would have been the more important
and would have contained the castle's living quarters, kitchens and
offices together with the all important great hall. Today the inner

court merely performs the function of garden to a modernized seventeenth-century house situated in the outer court.

In fact these modern-day features of the castle look rather incongruous. The massive gatehouse of the outer court is the rather extravagant entrance to a driveway. The house, itself, which looks more than a little out of place, fills most of the outer court and quickly destroys the romantic image with which most medieval castles are blessed. The garden of the inner court comes as a light relief with its weeping willows and patterned lawns.

The castle can be dated to the year 1381 when its building was initiated at the behest of John, the third Baron of Cobham. Cobham's reason for the construction of Cooling can be traced to the serious situation which then prevailed in the country.

In the early part of the fourteenth century England had been at the peak of its fortunes. An army had invaded France and inflicted several crushing blows against the might of the French. At battles such as Crecy and Poitiers the English longbow had reigned supreme. Furthermore, the Scots had been revenged, following the embarrassment of Bannockburn.

These successes, though, did not last long. The French, for one thing, changed their tactics and reversed many of the early English successes. By the year 1377, when the ten-year-old Richard II ascended the throne of England, things had reached a climax.

The chronicler known as the 'Monk of Evesham', gives a clear concise account of just how matters had deteriorated in that year:

'In this year, at about the feast of the birth of John the Baptist, there was a complete collapse of peace negotiations; for the French refused to keep the peace unless an agreement highly favourable to themselves could be reached ... During this same period the Scots burnt the town of Roxburgh ... Afterwards the French landed in the Isle of Wight on 21 August: when they had looted and set fire to several places, they took a thousand marks as ransom for the island. Then they returned to the sea and sailed along the English coastline continuously until Michaelmas. They burnt many places and killed, especially in the southern areas all the people they could find.'

A number of other important south coast towns were also attacked during this period, and the English government seemed quite impotent in dealing with the threat.

One of the first actions the new government took, in the name of Richard II, was the establishment of beacons along the coastline. Many in England were certain that the French would invade and these beacons were to be lit if such circumstances arose. Along the shore line of the Hoo Peninsula beacons were established at Cliffe and Hoo.

If things looked bleak in the first year of Richard's reign the situation soon became worse in the following years. French coastal raiders quickly became a habit that the south coast had to live with. These raiders even travelled up the Thames estuary.

In August 1380, a number of ships carrying French and Spanish mercenaries reached as far as Gravesend. According to the chroniclers of the time, they burnt and plundered most of the Thameside villages. At least one of these must have been on the Peninsula. Having reached Gravesend, the raiders soon put much of it to flame.

One of the landholders affected by this raid was John de Cobham, the third Baron of that title. His lands, stretching right across the Peninsula, and on towards Gravesend, must have suffered particularly badly. Leastways, he decided that this area of the Thames must be defended to stop any such occurrence happening again.

Work on Cooling castle started in the year 1381. In February of that year, Cobham received royal permission to crenellate the walls. To oversee the work, Cobham obtained the services of the country's premier architect, Henry Yvele.

Yvele was the king's master builder and was already employed in the reconstruction of Westminster Abbey. Among Yvele's other works can be included the highly praised medieval bridge at Rochester and the superbly proportioned nave of Canterbury Cathedral. The employment of Yvele clearly showed that Cobham was intent on perfection and not just the throwing up of four walls enclosing the occasional building.

By November 1382 the great gatehouse to the outer ward had been completed. Accounts, preserved in the British Library, from that period of the castle's history, show that the mason employed on the gatehouse was one Thomas Crompe and he received the sum total of £8 for his work.

Following the gatehouse the curtain walls were completed and in September 1384 it is further recorded that two masons, Thomas Crompe and William Sharnall, received the sum of seventy-eight shillings as payment for 650 quarters of lime. The castle was not completed for another year, however, for it is in September 1385 that Crompe received his final payment.

Henry de Cobham was head of the most powerful family in Kent and a family of numerous associations with the Hoo Peninsula. As a family they took their name from the village of Cobham where, in the twelfth century, Serlo de Cobham was recorded as being a landholder. By the next generation they had acquired the manor of Cobham and from that point onwards rarely looked back. They continuously acquired land in the style of a twentieth-century property developer.

One branch of the family acquired the manor of Beluncle and was associated with it until 1708, when Richard Cobham died without male issue.

By the fourteenth century, the main branch of the family had accumulated property at Hoo, Stoke, High Halstow, Cooling and Grain.

In 1355 Henry de Cobham succeeded to the family title. According to the poet Gower:

'He was worthy, patient, pious, and liberal, provident and just, strong in the virtue of manners; he was not an indirect but a true friend of the kingdom.'

Four years later he joined his first expedition to France, where he gained much credit for the family name. shortly after his return, he founded a chantry at Cobham which gained him the epitaph of 'Founder'. To help keep this chantry for all time, he granted certain lands for its upkeep. These lands included 250 acres of marshland situated near Hoo and an estate in High Halstow.

When Richard II came to the throne, Henry de Cobham was immediately ordered to repair the defences of Kent, ready to repel the expected French invasion. At this time he was engaged upon essential work on the upkeep of the manor house at Cooling, in order to make it habitable. This repair work seems to have been going on for quite some time. In 1384, a London plumber received forty-eight shillings and ten pence for work carried out whilst in 1379 Thomas Wrek, a London mason, received £5.

The original plan for the manor house at Cooling was dramatically altered following the French raid upon Gravesend and the various Thameside villages. Cobham obviously felt that an undefended manor house was useless in this time of crisis. Instead of continuing repairs on the manor house, work started on a full blown castle.

Shortly after the completion of Cooling castle, Cobham became involved in a second major building project – the reconstruction of Rochester bridge. It is not known exactly when a bridge first spanned the Medway at Rochester but it is known that the Saxons built just such a bridge. It was this bridge which, by the fourteenth century, was in such a state of disrepair that the citizens of Rochester determined on the building of a new bridge. A decision which was much easier said than done, for there was just not sufficient money.

Repairs to the old Saxon bridge had been carried out by levying a sort of tax on the surrounding areas. Thus, a document of A.D. 960 states:

'The seventh and eighth piers belong to the men of Hundred of Hoo; six beams to lay and four yards and a half to plank.'

Quite simply, this meant that for any repair necessary to the seventh and eighth piers the money had to be raised from amongst those living in this Hundred. Cliffe, together with a number of other parishes, was responsible for the ninth pier and Grain (as part of the Hundred of Chatham and Gillingham) took part responsibility for the second pier. This rather complex system, though, had long shown its inabilities to raise sufficient monies for even fairly minor repairs; much less the complete rebuilding of Rochester bridge.

It was at this point that Henry Cobham came forward, together with another Kentish knight – Sir Robert Knolles. It was Sir Robert who chiefly financed the building of the bridge whilst Cobham donated land in trust whose rent was to be used for repairing the bridge in future years. In fact, the revenue from these lands is still collected by the Rochester Bridge Wardens trust and has been used to finance new bridges in 1856, 1914 and 1970.

Amongst the lands so donated by Cobham was the Manor of Rose Court, on the Isle of Grain, and Eastwick marsh in Hoo. At this particular time Rose Court consisted of 895 acres which stretched right across the whole northern part of Grain, and extended as far south as the church. In 1399 the rent paid to the Bridge Wardens amounted to £10 13s. 4d. of which most came from sheep farmers who paid 3d. per sheep grazed on the lands of Rose Court Manor. Today, Rose Court is still owned by the Bridge Wardens and is the only piece of land on the Peninsula which has remained in the same hands for nearly six hundred years.

Baron de Cobham had now entered the busiest years of his long life. As a powerful nobleman, he must have been heartily sickened by the great decline in the country's affairs of state. Even in that same year, as work had been started on Cooling castle, many of his own tenants had joined the great peasant uprising which had marched on London demanding better government and freedom from their landlords.

Highly disturbed by these events, Cobham, together with other powerful noblemen, gently wrested the reins of power away from the hands of King Richard and his advisers. Unfortunately, this government of noblemen faired little better and Richard was soon returned to power. Cobham, not unexpectedly, suffered. His death was ordered by hanging, drawing and quartering. In an age of brutality this was the normal sentence passed on traitors, but a spark of humanity did exist, and in view of Cobham's great age – he was now in his eighties – this penalty was revoked and he was banished instead.

In 1396, Cobham found himself on that rather pleasant island of Jersey. It is unlikely that Cobham noticed any pleasantries here, for he was undoubtedly pining for his confiscated properties. However, banishment lasted but a few years. In 1399 Richard II was removed from power by Henry Bolinbroke who was later crowned as Henry VI. The Cobham's property was returned in full and Henry de Cobham was allowed to die peacefully in January 1408.

The Cobham fortune now passed into the hands of Henry de Cobham's much married granddaughter, Joan de la Pole. Within eighteen months of the Baron's death, she had outlived three husbands and was married to a fourth. This was Sir John Oldcastle who took the title of fourth Baron de Cobham on marrying Joan. He is probably the most well known of all the residents of Cooling castle.

He has partly been made famous by William Shakespeare. One

of the playwright's better remembered characters, is the drunken, cowardly, garrulous and obese Falstaff. This same Falstaff was modelled on Sir John Oldcastle.

However, one must quickly add that Sir John had little in common with Falstaff. Sir John Oldcastle was a fine soldier, slim of build and careful in drink. The association is greater in Shakespeare's mind.

Shakespeare presumed that because Oldcastle and the young Prince Hal were friends of youth, then Oldcastle must have been one of the Prince's early drinking companions; a mistake which could not be further from the truth. In the original manuscripts to the play *Henry IV*, Shakespeare went so far as to name the Falstaff character Oldcastle. Thus, when the play appeared Oldcastle's descendants wrung this apology out of Shakespeare and it appears at the end of the play:

'... Falstaff shall die of a sweat, unless he already be killed with your hard opinions; for Oldcastle died a martyr, and this is not the man.'

Oldcastle was strongly prompted by religious convictions. He was a Lollard and a supporter of Wycliffe. He firmly believed that many of the teachings of orthodox catholicism were false. Upon his marriage with Joan de la Pole, he introduced a Lollard preacher into the churches of Hoo, High Halstow and Cooling. It is this which first got Oldcastle into trouble with the religious authorities. The suspect preachings of this priest were sufficient to have all three parishes placed under a two-day interdict.

In 1414, Sir John was arrested for his unorthodox religious beliefs and was sent to the Tower of London. Even his friendship with Henry V could not save him. Instead he arranged an escape and returned to his Lollard friends.

Temporarily safe, he began to organize a rebellion to overthrow his one time friend. It was not a well thought out affair, and little attention seems to have been given as to how the country should be run if the rebellion proved successful. The rebellion, as planned, was two pronged. Lollards from all over the country were beseeched to march on London and meet outside the city walls, from whence they could quickly take possession.

At the very same time a daring plan was put into operation to kidnap the entire royal family during the Christmas festivities of 1414.

Agents of the king soon discovered the plot. The would-be kidnappers were quickly arrested whilst a large army was assembled outside of London. Many Lollards on their way to London were arrested en route, whilst those who reached the rendezvous point soon found themselves under attack. The one-sided fight was over almost as soon as it began.

Oldcastle managed to escape arrest and remained free for another two years, when he was eventually captured and the death sentence passed upon him. Unlike his predecessor, he was unfortunate enough to have the sentence carried out. In the Autumn of 1417, he was hanged and then burnt whilst still hanging in St. Giles Field, London.

Amongst those rebels of 1414, there was only one man from Kent, and he came from Dover. This is of interest because it was the Lollard preacher in those three churches of the Hoo Peninsula, that first got Oldcastle into trouble with the authorities. It was a sacrifice in vain for the preacher was unable to influence the people of the Peninsula to take the Lollard preachings to their hearts.

CHAPTER SIX

CLIFFE: A SMALL MEDIEVAL TOWN
AND ITS CONNECTIONS WITH THE MONKS OF
CANTERBURY CATHEDRAL

'The towne is large, and hath thereto a great parish
church: and (as I have beene tolde) many of the houses
were casually burned (about the same time that the
Emperour Charles came into this realme to visit King
Henrie the eight) of which hurt it was never yet
thorowly cured'.

Lambarde: *A Perambulation of Kent* (1576)

Throughout the Middle Ages the roads in Kent were in a totally
abysmal condition. Heavily rutted tracks in summer, and quag-
mires during the winter months, they clearly hindered travel rather
than encouraged it. Most people doubtless reached the conclusion
that by far the quickest way between one village and another was
simply to avoid the roads.

For the transportation of bulky goods, rivers provided a much
faster and more efficient way of access to most important towns
and villages. Moreover, while this state of affairs continued it
meant that the Hoo Peninsula, bounded by the Thames and
Medway, was far less of a backwater than it was later to become.

On the Peninsula, the original location of many village
settlements was the result of a desire to be near either one of the
two rivers. Medieval Hoo St. Werburgh, for instance, was on
the banks of the Medway but modern development has drifted
further north-east and away from the original village site.

Cooling, too, was once much closer to water. A creek, running
from the Thames, once ran close to the village. It is also the
existence of this creek which explains the positioning of Cooling
castle. St. James village, on the Isle of Grain, together with
Allhallows, were also sited as the result of the rivers.

However, it was Cliffe which most directly benefited from its
proximity to water. During the Middle Ages it appears to have
reached the status of a town and was endowed with a small port.

Evidence for this comes from a number of sources, and a not inconsiderable clue to the existence of a port is the presence of the now land-locked Wharf Lane. At some time, this tiny lane once meandered its way to a small anchorage with a number of boats carrying out a regular trade.

Documentary evidence for some sort of harbourage also exists. In March 1301 it is recorded that King Edward I ordered a general levy of ships to be sent into Scottish waters as part of his campaign to subdue this constant thorn in English diplomacy. Amongst the ports mentioned, was that of Cliffe which had to supply one vessel.

As such, no medieval navy existed. If a king required ships for a campaign, he had to hire them from merchants. There was no such thing as a purpose-built warship; instead ordinary trading vessels – known as 'cogs' – were given a simple conversion. Basically this consisted of placing a tower-like structure on the fore and aft ends. With this additional height the ship would be crammed with archers who would be able to fire a rain of arrows upon enemy vessels.

This conversion, however, made the merchant ships extremely unstable – not that they were particularly stable, or even seaworthy, to begin with. The medieval merchantman was a tub-like affair whose length was only a little greater than her beam. Battle tactics were merely an extension of land warfare. Archers would oppose archers, as combatant boats converged upon each other. Once they were in close proximity grappling hooks were thrown out and soldiers boarded. Hand to hand fighting then ensued.

In a number of following campaigns, Cliffe was called upon to supply vessels for warlike purposes. In 1346, the English mounted a successful invasion of France, which culminated in a spectacular land victory at Crecy. Prior to this campaign Edward III had assembled a fleet of well over 1,500 vessels, and it is recorded that amongst this truly massive fleet were two ships from Cliffe.

Throughout the Crecy campaign these two ships were doubtless involved in transporting supplies. They may also have been involved in the blockade of Calais.

Following this victory at Crecy, Edward turned his armies towards the important coastal town of Calais. For an entire year, the town remained beseiged by the English and a large part of the fleet was engaged in preventing the French supplying the town by sea. Eventually, Calais fell and was to remain in English hands for over two hundred years.

In the year 1326, Cliffe was mentioned as a port and, again, in 1380, when it was recorded as having one 80–ton vessel stationed there. Finally, in 1417, two ships were hired from Cliffe as part of Henry V's successful campaign in France.

Although the port of Cliffe was no doubt small and the town no more than an outsize village, it definitely had some wealth accruing to it. The size, and frequent rebuilding of the church, would indicate this. The church, itself, is not an inconsiderable clue to the riches once associated with Cliffe. As one of the largest parish churches in the country, it was the frequent beneficiary of a great many gifts bestowed upon it by the moderately rich merchants who inhabited the town. How else can one explain the frequent, and expensive, additions to the church? Only a town church could afford these luxuries. As a town, Cliffe was growing throughout the early Middle Ages, and as the town grew, so did the parish church.

Like other towns, Cliffe also had a fair. Fairs, during this period were very important and would have gone a long way in attracting trade. With a port, and close to a number of towns with large fairs, a number of traders would probably have been attracted to the town. During the period of the fair, such varied goods as Continental wines and cloth, as well as oriental spices, would have been on sale to anyone wishing to purchase.

Depending on how popular the fair was, the streets of Cliffe would have been crowded with people vying with one another to buy and sell. Local landholders and traders would benefit in particular, being able to sell, or exchange their produce, at competitive rates. For those less intent upon commercial transactions, there were many varied entertainments such as ballad singers, dancing bears and jugglers.

The exact date for the establishment of a fair at Cliffe is much in dispute. Alternative dates include 1109 and 1327. However, many years ago the *Chatham News* produced a document which purports to be the original royal charter setting up a fair at Cliffe. It is dated 1247:

'Know ye that we have granted and by this Our Charter have confirmed to Sir Hugo of the Dead Sea the parson of the church at Cliffe, the request that he and his successors be allowed to hold a Fair at Cliffe every year lasting three days, that is to say on the Vigil, the feast, of St. Aigidius unless that fair fall on the night next to another fair. Wherefore we are willing to allow the Fair with all liberties and free customs pertaining.'

This, of course, is a translation from the Latin.

As towns go, however, Cliffe's pre-eminence was remarkably short lived. A number of writers give a disastrous fire, in the year 1520, as the reason for the town's decline. In this one conflagration, most of the town is supposed to have been completely gutted. Once started, such a fire could easily have got out of control, for nearly all the buildings would have been of wood and other combustible materials. Up to the present time, however, there has been no archaeological evidence for such a fire. Further, there is a second view that Cliffe's decline as a town was not the result of a fire, but other factors instead. These include the silting up of the port, constant flooding of the surrounding farmlands – due to poor maintenance of sea walls, and the increasing incidence of 'ague' or 'marsh fever'. Of this last named factor, much more will be said later.

However large Cliffe was during the Middle Ages, it was still very much dominated by agriculture. Merchants and craftsmen would certainly have lived in the town, but by far and away the largest number of inhabitants would have worked on the land.

Throughout this period, the largest single landholder in the area was Christ Church Priory and it is because of this that we know more about Cliffe, during this period, than any other part of the Peninsula. The monks were not only literate, but excellent record keepers, whose records are still contained in the library at Canterbury Cathedral.

Writing at the end of the eighteenth century, Edward Hasted tells us:

'The Manor of Cliffe, with its appurtenances, was given to the Priory of Christ church, in Canterbury, in the time of the Saxon heptarchy, and its possessions were afterwards increased here by King Offa, who in the year 791, gave Dunmalingdene (Mallingden), and by Queen Ediva, who in the year 860, gave Oisterland (Stoke), and by other benefactors to it.'

In the year 1070 there was a general redistribution of church property when Archbishop Lanfranc took away some of the priory's lands, leaving them with the Manor of Cliffe but not Oysterland, in Stoke, which he retained for the see of Canterbury. In the survey of church property known as *Domesday Monarchorum*, we are told that the revenue from the Manor of Cliffe was used by the monks for the purchase of material for clothing.

All the manors of Christ Church Priory were placed into geographical groupings, for which one monk, known as a warden, was responsible. He made regular visits during which he advised on buying and selling, as well as upon the crops to be sown and when. The day-to-day running of the manor, however, was left in the hands of a bailiff. This was not a monk, but a lay person specially employed for the purpose.

Similar to the other manors on the Peninsula, there were villeins and cottars who rendered services in exchange for land. The monks, however, preferred to exchange these services for a money payment. For instance, one document in the Cathedral library records that a number of serfs were responsible for transporting hay to the nearby manor of Meopham. This service was replaced by an annual rent of £1 13s. 2¼d., paid by the peasants.

The monks, like so many other landholders, found the use of unfree labour quite uneconomic. A villein, forced to work on the lord's land not only worked slowly, but most inefficiently. It was far quicker to employ wage labourers and exchange the services the villeins performed for a money rent.

The monks of Christ Church, like most medieval monks, were pioneers in agriculture. Unlike their neighbours, they just did not grow the first crop that came to hand. They approached the whole process in a much more scientific way. By making a careful study of crop yields and market prices, they produced the most economic crop for the soil in question.

During the thirteenth century barley (a crop useful for brewing!) appears predominant with oats, rye, beans and peas also being grown. However, with market fluctuations, the acreage under wheat, barley and oats were all steadily increased during the following century.

Animals rarely feature as a major part of the manor at Cliffe – with the exception of sheep. The monks of Christ Church were among the larger landholders in the country owning manors throughout Kent and in most of the south-eastern counties. As such, they could afford to have each manor specializing so that some manors tended to be arable and others pasture. The manor, of Cliffe, however, was an exception. Some of its area was marshland which was used extensively for sheep. In 1322, the manor of Cliffe was recorded as possessing 120 sheep. These sheep would not only have been kept for wool; their milk would have been used for the manufacture of cheese and butter, whilst the dung was a valued manure.

In small numbers, horses would also have been kept for draught purposes. Cows, oxen, poultry and pigs may also have been kept, again, in small numbers.

The monks of Christ Church were also noted for the great effort they put into land reclamation. A number of their manors were situated close to marshlands, and whenever this was the case, they built numerous seas walls, in order to extend the lands they owned. The Manor of Cliffe was no exception in this respect. A number of the early sea walls in the Cliffe area are the result of work carried out under the supervision of the monks.

Land reclaimed in this fashion was usually rented out, and subsequently enclosed, rather than being farmed directly by the Priory. Indeed, as time went on, this side of the manor's income became by far the most important. From the late fourteenth century onwards, increasingly large amounts of land were leased out for rent, and more frequently, this land included parts of the original manor.

The tendency to lease lands at Cliffe, rather than to farm them direct, was symptomatic of a more serious problem. The monks of Christ Church Priory had lost their zeal for agricultural progress, and they were now quite happy to let their lands be farmed by others, whilst they merely collected the rent. This was eventually to create certain problems for the once prospering town of Cliffe.

The monks had taken responsibility for the sea walls and, with their virtual retreat from direct farming, they had less incentive to maintain the walls. The result was frequent floodings of the Cliffe marshes. These floods not only affected the farmlands but must also have encroached upon the town itself.

Already Cliffe was heading for economic decline. The floods merely exacerbated the problem. The better farmers began to leave the area and, with the silting up of the port, they were soon joined by the merchants. Both trading and farming, in this area of the Peninsula, now entered into a long period of stagnation. Maybe there was a fire in 1520 but this almost certainly was not, as Lambarde was informed, the cause of the town's decline.

CHAPTER SEVEN

THE REFORMATION

'Mary, Mary, quite contrary,
How does your garden grow?
With silver bells and cockle shells,
And pretty maids all in a row.'
The Protestant version of Mary Tudor's reign.

For England, the sixteenth century was the age of the Tudor monarchs. Of all the Tudors, though, it is Henry VIII who seems to have dominated the century. With the creation of the Church of England, and the break with Rome, he clearly paved the way for the Protestant revolution which could not but influence his three successors of the Tudor lineage.

King Henry's far-reaching decision was the result of the Pope's refusal to grant him a divorce. In the end, the divorce was achieved, but only after the creation of a much more pliable Anglican church. In doing so, however, the king also opened the floodgates to a religious controversy which was already in the process of tearing apart many of his continental neighbours.

Protestantism was nothing new to the Hoo Peninsula. When Sir John Oldcastle occupied Cooling castle for that very short period of time, he introduced a Lollard* preacher to the area. The success of his Lollard preachings can hardly be said to have had a considerable effect, though.

Under Henry VIII, church services ceased to be in Latin, whilst the monasteries were dissolved and their lands confiscated. On the Peninsula the lands of Christ Church Priory at Cliffe, together with those of Boxley Abbey at Hoo, fell into the hands of the Crown. Within a short space of time these lands were sold to new owners. The Manor of Cliffe came into the hands of the Cobhams, whilst the Manor of Little Hoo became the property of the Wyatt family.

The drift towards Protestantism was slow and carefully controlled whilst Henry VIII remained alive. His successor was his

---

* Lollardy being one of the earliest Protestant movements in England.

only son, Edward, who was rather sickly and much too young to run the kingdom himself. Instead, affairs of state were directed by a council of regents, headed at different times, by two Protectors. Both were very strong for the Protestant cause and firmly drove the kingdom of England in this direction.

For twenty years, England was set on a path leading her further and further away from the Roman Catholic church. Then, in 1553, Edward Tudor died and he was succeeded by his elder sister – Mary Tudor.

Mary had remained, throughout her life, a Catholic and it was not long before she made her feelings felt. Not only did she reverse all of the religious laws made during the reign of Edward, but she also reintroduced Latin into church services, and accepted the supremacy of the Pope in all things religious. Moreover, she showed her complete contempt for the Protestant community by burning over 300 sympathizers of that religion.

At the outset of her reign much of this could only be guessed. It was known that she was a Catholic, but it was not clear how far she was prepared to go. Anyway, she was the legitimate heir to the throne and few were prepared to stand in her way. However, when she also declared that she was going to marry Prince Philip of Spain, this, for many people, changed matters overnight. It was one thing to have a Catholic monarch, it was quite another for her to be taking her orders from the most militant of all Catholic countries.

Kent, in particular, resented such a move. A great number of the populace had clearly accepted the new religion and were hoping that Mary might be tolerant towards them. When news of the Spanish marriage reached them, their thoughts immediately turned to that country's use of the inquisition and its general treatment of Protestants. For them, the Spanish marriage had to be stopped at all costs.

A man who was particularly opposed to the Spanish match was one of the Peninsula's new landowners, Sir Thomas Wyatt. Wyatt had every reason for hating the Spanish as, for seven years, he had been fighting them in the Netherlands and was well aware of the way they dealt with those who professed any other religion than that that of Roman Catholicism.

The Wyatts were a northern family, who had recently settled in Kent. Their first land purchase in the area was the Allington castle estate, which was followed shortly afterwards by the acquisition of the lands belonging to Boxley Abbey. Determined upon making their way within the county Sir Thomas Wyatt's father had married into the Cobham family and, as a result, Sir George Brooke Cobham – the then occupier of Cooling castle – was Sir Thomas's uncle.

At this period in time, rebellion was the only way to change government policy, and it was with this view in mind, that Sir Thomas Wyatt joined with a number of other like-minded nobles, and they began to organize four simultaneous risings to take place in Devonshire, Leicestershire, Hertfordshire and Kent. Originally planned for March 1554, the risings were brought forward to January, when news of their plans began to reach government circles.

It was because of the change of date that the risings, when they did occur, were very badly co-ordinated. In Devon and Leicester the flag of rebellion was very poorly supported and the organizers decided to abandon the whole affair. In Hertfordshire there was no rising at all. It was only in Kent that there appeared to be any chance.

On January 25th, Wyatt left Allington castle and raised his standard in Maidstone. Being market day the town was particularly crowded. Within the hour he expected to know just what chance his enterprise had, and within the hour, he had his answer. Flocking to his support came well over 1,500 men ready to die for the cause.

From Maidstone, he marched to Rochester where he gained even more supporters. Amongst those who joined him at Rochester, were probably a number of persons living in Stoke and Grain who are recorded as having joined the rebels.* Soon he could rely on two thousand supporters, with more promised from Tonbridge and Sevenoaks. Things looked promising.

Whilst he was quartered at Rochester, Wyatt received news that some of the London militia had been despatched and were on their way to deal with him. On January 29th this force left Gravesend, moving towards Rochester. Under the command of the ageing Duke of Norfolk it was a force of over 600 trained men, bringing with them some six cannon.

* See *Tudor Rebellions*, Anthony Fletcher.

At Strood, the two opposing forces confronted each other and to an onlooker it must have seemed that high casualties would be the order of the day. But all this changed in a moment. Before Norfolk's men had taken up their positions,the cry of 'we are all Englishmen' went up and, by prearranged signal, the London militia defected to the rebel cause. Not a shot was fired or a sword raised in anger.

With this massive desertion, the road to London now lay wide open and, it is possible, that had the rebels speeded along this road they might well have been able to capture the city. That they did not, was supreme military folly. Instead, Wyatt directed his followers towards the small village of Cooling where they proceeded to lay siege to the castle.

It is unlikely that we will ever know the real reason for this manoeuvre. Many suggestions have been made. These range from the idea that Wyatt wanted revenge against his uncle, Lord Cobham, for not supporting the rebellion, to the view that Wyatt wished to use Lord Cobham as the figurehead of the rebellion.

All this, however, is speculation. The facts are as follows. Wyatt had, for several days, been trying to persuade Lord Cobham to join the rebellion, but he chose not to get involved. Indeed, when the Duke of Norfolk arrived at Gravesend, he received considerable assistance and advice from Cobham.

By marching on Cooling, Wyatt was clearly taking a serious gamble. Once on the Peninsula, he was in a natural cul de sac. If the loyalist supporters in Kent – and there were still a great number despite Wyatt's success – could have mustered some sort of army, Wyatt would have been trapped.

So it was at eleven o'clock on Tuesday, January 30th that the rebels took up position outside the walls of Cooling castle. Amongst the weapons they brought were two of the cannon acquired from Norfolk's men, which they immediately placed close to the castle's main gate.

Only one original account of the siege exists. This is in the form of a letter written by Lord Cobham shortly after the siege ended. It is addressed to Queen Mary and is obviously an attempt to explain to her why Cooling castle only managed to hold out for six hours.

Cobham was most concerned that his version of the siege should be the first to reach the Queen. This certainly comes out in the instructions placed on the front of the letter:

'To the Quene's most
excellent majestie,
hast hast,
post,
hast,
with all dyligence possible,
for the lyfe,
for the lyfe.'

And Cobham must have believed it was 'for the lyfe' as dereliction
of duty, which his failure to hold Cooling castle could easily be
called, was the cause of many a noble's execution. Even after Mary
read Lord Cobham's version of the siege it did not prevent him
from being thrown into the tower once the rebellion was quelled.

Anyway, according to the letter:

'The rebells perceyving that I was bent to resystt theym,
havyng ii great pieces of ordynnaunce that the Duke of Norfolk
left amongs them at his retyre, layd battery to the gate of the
castell and the gates, that without that they could never have
prevayled, at which assault iiii or v of my men were slayne and
divers hurt, which did so discorage the comons that I had thyre
assembled for the servyce of your highnes, that they begonne to
mutiney and whisper one to another.'

Throughout the letter, Lord Cobham clearly emphasizes his limited
resources, the strength of the opposition and his own determination
to defend the castle for his Queen. The end, though, could not be in
doubt:

'... defendying my castell with such power as I had untill v of
the clok after none, having no other munycions or wepons but iiii
or v hand gones, pykes, and the rest blakbylls ...'

Despite all this, Cobham continues that he and his sons were ready
to die for Mary, but with the drawbridge battered and burnt down
and his men unwilling to fight, further resistance was quite useless.

So, at five o'clock that afternoon, Cooling castle fell to the
rebels. That night Lord Cobham was given his chance to write and
despatch his letter, whilst the rebels encamped around the castle
grounds.

The following day, Wyatt and his fellow rebels started their
march on London. Queen Mary, in the meantime, used the days
between Norfolk's defeat and Wyatt's arrival outside London, to

rally her supporters. She made a brilliant speech at the Guildhall which went more than a little way to pursuade many a wavering Londoner to support her cause.

As a result of these events, Wyatt found every one of London's gates shut against him. Had he been able to arrive earlier, this might not have been the case and the whole story of his rebellion would have been so different.

For a few days the rebels marched aimlessly around the walls of London, before making an attack upon Ludgate. The Londoners stoutly defended this gate and Wyatt was eventually forced to surrender.

The Queen chose to pardon most of the rebels but not, of course, its leaders. Wyatt was subsequently beheaded on April 11th. Of Lord Cobham, his letter seemed to do him little good as he was thrown into the Tower where he used the opportunity to scratch his name on one of the windows – this can still be seen today.

Cobham, however, was eventually pardoned but he never returned to his castle at Cooling. It was no longer fit to be occupied. The walls, together with the living accommodation, were too badly damaged. The once proud castle was left unrepaired. Over the years decay set in and helped undermine some of the remaining walls.

A further insight into this period can be gleaned from a series of documents concerning the village of Allhallows. At the beginning of this century, when the Reverend F. J. Hammond was the vicar there, he discovered the Churchwarden's Account Book for 1555 to 1649, together with the Overseer's Book for 1601 to 1760.

It appears that these two documents had been lying at the bottom of an iron safe in the church vestry. Previous encumbents must have known of the safe, but took no interest in its contents. So, for well over a century, these papers remained undisturbed until rescued from further oblivion by the Rev. Hammond. When he found them they were little more than soggy rags. In some places the writing had completely perished but, in others, it miraculously remained virtually as clear as the day it was written.

The Overseer's Book will be left to a later section, for it is the Churchwarden's Accounts which interest us here. Mainly, they contain notes concerning all church income and expenditure. From them, we can see the exact needs of a small village church during this time. Moreover, as this account book covers much of the period of the Reformation, we can also see what demands were made upon such a church by various royal decrees.

During this time, the accounts tell us that the church was mostly financed through bequests of land made by parishioners. No mention is made of church collections. Once given to the church, these lands were rented out. In 1556, the following list of receipts appears in the account book:

'Received of

Thomas Franke for farme of x shepe	. . .	iis iid
John Davy for farme of shepe	. . . . .	iis iid
John Smyth for farme of xxvi shepe	. . .	vis vid'

Another source of income was as payment for services carried out by the church. One such example comes from the year 1555:

'Received of Mystrys Copynge for her dowters
buryale   . . . . vis viiid'

Against this was set the expenditure. Money was needed by the churchwarden for maintenance of the church, purchase of vestments, wine and so forth, and even washing of the surplices. The latter can be seen for an entry in 1555:

'To Peter's wyf for wasshyng the lynnen   . . . . . iid'

Sometimes quite considerable maintenance work had to be carried out. Once again, from the year 1555, it appears that repair work was carried out on the church steeple. At this time Allhallows had quite a large tower with a steeple and the foundations for this have been found in the churchyard. The work carried out in this year including the shingling of the tower steeple (at a cost of 4/9d); the mending of the bell frame and the purchase of fifty boards.

The year 1555 was the first year of the account books. For Queen Mary, this was the second full year of her reign and the first in which she had Protestants burnt. Before the end of her reign there were to be over 300 burnings of which, 58 took place in Kent. Despite the fact that she had been on the throne for such a short period, she had done much to revert England to Catholicism.

During the reign of King Edward varying decrees had meant the wholesale destruction of church fineries, such as elaborate crosses, church plate and statues. The large stone altars had also been torn out and replaced by simple tables which were supposed to resemble much more closely the one used in the last supper. In some churches the chancel was totally blocked off and the communion table taken to the centre of the church where it was deemed more able to bring the rituals of church service closer to the congregation.

Under Mary all this was reversed. Stone altars were rebuilt, certain items of church plate had to be repurchased for the Catholic style service, and crosses and saints' statues were once again permitted. All this, of course, put the small parish churches to a great expenses for which they received no help from the government whose demands they were carrying out.

In 1557, the services of the local stone mason was purchased in order to build a stone altar to replace the one removed under Edward. The following year saw another expenditure related to the Reformation:

the rowde and mary and john   .   .   .   xxviiis   viiid

The rood was an elaborate cross (rood being old English for cross) which was placed at the very centre of the church. In the case of Allhallows, it was situated on the chancel screen. Carved and painted, it would have dominated the church. To the right of the cross would have been a statue of the Virgin Mary, and on the left, St. John the Evangelist.

For the Protestants these were prime targets and an order had been made in 1547 for the removal of such images. The rood at Allhallows dated well back to the fifteenth century and there are references to it in 1468.

The revival of roods, though, was very temporary, for under Queen Elizabeth they were once again ordered to be removed. At Allhallows, all that remains is the fourteenth-century screen upon which it once stood, together with the sockets in which the rood and accompanying images were once placed.

At Cliffe, there are also a considerable number of references to a rood. Though here it was much grander than at Allhallows, and was accompanied not only by the statues of John and Mary, but also there was a complete rood loft on top of the special rood screen. The rood loft was a beautifully carved gallery designed to fill the space above the screen. It no longer exists, as it was torn down during the reign of Queen Elizabeth. Part of the rood screen, though, does still exist, together with the doorway that once led to the loft.

In the same year as Allhallows gained its new rood Queen Mary died. She was succeeded by her Protestant half-sister, Elizabeth. Determined to reintroduce the Protestant religion she also desired not to completely alienate the Catholic community. Religious changes during her reign came much more slowly and, as such, were much more acceptable to the majority.

Many of the changes in her reign came not as a result of direct royal decrees, but as instructions from local bishops. Thus there were dramatic changes in some dioceses but little alteration in others. Rochester was one of the former. In 1559, Elizabeth appointed Edmund Gheast as Bishop of Rochester. He was a puritan, and from 1559 to 1571 when he was transferred to Salisbury, he issued a number of injunctions directly affecting every church in his diocese.

During his twelve years as Bishop, Gheast insisted that all encumbents should be examined upon the Epistle to the Corinthians whilst no man was allowed to take communion unless he knew the Creed, the Lord's Prayer and the Ten Commandments.

In 1565 he issued the following injunction:

'Item, that the chalice of every parish church be altered into a decent communion cup therewith to minister the Holy Communion, taking away no more thereof but only so much as shall pay for the altering of the same cup. And they said cup to be provided in every parish within the said diocese by or on the side of the feast of Saint Michael the Archangel next coming after the date thereof.'

This injunction goes to the very heart of the Reformation. Under Queen Mary and the return to Catholicism the communion wine had been withheld from the laity. For the Protestants this was one of their major reforms, as they wished to see the laity partake of the communion wine. To do this they also felt it necessary to replace the Catholic communion chalice, which only a priest used, for a cup which could be used to administer the wine to everyone.

In Allhallows this injunction was obeyed immediately for, in the same year as the bishop issued his instructions, the following expenditure appears in the account book:

'For reformyng the chalys intoa cuppe according to the Lord
Bysshop's commandment . . . . iiis vd

Unfortunately, Allhallows church no longer possess its Elizabethan
cup, for it appears this was sold in 1835, with an Elizabethan
paten. It is possible, though, that the cup was not unlike the two
other Elizabethan communion cups still to be found on the
Peninsula. These are at Grain and St. Mary's Hoo. Both are rather
small and plain in design. The one at Grain was made by the
London goldsmith whose mark was IP.

Mention has been made of the paten at Allhallows which also
dates back to the reign of Elizabeth. A paten was the shallow dish
upon which the bread for communion was carried. For Catholics
the communion bread consisted of thin wafers, but for the
Puritans, the thin wafer was replaced by ordinary household bread.
Because of this, patens had to be greatly enlarged to carry the
larger bread. This may be the reason why, in 1576, the churchwarden records the purchase of a paten.

It is because of this enlargement of patens that a prereformation
paten is extremely rare. In fact, there are only fifty of them still
surviving in this country. One of these, interestingly enough, is at
Cliffe church. The paten here may have been used for church
collections, as it is slightly damaged. It is of gilt with an enamel
inscription and dates to the year 1520.

Probably as a result of Bishop Gheast's influence, the churchwarden at Allhallows records, in 1571, the sale of church
vestments. These were a particular target of the Puritans, as they
were considered to have much too close an association with the
Catholic church.

On the accession of Queen Elizabeth, communion tables were
once again in vogue. In 1564, it was declared that altars should be
replaced by communion tables placed in the centre of the church.
It was left to the bishops to actually enforce this. Some chose to do
little more than publicize this decree while others, such as Gheast,
did their best to see these instructions were faithfully carried out.
As a result, it is not long before the churchwarden's accounts start
to contain references to the communion table.

It is this same communion table which now stands at the back
of the church. The Rev. Hammond rescued it from the Rose and

Crown inn, where it had been in use for many years after the church had finished with it.

To make sure these injunctions were carried out, Bishop Gheast sent representatives to all of the parish churches in his diocese for this purpose. They would have spoken to the vicar and church-warden, checked his accounts and examined the church. Again, we know this happened in Allhallows as it incurred a few expenses for the churchwarden to enter up into the accounts.

It was also during the Reformation period that the church walls began to be whitewashed:

1582: 'Item to Weekes the mason for whitewashing the church, in part payment . . . . viiis'

Of course, we do not know if this was the first time the church was whitewashed as it may have been carried out during Edward's reign. It is probable though that the church wall had various paintings which the whitewashing was intended to cover up. Certainly we know the church had some colourful decorations, as these can be seen on some of the nave pillars.

With the reference to whitewashing, we have virtually reached the last of those items in the accounts which refer to the reformation. The rest of the entries mostly refer to the daily running of the church. One exception appears in 1604, when the new Prayer Book was purchased.

From the accounts, we have seen the church go through a series of changes. It started off as a highly decorated and rather ornate building, with services in Latin and a congregation who neither participated, nor understand what was going on. By the end of the period, the congregation not only participated but probably had a much greater understanding of the service. Nevertheless, all the fineries of the church had been removed and the building of which the parishioners were once so proud, had become somewhat drab.

As time proceeded, however, the pendulum was inclined to swing back again. In the seventeenth century the altar table returned to the chancel and some fine altar rails were purchased. Later, a carved Jacobean style pew appeared for the use of the vicar. But all this came slowly,, and it was not until the beginning of the following century that the church received its much heralded pulpit.

Times were once again changing.

CHAPTER EIGHT

THE DUTCH IN THE MEDWAY

'The last shot and the last charges of powder in the battery were fired at the hindmost ship – a laggard fire ship which had been afraid to run the gauntlet, and which blew up off Oakham-Ness before she got out of sight.'

From: *The Dutch in the Medway* by Charles MacFarlane.

Early on Monday, June 10th, 1667, inhabitants on the Isle of Grain awoke to find their island invaded. England's long-time enemy, the Dutch, had sent a large fleet into the Thames and the crew of one of these vessels had landed and captured the island.

Already these same islanders – for in those days Grain was truly an island – had witnessed the comings and goings of the Dutch warships on the Thames. With no English opposition, the Dutch had simply sailed into the Thames and taken control of this, the most important river in the entire kingdom.

Certainly it must have come as quite a shock for the inhabitants of Grain to find themselves so occupied. There seemed no rhyme or reason for this action. Nevertheless, the one thing they could be sure of was that they were occupied, and by a pretty desperate bunch of seamen. Nobody's life seemed secure on that particular Monday. Were they all to be killed and their homes put to flame? Perhaps some of them had seen the fires on Canvey Island, just across the Thames, which had been visited that previous night by these same invaders.

Some of the more stout-hearted villagers made their way to Cockleshell Beach and began waving their arms in order to attract the attention of the troops stationed just the other side of the Medway, at Sheerness. From Sheerness a boat was quickly despatched. From the frantic villagers standing on Cockleshell Beach, they soon learnt of the Dutch landing. With great haste, the boat recrossed the Medway and Sir Edward Spragge, commander of the troops at Sheerness, was informed. Spragge responded by despatching twenty-six musketeers of the Royal Scots to deal with the landing. A battle royal looked to be in the offing.

While these events were occurring, local tradition holds that the Dutch seamen revealed the purpose of their landing. A number of them marched towards the church where they showed their intentions of looting it. On arrival, they found that the building had a massive oak door which was carefully secured. Prepared for such an eventuality, they began to smash at the door with axes and anything else handy. But the door held well against this onslaught.

In all probability it is at this point that lookouts warned their comrades of the approaching musketeers. At any rate, these foreign invaders did not finish their task of breaking into the church; nor did they stay to fight the English rescuing force. The reason for their hasty retreat was probably lack of time. All Dutch seamen had been given specific instructions that looting would be punished by hanging. Aware that any delay might cause their superiors to suspect a landing, the Dutch seamen decided to return to their anchored vessel. No fight then, occurred on Grain, and the only memento of the Dutch visit is a much battered oak door, which can still be seen at the village church.

For a number of years the Dutch and English had been at war. Basically, this hostility grew out of commercial rivalry. Both countries were competing for trade in similar areas of the world, and, in addition, both disputed the other's right to freely use the high seas. Inevitably, clashes occurred which eventually, as the seriousness of these clashes increased, developed into a full blown war. A number of battles took place between opposing fleets but, on the whole, neither nation emerged as victor. By the beginning of 1667, the Dutch were looking round for a bold stroke which would both bring the war to an end and also give them victory. It is with these two aims in view, that the Dutch government sanctioned plans for a fleet to sail into the Thames in order to create as much damage and disruption as possible. In addition, it was felt that this same fleet might dare a sudden raid on the Medway itself, and catch a number of English warships still at anchor.

Throughout the early part of that year, the various components of the plan were assembled. English seamen, with a knowledge of the Medway, were recruited from Dutch gaols; a force of over 3,000 soldiers was assembled, whilst a fleet of well over eighty ships (including fifty-one men-of-war) was made ready.

To confuse the English as to the purpose of all these preparations, a small squadron of ships began a series of raids on the Firth of Forth area. The English, suitably misdirected, kept a number of ships in the North, to forestall any future Dutch action in this area.

It was on June 4th, 1667, that the main Dutch fleet left the port of Schooneveld and headed towards the Thames estuary. After a short delay, due to storms, the fleet arrived at the mouth of the Thames on Friday, June 7th.

Most of the Saturday was taken up with discussing a number of alternative plans. Eventually it was decided that a small squadron should be detached from the main fleet to sail further up the Thames, as far as Gravesend. The attraction was a number of merchantmen known to be anchored in the vicinity of Cliffe.

On Sunday the 9th, this sqaudron, under the command of Lieutenant-Admiral Willem van Ghent, made its move. However, news of Dutch intentions proceeded Van Ghent and the merchantmen were quickly moved to a safer anchorage. That night van Ghent anchored close to Canvey Island where a number of Dutchmen landed, setting fire to houses and stealing some sheep. Originally, van Ghent had intended to return to the fleet still anchored at the mouth of the Thames. However, on board the flag ship was Cornelis de Witt, political adviser to the fleet, and he persuaded van Ghent to take action against the garrison at Sheerness, and then, if successful, to proceed as far up the Medway as possible.

So, later on the same day as Grain received its Dutch visitors, van Ghent's squadron prepared to capture the fortress at Sheerness. In many ways, this was not a particularly difficult task. Works on constructing this particular fortification had only just been started, and, in addition, it was hopelessly undermanned and quite incapable of withstanding the concerted attack which the Dutch now mounted.

At about 5 o'clock on that Monday evening, a number of Dutch men-of-war closed in on the fortress. The defenders tried to put up what resistance they could. However, of the sixteen guns, only seven were probably mounted. The recoil action of the others drove them straight into the earth.

With little return fire, the Dutch ships had no difficulty in maintaning a withering and accurate fire, which was soon to take a toll of the defenders. The outcome of the battle was a foregone conclusion made even more certain by a landing of eight hundred Dutch soldiers a mile away from the fortress. Not wishing to be outflanked, the defenders at Sheerness left their guns and retreated.

It was the possibility of such a raid on the Medway that had originally led to the building of the fortress at Sheerness. The fortress there was also to perform the dual purpose of providing defence for a new naval dockyard to be built at Sheerness. The first step in all this, unfortunately, was not taken until 1665 when the exact site for the dockyard was chosen by King Charles II himself. On this occasion the diarist Samuel Pepys accompanied the monarch:

> '1665 August 18th. To Sheernesse, where we walked up and down, laying out the ground to be taken in for a yard to lay provision for cleaning and repairing of ships, and a most proper place it is for this purpose.'

From this date onwards, the building of the fort went ahead at a very slow pace, even though numerous attempts were made to hurry things along. Lack of labour and finance, though, meant the fort was substantially unbuilt by June 1667.

Further along the Medway, the defences were equally as neglected. A small fort at Swaleness had been allowed to fall into decay, whilst two small forts, Bay and Warham sconces, close to Upnor, had also been allowed to fall into disrepair. It was only at Upnor that a building remained capable of putting up any sort of resistance. This was the castle which had been built during the reign of Queen Elizabeth. But even this building was partially used for storage and most of the garrison had been paid off.

There was, however, one other line of defence. This was a chain stretching across the Medway from Gillingham to Hoo Ness. Once raised, it was supposed to prevent any hostile shipping proceeding further up the Medway. The first records that exist referring to a chain on the Medway, date to 1585, when one was fitted at the instruction of Sir John Hawkins at a cost of £170 5s. 0d. This, though, had long been dispensed with and, at the outset of the year 1667, no chain existed. During the early part of the year, however, it was decided that, as a Dutch raid upon the Medway was a distinct possibility, a new chain should be commissioned.

Although it was supposed to have been completed by April, this new chain was not ready until late in May. Constructed by John Ruffhead, anchor smith of Chatham dockyard, at a cost of

£573 8s. 11d. it was a massive affair weighing in excess of fourteen tons. Each link was something like two inches thick and to ensure that the whole thing could remain above water it was attacked to four floating stages.

Once completed, the chain was installed across the river. At both the Gillingham and the Hoo Ness end, simple cranes were installed to draw the chain tight in time of need. Finally, the chain was strengthened by a number of ship's cables.

Mention, in this chapter, has already been made of Samuel Pepys, the famous seventeenth-century diarist. At the time of the Dutch raid, he was closely connected with naval administration being, as he was secretary to the Navy Board. As such, his diary for the year 1667 gives us a clear and unique insight of the events occurring on the Medway.

On June 10th, the day of the Dutch attack on Sheerness, Pepys journeyed to Gravesend on naval business. On this occasion, it was his job to collect first hand reports of Dutch movements on the Thames. For this day he made the following note in his diary:

> 'Down to Gravesend, where I find the Duke of Albemarle (Lord High Admiral) just come with a great many idle lords and gentlemen, with their pistols and fooleries; but the Bulwark not able to have withstood half an hour had they come up; but the Dutch are fallen down from the Hope and Shellhaven as low as Sheerness, and we do plainly at this time hear the guns play.'

Panic seemed the order of the day at Gravesend, for he continues:

> 'I find the town had removed most of their goods out of the town, for fear of the Dutch coming up to them; and from Sir John Griffen (Governor of Gravesend fort) that last night there was not twelve men to be got in the town to defend it ...'

It was not until the 11th, that Pepys actually learnt of the loss of Sheerness and he records the news as being very sad 'and puts us in great fears of Chatham'.

With the Dutch in possession of Sheerness, and in control of the Isle of Sheppey, some very hasty measures were taken to strengthen the River against further progress by van Ghent. The chain was duly raised and three large ships – the *Unity*, *Mathias* and *Charles V* – were placed close to the chain in order to prevent the Dutch capturing and lowering it. In addition, a battery of guns was hastily constructed on either side of the chain. As a further defence, a number of ships were placed along the banks of the Medway to further hinder the Dutch.

Clearly, though, there was much confusion as to Dutch intentions and near panic had taken over the Admiralty. Troops were marched first to one destination, then to another. At Gravesend Pepys records:

> 'And strange our confusion that among them that are sunk, they have gone and sunk the *Franklin*, one of the king's ships, laden with stores to a very considerable value; they speak also of another ship laden to the value of eighty thousand pounds sunk with the goods in her ...'

On Tuesday 11th, a small number of van Ghent's ships tentatively sailed up the Medway to test out the defences, and to clear a navigable channel through a number of sunken ships. This day of respite was taken as a sign that the Dutch had decided that the Medway was too well defended. From Lord Albemarle Pepys hears this news:

> '... all is safe as to the great ships against any assault, the boom and chaine being so fortified; which put my heart in great joy'.

However, this good news was soon dispelled for on the 12th he records:

> 'Ill news is come of the Dutch breaking the Chaine at Chatham; which struck me at the heart ... Home, where all our hearts do now ake; for the news is true, that the Dutch have broke the chaine and burned our ships, and particularly the *Royal Charles* ... and the truth is I do fear so mach that the whole kingdom is undone ...'

The news was certainly true. On June 12th, van Ghent left Sheerness and sailed down the Medway. Before leaving the fort there, he had the guns carried on board his own ships, whilst the fort itself was completely dismantled.

The Dutch squadron sailed line astern down the narrow passage of the Medway as far as the chain. Here they were met by considerable opposition as they came within the range of numerous guns. Indeed, at one point, van Ghent decided that retreat would be the best and only possible course. However, he reckoned without one of his captains – van Brakel. This particular captain had been imprisoned the previous evening for disobeying instructions. Van Brackel saw his opportunity of gaining freedom and, as a result, he volunteered to take his ship up to the chain and engage the *Unity*, one of the ships guarding the chain. Whilst he was doing this, a number of fire ships were to be rammed on to the chain in an effort to break it.

The plan worked perfectly. While van Brackel engaged the *Unity*, the second of the fire ships, upon hitting the chain, sailed straight over it. The chain had not actually broken, but had been freed from one of its floating stages and was lying far below the tide level. With the chain no longer in place, the fire ships then sailed on to the *Mathias* and *Charles V* and set each alight. In the meantime the *Unity* was captured with minimal losses.

All further resistance was soon quelled and, as the smoke began to subside, the Dutch found a major prize within their grasp. The one hundred gun *Royal Charles,* described as one of the finest ships in the world, was anchored totally abandoned and quite unprotected. All the Dutch had to was simply board her and strike her flag. Pepys later described the loss of the *Royal Charles* as the most serious incidence of the whole raid. His diary entry for June 22nd describes the event:

'... that nothing but carelessness lost the ship, for they might have saved her the very tide that the Dutch came up, if they would have but used means and had had but boats ... That the Dutch did take her with a boat of nine men, who found not a man on board her – and her laying so near them was a main temptation to them to come on.'

The capturing of the *Royal Charles* was that day's final action by the Dutch. Overnight, they anchored in the Medway and finalised plans for the following day. With five fireships left, it was decided to use them in one all out effort to cause as much damage as possible.

It was not until noon the following day, that the Dutch embarked on the final phase of their plan. The fireships, together with an escort of heavily armed men-of-war, sailed as far as Upnor. Here further passage was disputed by the guns of the castle, with those of a number of hastily constructed batteries.

A hotly contested battle ensued during which the Dutch fireships were able to sneak past and make for a number of suitable targets. Placing themselves alongside the *Royal Oak, Royal James* and *Loyal London* they soon had these vessels ablaze. Of this incident, one naval officer later wrote:

'The destruction of these three stately and glorious ships of ours was the most dismall spectacle my eyes ever beheld, and it certainly made the heart of every true Englishman bleede.'

This final fling brought the Dutch endeavours to an end. They decided to go no further. This was partly because of the opposition they now faced from the guns at Upnor, as well as a number of heavy guns on the opposite shore. Further, the Dutch had now expended all their fireships.

On the 14th, van Ghent's squadron carefully sailed its way down river and into the Thames estuary, where it rendezvoused with the main Dutch fleet now anchored off Sheerness.

This, though, was not quite the end of the Dutch enterprise. Having rubbed English noses well and truly in the dirt, the Dutch government still required its fleet to keep up the pressure. Thus, the fleet did not return to its home port but remained anchored in the Thames and proceeded to blockade the river, thereby preventing supplies reaching London. This blockade continued well into July when a peace treaty, most unfavourable to England, was signed between the two countries. The Dutch raid had certainly served its purpose.

To these events on the Medway, the inhabitants could be little more than spectators. With the sound of gun fire constantly drawing their attention, few would have inclined to carry out their normal day's work. Instead, they headed for the many vantage points around the Peninsula that allowed them to observe the battle. Some of the men may have volunteered their services to fight the Dutch and some may have been conscripted. The majority, though, were just distant spectators watching a sight, the likes of which they would never see again. For one Peninsula inhabitant, the events did not prove as distant as he might have hoped. Perched on the high ground just beyond Hoo village he became the victim of a stray canon shot.

When Samuel Pepys visited the scene of the Dutch raid on June 30th he was told of this unfortunate man's death:

'But here (Chatham dockyard) I was told that in all the late attempt there was but one man that I know killed on shore; and that was a man that had laid upon his belly, upon one of the hills on the other side of the River, to see the action; and a bullet came and took the ground away just under his belly, and ripped up his belly, and so was killed.'

The Dutch raid is obviously a fascinating subject for the historical novelist, presenting the writer with a great deal of the excitement which is so necessary for the success of such a book. One piece of fiction, written as early as 1845, by Charles MacFarlane and entitled *The Dutch in the Medway*, gives a totally different picture of the activities of the Peninsula dwellers. For one thing, the women are carefully taken to the centre of the Peninsula, somewhere near Cooling, where it is considered they will be safest. The men in the meantime band together ready to repel any Dutch invaders. A number go off in search of weapons and eventually return from Cooling Castle where:

'... they had found a few old brass guns; and in some other places nearer the water they had furnished themselves with a few old ship guns, and with a considerable quantity of powder and suitable ball. A few sailors had joined them, after explaining the confusion which prevailed in the upper part of the river, especially at Upnor catle, together with the faults of construction, and the other causes which would render the fire of that castle so very useless a waste of powder and shot, these mariners had recommended the construction of a battery on the bank below Hoo, where, on account of sandbanks and shallows, the Dutch would be obliged to sail very close to the shore.

'... As they worked might and main, a number of peasants came and joined them from Stoke and from other villages. Women and children, and tottering old men, came flocking to Hoo and to the river bank beneath, bringing spades and mattocks, and meat and drink, and then lending their hands to the digging.'

Throughout what I imagine is June 12th the battery is constructed and, sometime on the following day, is ready for use. It is on this particular day it comes into operation. The Dutch have successfully passed over the chain and have also destroyed a considerable amount of shipping. Having expended all their fire boats they return down river, passing close to Hoo:

'As the foremost Dutch ship approached, sounding her trumpets in triumph, and apprehending no further hindrance or harm, our heroes stood to their guns with lighted matches, and when she was at the closest to the bank, without any proceeding shout or cheer they gave fire. Every ball told, and hit the ship between wind and water. The trumpets left off trumpeting that there was a rent in England's honour, and there was evidently astonishment not unmixed with confusion among the crew. They could neither recede not cast anchor and stop, for, at that spot there was not room enough for the ship to swing; so they put out sweepers and glided past the battery, which they could still only see by the smoke of its guns; but before they get out of reach their ship was hit again and again ...'

A large portion of the book is devoted to this entirely fictitious action. The Dutch, on learning that a battery was preventing their safe return down river, landed a force of soldiers to carry the battery. Ready for such a move, the improvised army made ready to repel the Dutch; a manoeuvre which proved entirely successful.

'The Dutch, dreading to be left aground by the receding tide, had, after some of their habitual hesitation, resolved not to land any more men or make any further attempt at carrying the battery, but to drop down with the current and get out of reach as quickly as possible. And they now came down in close line, without any insolent trumpetings. Each ship as it passed presented her broadside so near to the battery that every gun fired ... had a smashing effect on her sheathings; but not one of the many guns discharged by the Dutch did the least harm on the shore, for they were too near too the bank and in much too great a hurry to depress their guns.'

Finally the Dutch, after receiving a great many injuries, passed out of range of the battery. In triumph, those who had manned the battery marched back to their wives and children.

'There were tender greetings, and overflowing joys expressed by silent tears, when our returning Kentish men met their wives and children on this spot. Every loving wife among them had thought that her own husband at least must perish; but here they were all back, husbands, brothers, and sons, and no one killed, and scarecely six slightly wounded among them all.'

In fact, from reading MacFarlane's version of the raid on the

Medway it seems more like an English victory rather than one of England's greatest defeats.

As well as the above MacFarlane also gives some interesting descriptions of the area, which were probably true of the time he was writing:

> 'The district was rarely visited by the stranger; and although it was so near to Chatham, the sight of an officer or any servant of Government was so uncommon and distasteful, that the mischievous little boys generally pelted such a visitant with Hoo mud.'

Once the Dutch were out of the Medway, the cost had to be counted and the stable door securely bolted to prevent any further repetition. In his official capacity of secretary to the Navy Board, Pepys was sent to Chatham on June 30th to get a complete picture of damage done. Faithfully he records this visit in his diary:

> 'Thence by barge, it raining hard, down to the Chain; and in our way did see the sad wrecks of the poor *Royal Oak, James* and *London,* and several other of our ships sunk by us; and several of the enemy's, whereof three men of war, that they could not get off and so burned. We did also see several dead bodies lie by the sides of the water. I do not see that Upnor Castle hath received any hurt, though they played long against it, and they themselves shot till they have hardly a gun left upon the carriages, so badly provided they were; they have now made two batteries on that side, which will be very good and do good service.'

To repair the damage, Prince Rupert, the famous cavalry leader of the English Civil war, was despatched to the Medway in his capacity of senior admiral. It was his job to give overall direction to the new defences to be built on the river.

Long term plans were now made for the construction of forts at Gillingham, Sheerness and Cockham Wood. As well as these, a number of batteries were to be placed along the banks of the Medway. More immediately, the existing defences were strengthened and a new chain was placed across the river.

The three new forts were the main backbone for the redesigned defences. All three were similar in principal, being designed to protect both the Medway and the landward side of where they stood. Work on the forts started as soon as was practicable, and all were under construction by 1669. In September of that year, Major Manley, in charge of the actual construction of the forts, wrote to the Duke of Lennox concerning progress:

'... this summer there hath beene made a goode progress in ye works att Sheerness and the forts att Gillingham and Cockham Wood side, both these are like to have towers in them which besides keeping of stores are to bee a retreat to the soldiers in case of necessity; they are to have fifty pieces of cannon in each of them, the least of which is to carry twenty-four pound ball.'

Of these three forts, only the one at Cockham Wood rightly falls into the area of this book, built, as it was, just inside the parish of Hoo and about a mile down river from Upnor castle. Construction of this fort was not completed until the year 1700. Designed by Sir Bernard de Gomme, an eminent military engineer of that period, it had some forty-eight guns when eventually completed. Nowadays, little remains of the fort except for a few stones merely marking the site where it once stood.

On the Isle of Grain, three gun batteries were constructed. These were Buda Battery, Middle Battery and Quaker's Battery and were all situated on the beach area immediately in front of Smithfield Marshes. These were all fairly simple affairs being little more than earth ramparts thrown up to protect a number of guns.

On Hoo Ness a further battery was constructed to give further protection to the chain. After the Dutch raid, the chain had been renewed and it probably remained until about 1688, when the Navy Board decided that the chain would serve no useful purpose as the new defences were quite adequate.

It is, in concluding this chapter, interesting to note that the lesson that the Dutch had taught England was soon forgotten. The defences hardly reached the turn of the century before planners decided that economies could be made in the Medway's defences. On numerous occasions garrisons were reduced and guns transferred elsewhere. In 1716 a large number of guns were taken from Cockham Wood fort and it was not long after that all the rest of the guns were taken away and the fort abandoned. The same happened elsewhere for the batteries at Hoo Ness and the Isle of Grain were also abandoned sometime during the eighteenth century.

Indeed, if at the end of the eighteenth century, Napoleon had wished to emulate the Dutch he would have probably met with as a great a success as van Ghent. And in 1825 it was reported that 'Sheerness was inadequate to resist a coup-de-main'. The only thing that saved the Medway from receiving a second mauling, was that Napoleon was quite unaware of the very weak state that the Medway's defences had once again fallen into.

CHAPTER NINE

THE PASSING YEARS:
SOCIAL AND ECONOMIC LIFE ON THE PENINSULA 1600–1800

'Nor is there a gentleman's house, or a clergyman residing, in it, owing to the depth of the soil, the dirtiness of the roads, and the unwholesome air from the neighbouring marshes.'

Ireland: *A New and Complete History of the County of Kent* (1830)

Towards the end of the Middle Ages the Hoo Peninsula entered a period of steady economic decline: a decline which was not to be reversed, until the middle of the nineteenth century. The reason for this fluctuation of fortunes was a small parasitic insect with the very impressive name of *Anopheles maculipennis atroparvus*. This, more simply, is a variety of mosquito. No ordinary mosquito, though, as this is one of the varieties that is capable of carrying and transmitting malaria.

For a period of over four centuries the marshlands of the Hoo Peninsula provided this mosquito with an ideal breeding ground. During this period, malaria became an everyday hazard and the area gained for itself a reputation as a place of disease and early death.

During these years the history of the Peninsula is partly filled by the names of the numerous wealthy families who chose to forsake the Peninsula for more healthy climes. Those who remained on the Peninsula were those who could not afford to move away. Yet, even amongst the ranks of the poor their numbers were greatly depleted for the disease took a particularly heavy toll amongst children. The result was that the Peninsula was heavily under-populated. During the seventeenth century its average population was less than twelve people per acre. This compares most unfavourably with the Thanet or Medway valley areas both of which, at this time, had populations well in excess of thirty-five per acre. Commenting on this Edward Hasted, the author of *The History and Topographical Survey of the County of Kent* written during the 1760s, says of the area:

'Formerly it used to be noted for the wealth of the yeomen who inhabited it, but there are now few but bailiffs and lookers who live in it, the farmers and occupiers of the lands dwelling at Rochester, Stroud and elsewhere.'

The cause of malaria was not discovered until the 1890s. Prior to this date it was generally supposed that the spread of the disease was caused by foul air being emitted from marshland areas. The word malaria, although not introduced into this country until 1840, actually means 'bad air'. The illness was given a wide variety of names, all of which have some association with at least one characteristic of malaria. Included amongst these names are ague (which quite simply means acute), marsh fever, coast fever and autumnal intermittents. The last name refers to the frequent occurrence of the disease during autumn.

Not only the Peninsula marshlands were cursed with the illness but also the whole of the North Kent marshes, as can be gleaned from a further reference to Hasted's history and topographical study:

'On the north side of the great road leading from London to Dover almost as far as Canterbury ... there is a long space of country lying near the banks of the Thames and Medway along the Swale and adjoining to the river Stour below Canterbury, in which the air is gross, foggy and much subject to intermittents, owing to large tracts of low swampy marsh ground among which are such quantities of stagnating water as render the country near them exceedingly unwholesome, especially in the Autumnal quarter.'

In addition to the North Kent marshes, large expanses of Essex, most of East Anglia and the Westminster marshes were also subject to malaria. Among the prolific writings of Daniel Defoe are to be found references to the hazards faced by the London gentry when shooting on the Essex marshes. For, he says, they often returned with Essex ague; the results of which often proved a far heavier load than the fowl they had shot.

At the outset of the Middle Ages the Hoo Peninsula was quite free of malaria. Its arrival coincides with the building of sea walls around the coastline. The first walls on the Peninsula were probably built sometime during the eleventh or twelfth century. These early walls served the dual purpose of both reclaiming land

and preventing the sea flooding valuable grazing land. Intended to bring prosperity to the area, they brought about an opposite effect. By keeping the sea water off parts of the marshes, they created, within the marshes, pools of stagnant water which, at one time, would have been frequently washed by incoming tides. It was these pools of stagnating water which eventually became the breeding ground for our friendly *Anopheles* mosquito.

Two distinct groups of people were most in danger of contracting malaria. The first group was that of children born into the area. Parish records show a very high incidence of child deaths on the Peninsula whilst, in the churchyard at Cooling, there is a very vivid reminder of this aspect of Peninsula life. Here can be found thirteen lozenged shaped graves each belonging to various children of the Comport family. It is likely that these thirteen children were all the victims of malaria. The fame of these graves in the churchyard at Cooling has, in fact, spread far and wide as they feature in the opening chapter of Charles Dickens' famous novel *Great Expectations.*

The second group most at risk were visitors to the area. Native adults seemed to have acquired an immunity to the disease but this immunity did not, of course, spread to the visitor. It was because of this characteristic of malaria, that a local saying arose which stated that no husband need despair if he fell out of love with his bride – for, if she came from another area, she would be dead within the year!

It was this state of affairs that was driving the wealthier families out of the Peninsula. In 1799, the writer of the *Kentish Travellers Companion* commented:

'The parish of Cliffe is extensive and from the ruins of some buildings situated not far from the street the town is imagined to be larger than it is at present, the number of inhabitants are decreasing yearly and for want of them many houses are decaying fast.'

W. H. Ireland, in his history of Kent published in the year 1830, was able to comment:

'There is scarcely a gentleman's house, or even a clergyman living there, in consequence of the ... unwholesome air issuing from the neighbouring marshes.'

Malaria had snuffed out the very life blood of the area.

During the Middle Ages a number of richer and more powerful families had established themselves on the Peninsula. However, as the risk of malaria became greater, most of these families decided upon moving out of the area. Usually their houses became unoccupied and their lands divided into smaller portions. Such was the case concerning Newlands Farm situated in the parish of St. Mary's Hoo. This was owned by the substantial Somers family, one of whose members had been Chancellor of the Exchequer under Henry VI, whilst a later member had been a foreign ambassador under Queen Elizabeth. Having acquired Newlands Farm during the fourteenth century they sold these lands at about the time of the English Civil War. It was purchased by the trustees of the Chatham Chest and it was they who built the present day Newlands Farmhouse, sometimes around the year 1746.

It seems to have been quite a common practice for various trusts, and similar bodies, to purchase land on the Peninsula. They did not have to worry about the unhealthiness of the area, as they merely rented out the land in smaller lots. Sometimes, as in the case of Newlands Farm, they put in their own bailiff and built him a house. Other such bodies owning land on the Peninsula included the Dean and Chapter of Rochester who owned much land in Cliffe and Stoke, whilst Coombe Farm, St. Mary's Hoo, was owned by the trustees of St. George's Church, Bloomsbury.

Sometimes, of course, land when sold came into the hands of a land speculator who purchased the land solely in order to make a profit by renting it out in lots. This seems to have been the case with the land adjoining 'Allhallows Place House'. During the reign of Edward III this house was in the hands of Sir Thomas Pympe but, during the reign of Charles II came into the hands of the Grimston family. At this time the senior member of the family, Sir Harbottle Grimston, was speaker of the House of Commons. By all accounts, the house was quite a large mansion and was, for a time, a centre of Grimston family activity. The Grimston family chose to sell the house and land sometime during the eighteenth century and it came into the hands of one Samuel Fasham. It was he who obviously rented out the land for profit. Certainly he chose not to live in Allhallows Place House, as Hasted recalls the building as 'although much decayed was formerly of good account'.

One further type of property owner existed on the Peninsula.

This was the man who owned estates throughout the country and farmed through a bailiff. Such an example was the Earl of Jersey, whom Hasted records as owning the manors of Great and Little Hoo.

With no single major landholder resident on the Peninsula, the tendency towards economic regression was compounded. Both the roads and sea walls were in an appalling state, and further discouraged any meaningful investment in the area.

The upkeep of the roads was basically the province of the parish authorities. Occasionally the parish rate would be used to finance a gang of local men who would fill in the worst of the ruts and potholes. The presence of richer farmers in the area would have solved the problem, for it would have been to their advantage to have better roads for the transportation of their produce to market. Of the roads on the Peninsula Hasted notes:

'The roads are very deep and miry, and full of water.'

If a local farmer did have need of transporting large quantities, it was usual for him to resort to river transport. From the Peninsula, surpluses of corn and wool were sometimes shipped directly to London by hoy. At other times sheep might be taken into Rochester market by river. A further example of the use made of the river occurred in the year 1651 when George Maplisden, purveyor of goods for the dockyard at Chatham, brought a large quantity of elms from Cliffe and had them carried by water at a cost of three shillings.

Flooding during the seventeenth and eighteenth centuries became a further problem. since the end of the Roman occupation tide levels had been rising. The first floods occurred during the Middle Ages and prompted the building of sea walls. Among the years in which early floods happened were 1158, 1236 and 1309.

At this time flooding was neither frequent or particularly serious. To combat it, individual landholders simply erected a fairly small wall close to their house and around a favoured piece of grazing or farmland. These long abandoned walls are still to be found in many parts of the Peninsula. Later, these landholders grouped themselves together to build a system of much larger walls, which eventually formed a continuous barricade.

Initially, the financing of these walls was solely in the hands of the landholder who chose to build a wall. Later a scot tax was

introduced that was levied upon everyone living in the vicinity of
the walls.

The body responsible for the maintenance of sea walls was the
Commission of Sewers. Formed at the beginning of the seventeeth
century it was empowered to levy whatever money was necessary to
maintain the walls. This, at least, was the theory, but the general
impoverishment of the Peninsula tended to mean that the Commissioners had insufficient funds to properly maintain the walls.
This, combined with the increasing incidence of flood tides,
frequently saw the Peninsula under water.

The Isle of Grain suffered in particular during these years.
Sometime during this period a considerable area of the island was
lost due to erosion by the Thames. At one time, farm land on the
north side of the island stretched as far as the present day low
water mark. However, due to flooding by the Thames, this land
was permanently lost. It is possible that this was as a result of
serious flooding in the year 1724. So bad was it in that year, that
the Commissioners decided the best defence for the future would
be to sacrifice large tracts of land and build a completely new sea
wall. The land so sacrificed may have been the land already
referred to.

In February 1735 severe floods once again occurred. It appears
that on this occasion much of the low lying areas of the Peninsula
were underwater for several days, and the only way the area could
be drained was by driving large breeches into the walls. Of the
flooding in this particular year we have a copy of a letter, held in
the British Library, written by an eyewitness. Some believe the
account to be somewhat exaggerated, as the writer talks of many
deaths and we have no evidence from parish records, of flood
victims in this particular year. According to the writer the
floodwaters broke the walls so quickly that farmers were quite
unable to escape the onrushing waters. From their upper windows
many wives saw:

'... their husbands, sons and servants drowned as they were in
the fields at plough. What can be more shocking than to behold
such a sight?

'The Hundred is in a miserable condition. The names of the
persons, nor the number of cattle, cannot yet be learned, the
waters continuing so high upon the land ...'

The writer, himself, claims to have lost a son, two servants and a great number of sheep, cows, horses and swine.

It is recorded that a further major flood occurred in 1779 when the walls around High Halstow were breached. The last flood of this particular century occurred in the year 1791 though, of course, the problem continued into the following century. Indeed, the last major flood on the Peninsula was as late as 1953. On this occasion the entire East Coast of England was inundated with floodwater.

With malaria, flooding and quite inadequate roads, the Hoo Peninsula was rapidly becoming the most backward area in the midst of the country's most thriving county. Economic innovations simply by-passed the Peninsula. Such was the case with the movement to enclose farm fields.

It will be recalled that during the Middle Ages, farming on the Peninsula was based around the manorial system. Fields were unenclosed and divided into numerous strips. Each individual owned a number of these strips positioned throughout the various fields attached to the village. Long recognized as a most uneconomic method of farming, frequent attempts were made to locate several strips together and then to have them enclosed by some form of fencing.

In England, as a whole, the enclosure movement reached its peak sometime during the eighteenth century, though, in Kent, the movement peaked at a much earlier date. In fact, a number of historians believe that much of the present day Kentish landscape dates from the Middle Ages. However, on the Peninsula this was not the case; enclosure went on at a much slower pace.

Certainly some of the Peninsula was enclosed during the Middle Ages. For example, from the year 1447 we have records of at least one field being enclosed. In that year a certain Richard Bruyn, a tenant farmer, chose to enclose land in the area of 'Le Daynefeld' near the village of Hoo. We know of this because, in 1450 following the Cade Rising a number of his fellow villagers took him to court for he also enclosed with 'hedges and ditches' a 'certain royal path'.*

Elsewhere on the Peninsula, it is likely that many other fields were also enclosed. Apart from the collecting together of strips and enclosing these with a fence, it was common for villagers to move

* See Chapter 3.

out of the immediate vicinity of the manor and cultivate wasteland. If they did this there was absolutely no need for them to divide it into strips. However, whereas the enclosure movement in the rest of Kent continued until virtually every field in Kent was enclosed, this was not the case on the Peninsula. As far as the Peninsula was concerned, the impetus of the enclosure movement ran out of steam towards the end of the Middle Ages.

As late as 1778, Cliffe had the largest known open field in Kent being, in extent, some two thousand acres. The whole of this field was carefully divided into numerous rectangular strips. Also in Cliffe, at this time, was the unenclosed Redham Mead. This was divided into 174 parcels of land of varied shapes and sizes. The largest size being 7 acres and the smallest being 14 perches.

As well as Redham Mead, there were two other villages containing unenclosed meadow land. This was at Allhallows and Grain. Meadow land was particularly important to the village economy as each man in the village had a portion allotted to him and once the crop had been gathered in every villager was allowed to graze his animals on this land. Where villages in other parts of the Peninsula lost their meadow land it frequently meant that villagers were unable to keep animals, as there was insufficient grazing land. In this respect, the villagers of Cliffe, Grain and Allhallows were very fortunate.

Enclosure of fields usually came upon the initiation of wealthier farmers. It was the richer farmers who had most to benefit for, when enclosing of fields was carried out, the cottager frequently lost his land. This was because he had no documentary proof regarding his right to this land and the lord of the manor, or who ever held the land, no longer had need of his services. In those villages on the Peninsula where all the fields were enclosed it was often accompanied by tremendous poverty and upheaval for those at the bottom end of the social ladder.

Apart from farming, the other main industry on the Peninsula was fishing. All of the villages would have had at least one family engaged in fishing whilst the Slough area of Allhallows Parish was, made up totally of fishermen. In fact, it was often the fishermen who turned out to be amongst the richest on the Peninsula. Not because fishing proved to be remarkably thriving but because many of those so engaged had, during the eighteenth century, a small side line. But it was a side line that could reap huge profits for many of these fishermen were also smugglers.

The Hoo Peninsula does not compare with such smuggling centres as the Romney Marsh but, nevertheless, for local fishermen, it was an important aspect of their lives. Stories abound as to the extent of smuggling on the Peninsula. One story credits the Comport family of Cooling with being organizers of local smuggling. Goods smuggled in the Cooling area are also supposed to have been hidden under the pulpit of the church. Other stories tell of tunnels built for the smugglers. One supposedly runs from Allhallows church to the Rose and Crown while another, at Grain, runs from the Hogarth (originally the Chequer Ale House) down towards the beach.

The small fishing community of Slough, already referred to, was certainly one busy smuggling area. 'Run' goods were brought into Yantlett Creek during the darkest hours of the night. Here, they would be quickly unloaded by a waiting gang of men who would remove the smuggled goods to the Lobster Inn (this later became part of Aviary Farm) where they would be hidden overnight. There each helper would receive 5/-d, together with a small sample of the goods smuggled.

The 'run' goods would remain in the Lobster Inn before being taken to Rochester, via the turnpike road running from Chalk. Not all the goods would be sold in Rochester. Part of the consignment would be sold locally at ludicrously cheap rates. This was partly because goods such as rum and tea were taxed at such high rate that a profit could be easily be made on the lowest of prices. Besides which, it was always useful to sell goods to those living close by, as they were less likely to turn informer. Thus, most people in the area somehow benefited from smuggling. The fishermen, the local farmer and his labourers all had their share in the nefarious profession. The only loser was the exchequer and nobody on Hoo worried about that.

To combat 'moonlighting' the government appointed riding officers to patrol the beaches where smugglers could operate. As well as the riding officers, the government also invested in a number of patrol boats. However, insufficient finance was provided for these anti-smuggling activities. The government was quite happy to put taxes up and make the trade profitable, but it was quite unprepared to spend money on the counter-measures. The result, was that there were both insufficient patrol boats and riding officers. For the whole of the North Kent shore there were but three patrol boats, whilst for the Hoo Peninsula, with its many miles of open beaches and concealed bays there were but two riding officers.

The lot of the riding officer, to misquote Gilbert and Sullivan was not a happy one – particularly if you were allotted to the Hoo Peninsula. The riding officer worked alone among enemies. Because everyone in the area benefited from smuggling, all were prepared to watch the riding officer and report his every move. There was little real chance of him catching anything being smuggled. Nor is it likely that he wanted to catch any smugglers in the act. If he did, there would be a fight – a fight, on a lonely beach, where he was clearly outnumbered and hated.

During the eighteenth century, John Collier was surveyor-general of the Kent riding officers. It was his job to check that they were doing their job properly and every year they submitted to him an annual report. From these annual reports, held in the Customs and Excise library, we find some interesting information relating to the smugglers on the Hoo Peninsula.

As mentioned, there were two riding officers allotted to the Peninsula. In the year 1734, they were Frances Riggs, and John Tomlin both based at Stoke. In that year their annual report complains that smuggling is on the increase and that virtually every village was so engaged, although it was generally considered that Grain was probably the greatest problem. As a result of this report, in which they indicate that the Peninsula smugglers were using the turnpike road, Rigg was moved to Chalk to waylay smuggled goods entering Rochester.

In 1740, it is recorded that the following seizures were made by the Peninsula based officers: 16¾ lb. of tea, 5 dozen combs, 2 horses and 2 anchors of brandy.

The penalties for smuggling were tough. Hanging and transportation were frequently resorted to. But, of course, to implement these penalties, you had to catch your man. The smuggler on the Peninsula clearly had the upper hand. Whether it was by plain threats, or bribery, we do not know but, by 1742, although smuggling was still rife on the Peninsula, no arrests were made. It was patently obvious that the riding officers on the Peninsula were just not doing their job. In that year John Collier threatened the riding officers there with dismissal. This seems to have done the trick. For, following the all time low of 1742, the year 1743 saw some 205 seizures made in the Hoo area. However, this probably did not unduly worry the smuggler. They had one more card up their sleeve – the magistrate. It appears that the magistrates in this area were also involved with the smugglers, for Collier later reports that it is impossible to get them to convict.

It was not until after the Napoleonic War that the smuggler was given a run for his money. The government provided the Customs service with an unlimited supply of Royal Navy ships with which to reduce smuggling. This quickly paid dividends, and by the 1820s smuggling in North Kent had all but been annihilated.

CHAPTER TEN

THE POOR

'The Poor-house?' said the Secretary.

Mrs. Higden set that resolute old face of hers and darkly nodded yes.

'You dislike the mention of it.'

'Dislike the mention of it?' answered the old woman. 'Kill me sooner, than take me there. Throw this pretty child under cart-horses' feet and a loaded waggon, sooner than take him there. Come to us and find us all a-dying, and set a light to us all where we lie, and let us all blaze away with the house into a heap of cinders, sooner than move a corpse of us there!'

Our Mutual Friend, Charles Dickens

There can be little doubt that the vast majority of the Peninsula's population, up until the present century, could be considered poor. The concern of this chapter, however, is with those who fell below what is commonly called the 'bread line'. In other words the people who, for no fault of their own, had to seek some kind of assistance in order to acquire the basic essentials of life: food and shelter.

The problem of poverty was considerably less acute during the early middle ages. In times of need the manorial lord would often help his serfs to maintain themselves. Further, every family had their own land which they kept cultivated and, however bad harvests were, this would always provide them with sustenance. With the collapse of the manorial system, both these factors disappeared and most families came to rely totally upon wage labour. In an agricultural community, such as the Hoo Peninsula, this new economic arrangement provided a number of specific problems. Landless families became dependent upon the willingness, and ability, of landholders to employ them. Agriculture, though, rarely supplies secure employment as seasonal variations usually mean little work being available during the harsh winter months.

Prior to the sixteenth century, the government did very little in the way of helping the impoverished. Instead, it preferred the problem to be dealt with by the charitable gifts of individuals, the monasteries and occasional municipal authorities. This usually meant that relief of the poor was very unevenly distributed. When the government did take a hand, it only showed a complete lack of understanding. To be poor was considered the result of an unwillingness to work, and a number of statutes were introduced which prescribed such 'cures' as branding, flogging and hanging.

On the Peninsula, the earliest references to the poor are to be found amongst various wills and bequests made by parishioners. But the resources of most of those resident on the Peninsula was somewhat limited, and the amounts of many bequests are consequently very small. Yet, however tiny these amounts were, one cannot help but feel that such gifts were much better directed than the much more numerous bequests made towards the purchase of cups, chalices and spoons to already over endowed parish churches.

In 1532, this rather thoughtful bequest was made by one Giles Palmer, of St. Mary Hoo:

'Towardes ye marriage of poor maydons boorn wt in the hundred of Hoo. iiii^d.'

From John Fill of St. Margaret's parish in Rochester came, in 1540, a sum of money:

'To Halstowe parish to by shoes and gyue poore men on goodfryday'.

In the year 1552 came this bequest from John Golding, a farmer of High Halstow:

'I will there schalbe given to the poore people of Halstowe vi^s viii^d for one ycrc at iiii tymes in the yere that is to say at Hallowtyde at Crystymas, at Candilmas and Easter.'

And, finally, a bequest of William Colt, of Hoo St. Werburgh, made in the year 1516:

'An accar of land lying in Northefeld callyd Longland shall remayn to John my son and his heyrys on this condycon that he and hys heyrs every Goode Fryday for evermore do bake or cause to be bakyn a bushell of goode whete in washell brede, and every washell in valor of a ob. and so to be delyuered to poure people wher ned ys most or schalbe in the chyrche of Hoo'.

All these bequests fall within the early part of the sixteenth century. This is no coincidence. Admittedly, it is likely that earlier bequests have been lost to posterity but, during the period of the sixteenth century, poverty was dramatically increasing. This was a period of inflation and rising unemployment. The poor were becoming far more noticeable and, as a possible solution to the problem, the government was doing its best to encourage private individuals to make charitable gifts towards the poor of their own parish.

It is at the hands of the Cobham family that the most extensive aid was given to the poor of the Peninsula. In the year 1597, Sir William Brooke, Lord Cobham, left by his will £2,000 for the establishment of accomodation for twenty poor individuals. Each was to be drawn from amongst the various parishes in which the Cobham family owned land.

To be called 'The New College of Cobham' the charity was established in the village of Cobham on the site formerly occupied by a chantry. This chantry had been established in the year 1362 by Sir John Cobham but, during the reign of Henry VIII, it had been dissolved. Since then the building had been abandoned. By Sir William's will, the £2,000 was to be used to convert the chantry buildings into twenty separate lodgings. The money remaining was to be used to purchase land, whose rent in perpetuity, was to be used to maintain the college.

In all, some twelve parishes had the right to nominate their poorest members to the college. On the Peninsula the parishes of Cliffe and Cooling had the right to nominate one each and Hoo St. Werburgh three. The rules of the college laid down that nominations were to be made by the parish incumbent, church-wardens, sidesmen, overseers and constables.

The overall running of the college was placed in the hands of the Rochester Bridge Wardens, who subsequently took on the title of Presidents of the New College. From time to time, though, visits were also to be made by either the head of the Cobham family, or the Bishop of Rochester. As the governing body, it was the Presidents who laid down the rules and regulations concerning the daily life and behaviour of those resident in the college. For one thing, the building was not meant as an alternative to work and all those able to work were expected to take service with any local farmer in need of assistance. Fines were levied upon anyone refusing such work, and if the offence occurred three times, the rules laid down that such a person 'shall be expulsed the same college for ever'.

Residents of the college received a monthly pension of 6/8d. and free meals. They took their meals in the main hall, during which time they listened to readings. When outside the college each resident was expected to wear the college badge on their right shoulder and failure to do so led to being fined. Other rules stated that they were not to 'haunt any tippling houses within two miles of the college, nor to keep tippling or victualling within the college, nor to beg alms, to break any hedge, or carry wood or fuel unlawfully'. Swearing or giving 'any railing speech' against one another were both forbidden as was 'any stripe or blow to any other of them'. This last offence led to the loss of one month's pension.

Private gifts by charitable families were all very well, but could hardly solve a national problem that was daily getting worse. Only the government could take the ncessary action to relieve all the impoverished. Apart from an Act of 1388 which stated that the helpless poor had a right to relief in their own parish, the first tentative steps came during the time of Henry VIII. During his reign provision was made for the collection and distribution of funds for the poor. However, this did not prove very efficient as, once again, donations depended upon voluntary gifts. Later, though, Justices of the Peace were instructed to levy a small rate on all those living within their jurisdiction.

In 1598 came the most comprehensive law of all. Subsequently known as the Elizabethan Poor Law, it fixed a rate of contribution to be levied upon all able to pay; it provided for the compulsory apprenticeship of children of impoverished families; and it allowed for the appointment of 'Overseers of the Parish' whose job was the collection of the poor rate from every individual and the proper use of this money.

Before long, the new law reached the Peninsula. Each parish appointed its overseer but it was not until the eighteenth century that the first workhouses were established on the Peninsula. The legislation introduced in 1598 was renewed in 1601, and remained in force until 1834.

The Peninsula is most fortunate in having from the parish of Allhallows, a fairly complete collection of the account books kept by the parish overseer. They were amongst the documents discovered by the Reverend Hammond at the beginning of this century and are now mostly held in the County Records Office. The workings of the Elizabethan Poor Law can clearly be seen by reference to the Allhallows account books.

It was in 1601, that Allhallows fulfilled the requirements of the new law. In that year twenty-four residents of the parish were assessed for the new poor rate, together with an additional eleven who were non-resident landholders. In all, the total amount collected by the overseers amounted to £9 16s. 4d.

Of the impoverished in Allhallows the numbers were fairly small during this period. In the year 1604, only five different people are recorded as having need of assistance from the Overseer, though in the case of one family – that of John Wright and his daughter Alice – the help given was quite substantial. In that year the following payments were made in connection with the Wright family:

Item for Walter Wood for two neckinger for Alice Wright and twoe aprones	10d
Item for a pair of shoes for Alice Wright	10d
Item paid to Walter Wood the 10th February for keeping Alice Wright at 14d the weke	£3. 15s
Item paid to Thomas Davey the day abovesaid for keeping of John Wright at 12d the weke	57s
Item paid to James Nablet the 11th March for keping Alice Wright one month	3s 4d
Item paid for skynes to make John Wright cloathes	3s 4d.
Item paid for John Wright for canvas	3s

In that year of 1604, the total amount laid out by the Overseers was £8 2s. 9d., of which well over half went towards the upkeep of the Wrights, father and daughter. In the following year, though, one half of this problem was solved when Alice Wright went to live with Walter Woods at a cost of £3, and later she was apprenticed to James Nablett of St. Mary's Hoo. John Wright continued to be a burden on the poor rate for a good many years to come.

From the payments listed above it can be seen just what sort of use the Overseers put the poor rate too. But this, of course, does not cover every aspect of poor law assistance. Apart from rent and the direct purchase of clothes, the most common expenditure was towards raw materials in order to allow impoverished women to earn money from making clothes and other goods. Another common expenditure was for apprenticeships. Sometimes this involved payment out of the poor rate and at other times local craftsmen would be encouraged to take an apprentice without charge. In the first year of the Allhallows accounts James Joy was apprenticed:

Item payd to Robert Hawke of the pische of Stoak the 24th August in pte payment of amount payd for putting forth James Joy apprentice	£3
Item payd to Robert Hawk 14th February last for Joy his apprentice	£1
Item payd to Robert Hawk 20th March last being in full payment for putting forth Joy apprentice	£1 5s. 0d.

As well as the major items already mentioned there were numerous smaller items that were paid out of the poor rate from year to year. For instance, a fairly regular payment was 'to our constable for the gaol and marshalsey'. This refers to the London prison of Marshalsea. Although situated in London it housed criminals from all over the country and most parishes had to contribute towards its upkeep. The normal payment was eight shillings and eight pence.

Funerals of the impovershed also came out of the poor rate. In 1679, the following entries into the accounts can be found:

Item payed to Goody Cadluck for looking to a poor man in his sickness	3s
Item payd to ye Widow Prower for to help sork (prepare) him	6d
Item payd when ye poor man was put in ye ground	1s 4d
Item payd for a Blankett to put ye poor man in	2s 6d
Item payd to two men for going to Rochester about ye affidavit of ye poor man	4s

The accounts of the Overseers were annually audited by the Rochester justices and any mis-spending could be charged upon the Overseers. When turning to the end of the accounts, to the year 1832, one feels the Overseers of Allhallows were extremely lucky not to be picked up on the expenditure of the poor rate for a rather extravagent meal partaken at the 'Rose and Crown'. Seven people attended the meal. They were the two churchwardens, the two overseers of the parish and three others including a Mr. More. The bill for the meal appears in the account book:

29th March		£	s	d
1832	Butchers Bill	1	12	2½
	Plumb puddings		7	0
	Vitchls and Butter		3	0
	Bred and cheas		3	0
	Ale		2	6
	Desserts		3	0
	Tobacco		2	0
	Wine 3 bottles		15	0
	Punch 5 Boles	1	10	0
	Grog for More		1	6
	Servents		3	0
		4	11	2½

Naturally enough the account books are a considerable help in the assessment of poverty in the area. However, they do not tell us the full story, as the concern of the Parish Overseer, is clearly with those who needed assistance from the poor rate. Poverty, though, was not just restricted to these people. There was also a large group who were only just able to support themselves without recourse to parish support. To gauge their numbers, we must discard the account books and look elsewhere. In fact, for Kent, we must look to the year 1664. In that year a hearth tax was levied upon every family within the county. What makes this particular tax of interest at this point, is that it lists both those who paid together with the numbers exempt from payment. And these same people who were exempt from the hearth tax were also exempt from the poor rate; in other words they include those families who were poor but not poor enough to merit parish support.

Listed by parish, the tax returns held in the County Records Office, show for Allhallows, for instance, that of twenty-one families, nine were exempt from payment. In High Halstow, of thirty-four families ten were exempt. All in all, over the entire Peninsula, some thirty-three per cent of families were exempt from paying the tax and this figure represents, far more closely, the real incidence of poverty on the Peninsula.

Returning to the year 1832, we arrive at a time when the Elizabethan Poor Law was coming under heavy criticisim. It had been on the statute books for two hundred and thirty-four years and was clearly showing its age. For one thing, the Elizabethan Law was based on the parish and with the increased poverty which came in the wake of the Napoleonic wars many parishes were quite unable to deal with the problem. It was as a result of this that a Poor Law Commission was set up in 1832 to examine the situation and recommend immprovements. Two years later the commission reported. Its major recommendation was the compulsory amalgamation of parishes into a number of unions for the purpose of administering poor relief. The idea behind this was that the larger unions would lead to certain economies of scale as the result of the pooling of resources. Accepted by parliament the process of linking parishes went ahead immediately. In the case of the Peninsula, Allhallows, Cooling, Grain, High Halstow, Hoo St. Mary, Hoo St. Werburgh and Stoke were all amalgamated into the Hoo Union, whilst Cliffe joined the Aylesford Union.

To supervize the unions a Central Poor Law Committee was established. Subservient to this committee were a number of Assistant Poor Law Commissioners whose job was to regularly tour the Unions and report on their activities. The Central Poor Law Committee was directly responsible to Parliament, for which body it produced an annual report. The 1834, Poor Law also introduced Boards of Guardians. This was an elected body whose concern was the execution and administration of the new law within the area of each union. Guardians were to hold office for a period of three years after which new elections would be held.

In the year 1835 the parishes within the Hoo Union went to the polls and elected eight Guardians. These were: Peter Gunning (St. Mary Hoo), Richard Everist (Allhallows), William Henry Nicholson (Hoo St. Werburgh), Henry Everist (Hoo St. Werburgh), John Savage Smith (Grain), John Muton (Cooling), James Everist (Stoke) and Michael Comport (High Halstow).

The main idea behind the new poor law was the feeling that the increasing numbers in receipt of poor relief were not just victims of economic depression, but were encouraged into lethargy by the liberal attitude and kindness of the parish overseers. To overcome this, it was deemed that poor relief must not only be much harder to come by, but must also provide a standard of living below the most unpleasant means of earning a living. To help foster this, the government demanded that the bulk of poor relief should be given inside the workhouse. For the Guardians of the Hoo Union it was therefore necessary to build one very large workhouse to replace the various smaller ones dotted around the area for which they were responsible. After making some initial enquiries they eventually decided to purchase, for £150, Elm Meadow which lay just outside the village of Hoo and on the road to Strood. On this site was built the new workhouse at a cost of £2,300. (For those wishing to identify the exact location of the workhouse, it once stood to the left of Elm House and close to the Hoo Institute, in Main Road.) The workhouse was a two storey brick affair designed to accommodate 150 paupers in somewhat overcrowded conditions.

The Guardians did not have the necessary money to pay for the building of the new workhouse and it was necessary for them to raise a loan from the government. Some of the money, though, was re-couped more or less immediately when the poor law property belonging to the parishes was sold. The sale took place on October 27th, 1836, by auction in the Five Bells at Hoo and the seven buildings were described by the auctioneers as:

> 'one brick and tiled cottage situated near the Street at Hoo one tenement and garden next to the church at Allhallows two cottages and gardens opposite the Cock Inn at Grain two dwellings adjoining the church at High Halstow one brick house close to the church at St. Mary Hoo cottages adjoining church-yard, Upper Stoke twelve room tenement adjoining church-yard, Cooling'.

The workhouse at Hoo was completed by September 1836, and came into full operation in December 1836. Prior to these dates, adverts had appeared in various local papers offering the position of master and matron. A number of applications were received and after several interviews had been made, a Mr. and Mrs. Chiles were appointed to the posts at a salary of £25 per annum together with 'soap, candles and provisions of same quality as the paupers'.*

The Guardians carried out their duties to the very letter of the law. Under no circumstances was life in the workhouse to be pleasant. In the villages, the impoverished had had it too easy. This was to cease. Inside the workhouse at Hoo married couples were

---

* This quotation, together with much of the following information regarding the workhouse at Hoo comes from the minutes of the Hoo Union which are held at the County Records Office, Maidstone. They can be found under the reference G/Ho AM1–17.

permanently separated; parents had no right of access to their children and meals were to be taken in silence. Once inside the workhouse the sane found themselves in company with the insane; the violent with the non-violent; the sick with the able bodied and the old with the young. From the Charles Dickens' novel, *Oliver Twist* we find this revealing description of a workhouse. A description which was not that far removed from life in the Hoo Workhouse during these early years:

'So, they established the rule, that all poor people should have the alternative (for they would compel nobody, not they), of being starved by a gradual process in the house, or by a quick one out of it. With this view, they contracted with the water works to lay on an unlimited supply of water; and with a corn factor to supply periodically small quantities of oatmeal; and issued three meals of thin gruel a day, with an onion twice a week, and half a roll on Sundays.'

Only in one major respect did the Guardians of Hoo differ from those that Dickens described. At Hoo, they did not force every one into the workhouse. A system of relief payment was made to many people outside the workhouse. Examples of this out-relief can be gleaned by reference to the records kept by the Guardians. A fairly typical week was the second week of December 1835, when the Union minutes record:

'That two shillings and sixpence extra relief be given to Susan Bridges widow, thirty shillings to Mrs. Hazelton towards the expense of burying her father, Simon Langley. Three shillings per week to James Kemsley, fifteen shillings temporary relief to Sarah Logan formerly Wilson. Two shillings per week to James Rogers. Twenty shillings to Edward Gouge towards the expenses of burying his child and fourteen shillings to William Sanders for the like purpose.'

The new authority, like the old poor law structure, was financed by the poor rate. Having estimated how much was needed in the coming year, the Guardians informed the villages. The amounts varied according to the rateable value* of each village. For the financial year ending April 1837 the parishes of the Hoo Union paid the following amounts:

* The rateable value of the parishes within the Hoo Union stood, during this period, as follows: Hoo St. Werburgh £710; Grain £272; High Halstow £330; Hoo St. Mary £153; Stoke £305; Cooling £153.

Hoo St. Werburgh	£198. 2. 0d
Grain	£ 76
High Halstow	£ 95. 19. 8d
Hoo St. Mary	£ 68. 9. 0d
Stoke	£ 88. 14. 0d
Cooling	£ 43. 12. 0d

One point to the credit of the Hoo Union, though, was that in September 1835, having noted that no medical practitioner lived in any one of the parishes in their area they advertised for a medical officer. This, at least, was a step forward. Subsequently a Mr. William James McKay Cunningham was appointed to the office.

The Hoo Union workhouse was not to get off to a very auspicious start. Within a few years it had gained for itself a very bad reputation. This mainly due to the conduct of the successor to Mr. Chiles. In the year 1840, rumours began to reach the ears of the Guardians that all was not well as regards the conduct of the new master – James Miles. Rumours of the use of excessive brutality were rife. Towards the end of the year 1840, the Guardians resolved:

'That two Guardians inspect the workhouse each board day, before the other members assemble and report to the meeting the state of the establishment and visit it if possible at least once between board days.'

Making careful enquiries, they found that they had employed, in Miles, a sadist. Subsequently, in 1841 James Miles was dismissed as Master of the Hoo Union and a summons was taken out against him. He was charged with being 'in the habit of flogging the children, particularly the girls of the age of 13–14'. The minutes, however, do not give the outcome of the case, which was brought before the quarter sessions after the magistrates had found sufficient evidence to warrant his being brought before a higher authority.

Following the incident, the Guardians amended a number of the rules governing the workhouse:

'That the punishment allowed in the workhouse be solitary confinement, alterations of diet and corporal punishment (either with cane or rod).

'That corporal punishment be inflicted only on the back and shoulders and to be had in recourse to *as seldom as possible.* That it is never to be inflicted on any girl except by the matron or some female inmate of the house in her presence and under her direction.'

It was also laid down, that every case of punishment was to be written down and laid before the Guardians. The punishment book for the years 1851–1917 is held by the County record Office. For William Eastman who, on October 9th, 1851, refused 'to wash the potatoes' the punishment was the withholding of 'his pudding, cheese and butter for 48 hours'. It was observed that 'he has washed them ever since this punishment'. The most common punishments used were locking up and/or a bread and water diet. Swearing often resulted in the latter, whilst a theft of faggots in 1854 led to the culprit being locked up for nine hours. A case of indecent exposure in the wash room led to the man having his tobacco stopped for a week.

Not all misdemeanours were dealt with by the master. Sometimes the case was considered too grave or the offender had offended too often. In such cases they were brought either before the Guardians, or the local court. In September 1857, James Handford was reprimanded by the Guardians after violently beating another inmate. John Handford's wife also found herself in serious trouble. In October 1854, she found herself on a bread and cheese diet after swearing at the matron. At the beginning of November 1854 swearing and 'insolence' led to her getting a 48-hour bread and water diet. The crunch came in February 1855 when it was recorded in the punishment book:

'Violently assaulting and beating another inmate and using profane and obscene language. Committed to the county prison for seven days by the magistrates.'

She returned to the Poor House at the beginning of March but showed no improvement, as she refused to do any work. As a result, the magistrates committed her to a House of Correction for twenty-one days.

Another document held at Maidstone is the complaints book. Interestingly enough it contains but two entries. The first, 1870, complains of 'bad bread' and the second, of 1876, when John Hennery complained 'That he is neglected by the doctor, by not allowing him beer, and despised by the master and everybody because he is an Irishman'. Both complaints were investigated and the first was written off as 'trumpery' and the second 'this pauper is continually dissatisfied that the guardians take no notice of him'.

The County Records Office at Maidstone contains seventeen hefty volumes of the minutes of the Board of Guardians covering the entire period of their authority. That is from 1835, until the 6th March, 1930, when a new law and entire new procedure came into force. The majority of the minutes refer to payments made, minor alterations to the workhouse, changes in staff salaries and so on. Some of it is fascinating but some of it is deadly dull. It is for this reason that I intend skipping a period of eighty-eight years to the year 1923. The year in which the Guardians resolved to sell the workhouse.

Changing attitudes now meant that fewer families were being forced into the workhouse whenever it was avoidable. Moreover, the introduction of unemployment benefit also helped remove some of the pressures placed upon the Guardians. The result was that inmates at the Hoo Union workhouse tended to be drawn from amongst the ranks of two distinct groups of people. Firstly, there were the elderly, those who were too old to obtain either work or alternative accommodation. The second group were the vagrants who moved from one workhouse, to the next gaining accommodation overnight in what were termed the casual wards. It was because of this situation that the Hoo Guardians decided that it would be more economical to sell the workhouse and move the elderly permanent inmates to the Strood workhouse – in return for which the Hoo Guardians would pay a regular fee to cover accommodation costs. As a result the workhouse was sold in 1924. At its time of sale the building consisted of a garden with glasshouse, bedroom and rooms for the master and matron, washrooms, rooms for male and female inmates and a nursery.

For the Poor Law Unions, however, far more sweeping changes were on the way. The 1920s and 30s brought widespread poverty and unemployment. In the urban areas the Guardians were quite out of their depth and totally unable to handle the situation. It was as a result of this dire situation that the year 1929 saw an act passed by parliament which both abolished the Board of Guardians and handed their powers, in total, to the County Councils. Every County was told to set up special 'Public Assistance Committees' whose function was to carry out all those duties once administered by the Board of Guardians. In many ways it was not a very satisfactory piece of legislation as, by replacing the Poor Law Unions by a larger body with the same powers, it did nothing to remedy the actual cause of the crisis.

The Hoo Union being, as it was, a rural area, was quite in control of the situation. As a result, the Guardians did not approve of the new legislation. In 1929, they sent a copy of a resolution to the government calling the new legislation a retrograde step.

It was on March 6th 1931, that the Board of Guardians at Hoo held their last meeting. It was a meeting in which the following statement by the chairman was minuted. He:

'expressed the hope that the newly appointed body whose duty it would be to care for the deserving poor would exercise the same friendly attitude that had been adopted by the general body of Gentlemen who had this responsibility for nearly one hundred years.'

CHAPTER ELEVEN

PREPARING FOR WAR
THE VICTORIAN DEFENCES OF THE
HOO PENINSULA

'We also propose that a casemated battery should be
constructed on the Grain Spit, enclosing the present
tower, to oppose the entrance of ships ... To co-operate
and support this work, an open battery should be placed
on the Isle of Grain, the guns of which should bear on
the channel and across the Medway.'
Part of the report made by the 'Royal Commission
for the Defence of the United Kingdom' (1861)

By all accounts, it would appear that the lessons of the Dutch raid
were all but forgotten by the middle of the eighteenth century.
Although a great deal of money had been ploughed into defending
the Medway in those years immediately following the raid,
succeeding governments, in one economy drive after another, had
reduced these defences to a completely ineffectual condition. To
any reader familiar with the eighteenth century such a situation
must be incomprehensible. Rarely did a year go by, that the British
were not at war with at least one country, and usually several.

Evidence for the indiscriminate running down of the Medway
defences can be found in a number of sources. One of these sources
is Hasted's history of Kent. Writing of Upnor castle he says:

... for many years, there has not been a gun mounted in it for
service, nor yet a platform.
In the castle there is a magazine of powder, for the use of the
navy, &c for the security of which, here is an establishment of a
governor, store keeper, clerk of the cheque, a master gunner,
twelve other gunners &c.'

Of the batteries built in the Upnor area, immediately after the
Dutch raid, Hasted gives us some more very revealing information
(information, presumably, which would have been of invaluable use
to any enemy): 'One of these is the fort once called the 'Swamp',
now the Birdsnest; but there has not been a gun mounted on it
within remembrance, and the embrasures of earth have long since
mouldered away, and overrun with bushes and brambles.'

Finally, Hasted comments on the condition of one of the major
forts also built as a direct result of the Dutch raid:

'... Cockham Wood fort, about a mile below (Upnor) on the
same side of the Medway, is yet to be seen; but with all the guns
dismounted, and thrown on the ground, the shot &c lying in the
master gunner's house just by, which, as well as the fort, is
becoming very ruinous.'

Of the battery built on Hoo Ness Island, in the Medway river
itself, the story is the same:

'Hooness fort, commonly called the folly, is situated still lower
down on the same side of the river, where there are no guns
mounted; but there is a master gunner from Upnor castle, who
lives at it for a week at a time.'

Hasted's comments are confirmed by Thomas Blomefield, the
inspector of Royal Artillery who, between 1779 and 1793, carried
out a very comprehensive survey of the English coastal defences.
He certifies that Upnor Castle, Cockham Wood fort and Hoo Ness
battery are all depleted of any weapons – or almost:

'Upnor Castle is at present used only as a magazine. There
are, however, eleven very old nine pounders let into a frame of
wood to fire on Rejoicing Days. They are very dangerous guns, a
man has actually been killed in attempting to reload one of them
when His Majesty was at Chatham. It is proposed to remove
them entirely, as the neighbourhood of so large a magazine is
certainly a very improper place for a battery.'

Blomefield fails to make any note of Buda, Middle and Quaker
batteries. These were all, at one time, sited on the Isle of Grain and
so we can probably draw the conclusion that they had completely
disappeared by the time of Blomefield's survey. It is only at
Sheerness, though, that the Medway retained a fortress capable of
putting up any real resistance. Here, at least, care had been taken
to maintain a fortress of some strength. Certainly Sheerness had
suffered a few depletions as regards armament, but this had not
been taken to the lengths that have already been noted. By many,
Sheerness was considered the lynch pin for defending both the
Thames and Medway and, as such, had actually received a series
of new batteries during the seventeenth century.

From 1793 to 1815, Britain was once again at war with France. Prior to the Battle of Trafalgar, in 1805, there was a very real chance that the Emperor Napoleon would unleash an invasion army against British shores. Indeed, one historian has gone so far as to suggest that a landing point planned by Napoleon was one of the defenceless beaches of the Hoo Peninsula. During the wars with France, Upnor Castle was rearmed and a battery of four guns was built at Lower Hope Point for the defence of the Thames. Sheerness was, once again, singled out for special treatment. Further batteries were added here to protect an increasingly important naval dockyard.

The year 1815 brought the Battle of Waterloo and the beginning of an extensive period of peace. Once again defences were neglected. To try and shore up some of the breaches in the Medway's defences one report, made in the year 1825, recommended the building of a redoubt on the Isle of Grain – this was intended to stop an enemy capturing Grain and using it as a base to bombard Sheerness. In 1840, a further report appeared with the message that:

> 'Sheerness, if left in its present condition, will inevitably fall under any rapid enterprise which may precede or commence hostilities.'

This report recommended the positioning of a large battery on the Isle of Grain so that any large enemy vessels proceeding up the Medway could immediately be brought under cross-fire from both Grain and Sheerness.

Both these reports were more or less totally ignored. The only alteration to the Medway's defences during this period was the erection of a gun tower on Grain Spit. Often referred to as a 'Martello' tower, this is the structure which can still be seen at the mouth of the Medway, standing between the Isle of Grain and Sheerness. Construction of this tower probably started in 1849 when it is recorded that a local firm laid the foundations for the tower. The tower, itself, was built by the Lincolnshire firm of Kirk and Parry who encountered severe difficulties because of the exposed situation of the site. Nevertheless, the tower was completed by 1856, for it was in that year the *London Journal* gave a full description of the tower (which at that time had an armament of four smoothed bored guns):

'The tower is somewhat of an oval in form – being struck from seven different centres, in order to give additional solidity to the parts likely to be struck by shot in case of an enemy approaching within range of its guns.

'The dimensions are seventy-one feet by sixty-three feet, with a height of forty-two feet. The foundation is on piles, on which rest solid balks of timber, covered by a layer of cement six feet thick. The average thickness of the masonry is twelve feet. The basement and the twelve feet wall of masonry are lined with nine inch brickwork. The building contains rooms for ordnance, provisions, stores, and the magazines – the latter being cased over with asphalte. In the upper storey is barrack room for thirty gunners, and private apartments for officers.'

It was not until the 1850s that the government at last contemplated some sort of remedial action as to the poor state of the Medway's defences. In that decade, three factors came together which at last shook the government out of its complacent attitude towards coastal defence. The motivating forces in this complete transformation, were a rumoured threat of a French invasion, the dramatic improvement in the fire-power of large guns and the emergence of a revolutionary new warship known as an iron clad. Separately, these three components might have had no influence at all on government thinking; but combined, they produced the most serious threat imaginable to the nation's security. If the feared French invasion materialized, and they used the new guns fitted to iron clads then, in a few minutes, the type of defences in the Medway would be reduced to rubble.

However, as it transpired, the supposed invasion was a myth. A myth that emerged as a result of events in France. In December of 1851, France suffered a 'coup d'etat' which gave dictatorial powers to a man bearing the most feared name in Europe – Napoleon. Not, a reincarnation from the grave, but a nephew of the former French Emperor who took, for himself, the title of Napoleon III, Emperor of the French. Once this traumatic event had occurred in France, it was naturally assumed by every Englishman that this Napoleon was bound to emulate his uncle's objective of European domination: an objective which, if carried out, would require the complete subjugation of the United Kingdom.

Only a month after Napoleon's seizure of power, Prince Albert was able to confide to a German cousin that the British were 'occupied and bothered' by the possibility of a French invasion. It was also about this time, that a flood of pamphlets appeared, all warning the public of French intentions. One of these purported to be 'A History of the sudden and terrible invasion of England in May 1852' and told of how it only took the French, using modern weapons, fourteen days to cower the British into submission. This was made possible as the English army 'was annihilated before they could come within shot of the enemy'.

The invasion fear reached a new peak in 1858, when it was learnt that the French had laid down the first of a fleet of iron clads. This was the 'Gloire', a warship of 5,675 tons covered with four inch thick armour plating and backed by twenty-six inches of wood. Easily able to repel any projectile designed to be fired by British coastal guns, it was a serious threat to the belief that British defences were impregnable.

The last stimulant to the government's transformation, was the news that the French were also experimenting with the new design in guns. These guns, already known to the British, were rifle barrelled and breech loaded. They had an accuracy and range quite undreamed of a few years earlier. Whereas the coastal defence guns, then in service, had a range of only a few thousand yards, these new guns could propel a much heavier shell some ten miles. By rifling the barrel, a spinning shell could be fired, which had a much smoother flight and consequently greater accuracy. Breech loading meant that projectiles could be loaded and fired much quicker. The reason that the British government had not chosen to rearm with the new guns, was that no other government had previously shown an interest in the weapons and rearming with such guns would be an expensive process, at a time when economies in defence were again being looked for.

With the French introducing these new guns, something had to be done by the British. Not only had Britain to arm with such weapons, but British coastal defences must be made sufficiently strong to withstand an attack by vessels using such weapons. To consider the various aspects of the problem, the year 1859 saw the establishment of the 'Royal Commission for the Defence of the United Kingdom'.

Aware of the urgency of the matter, the members of the Royal commission took a comparatively short period of time in finalizing their report. It was presented to Parliament in 1860. In its preamble, the report stated that the Royal Navy, due to the great improvement in weapons, was no longer capable of preventing a determined invasion of British shores. It was necessary, the report continued, for the navy to be supported by a series of forts and gun batteries sited at various strategic points along the coastline. Having made all this clear, the commission's report then elaborated upon where these defences should be. Their recommendations for the Thames and Medway estuaries are all that need concern us here.

For the Medway, the commission reported the need for completely updating both the defences around the equally important repair and building yards at Chatham. For Sheerness, it recommended new gun batteries and a completely new fort. For Chatham, it saw the need for strengthening the Lines, together with a ring of new fortresses. The latter was subsequently cancelled. For the Hoo Peninsula, a new battery and fort were to be built at Grain, whilst two small forts were to be built at Oakham Ness and Burntwick Islands. As for the gun tower in the Medway, off Grain, the commmission reported that it should be strengthened by casemated work, though this was later cancelled through lack of finances, and the tower subsequently remained unaltered for a good many years. The report gave the reasons for strengthening the defences on the Isle of Grain as follows:

'... a casemated battery should be constructed on the Grain Spit, enclosing the present tower, to oppose the entrance of ships, and to flank the beach on Grain Island within its range. To co-operate with and support this work, an open battery should be placed on the Isle of Grain, the guns of which should bear down the channel and across the Medway. This battery will be secured against assault, by a work upon the rising ground in its rear, which will also deny the occupation of the island to an enemy ...'

On the Thames side of the Peninsula the commission recommended the building of forts at Slough and Cliffe. Slough fort would serve the dual purpose of preventing enemy ships entering the Thames and, according to the report, 'preventing the landing of an enemy on any part of the adjacent shore'. The fort at Cliffe was one of a number of forts designed to prevent an enemy fleet attempting to attack shipping, at anchor, in this area. Among the other forts co-operating with Cliffe were Tilbury, Coalhouse Creek, Shornmead and Gravesend.

Parliament accepted all the recommendations laid before it, and immediately set about raising an eleven million pound loan to cover the expenses entailed.

Although work on these forts and batteries was commenced almost immediately, one problem had not been solved. The commission had indicated that the new constructions should be heavily fortified, but no experiments, as yet, had been made into the types and thicknesses of materials most able to withstand shells fired by the new types of weapons. It was as a result of this, that a second commission was set up to examine and test iron plates. It was on the opposite bank of the Thames, at Shoeburyness, that this committee carried out much of its work. A number of thicknesses of iron plates were tested by the simple expediency of firing shells into them, from varying ranges. The committee presented its report in 1865, and recommended that all the forts then being built, should have metal plates inserted into their structure, whilst batteries should have casemates also of iron plates. The basic problem here, was that by the time the committee reported, many forts were partially completed and as a result numerous delays arose whilst the necessary alterations were made for the insertion of the plates.

Nor was this the only problem. Even as the forts were being built, more advances were being made in the construction of guns. Many of the forts and batteries had to have further alterations made to allow them to be fitted with even heavier guns than that for which they were originally designed. Because of these factors, forts which were scheduled for completion in 1864, were not in many cases, completed until 1873. Delays also arose over the arrival of ordnance. The sudden demand for so many of the new type of guns, which were in short supply anyway, completely inundated the armaments industry, and it was many years before they were able to supply sufficient guns of the correct calibre.

Construction of the fort at Grain started in 1861, and was completed by 1867. It was a large heptagonal affair with a continuous dry ditch running around the outside. Inside the fortress area, there was a large forecourt and a 'D'-shaped keep. This keep was two storeys high, and had a number of red brick buildings attached to it. These provided both storage and accommodation.

The keep, itself, was designed to withstand a siege and, as such, had an internal water supply.

Intended as a defence of both the Isle of Grain and the entrance of the Medway river, the fort was first equipped with large guns of ten-inch calibre, facing out to sea, and a number of smaller calibre guns facing inland. As a result of the delays already mentioned, these guns did not arrive until 1874 when it was reported in the *Sheerness Guardian*:

> 'The heavy guns (7 in., 10 in. and 9 in.) are now mounted on the fort at the Isle of Grain and the whole place is ready for use.'

The walls of Grain fort consisted of granite some twelve feet thick with an additional lining of brick. Armour shields recommended by the iron plates committee did not arrive until 1885. Then they were only fitted to the casemates and not to the walls as originally recommended.

A government report of 1869 makes the following comment, as to progress then being made at Grain:

> 'In the construction of the work no difficulty was experienced in obtaining a secure foundation. The earthen ramparts were at first made with a slope of one to one; this slope, from the nature of the material used, proved insufficient to give them stability ... and they have now been remodelled with a slope of one and three quarters to one. With this exception the work has been well and skilfully constructed. ... The amount expended to the 30th June, was £99,845 and the further sum required for its completion ... is £14,869, making a total of £114,714.'

One thousand yards down river from the fort, was the Isle of Grain battery. According to the 1869 progress report already mentioned:

> 'It was designed as an open battery for fourteen guns bearing on the defence of the Medway, and is 900 yards from the nearest point of deep water channel.'

Work started on this battery in 1868 when it was reported in the *Sheerness Guardian*:

> 'On 7th November about one hundred men of the Royal Inniskilling Fusiliers arrived at Sheerness and were at once taken to the Isle of Grain where they are to assist in the erection of certain fortifications there.'

Shortly after the work was started, subsidence difficulties were met and the original plan for fourteen guns had to be severely curtailed. When finally completed, the battery was of granite construction with armour shielded casemates. It received a number of eleven-inch guns during the 1870s.

As already mentioned, Grain tower was, at one time, scheduled to have its casemates strengthened and, in addition, it was to be rearmed. All of this was cancelled, due to financial difficulties and the belief that the two structures on the Isle of Grain would serve adequately. Despite this, the tower was retained in its original capacity, being armed with three smooth bored cannons of the type that it had probably received during the eighteen-fifties.

As for the two mid-river forts recommended for Oakham Ness and Burntwick Islands, test borings showed that the ground would be far too soft to support such structures. In the words of the 1869 report:

> 'It was subsequently determined to construct these works at Hoo (Ness) and Darnet, two projecting points below Gillingham Reach, commanding the winding channel at that part of the river.'

Even on their new sites, there were still considerable subsidence difficulties. The original plan for these two forts had called for two circular structures, each with two tiers of guns and each gun being protected by its own armour shield. Because of the subsidence difficulties the forts were both finished with only one tier of guns. Work was completed in 1874, when the following report appeared in the *Sheerness Guardian:*

> 'A detachment of Royal Artillery at Sheerness has been ordered to proceed to the new fort a Hoo Ness, one of two which have been constructed for the defence of the Medway and Chatham dockyards and stones are now being conveyed to the fort and one built on the opposite side of the river with the immense guns with which they will be armed. From the nature of the soil, the foundations of these forts proved very costly.'

Elsewhere on the Peninsula, were the forts of Slough and Cliffe. The one at Slough was designed to oppose enemy shipping moving up the thames, and also to prevent a landing of enemy troops in this area. It was originally planned to be armed with twenty guns but this number was later reduced to ten. It was a semi-circular structure of granite and armour plated casemates. Although completed on time, it seems to have been bereft of guns until as late as 1885, when it was recorded as awaiting both guns and shields. It was in 1890, that the fort was first armed. At this same time, four concrete emplacements were added to the fort, to strengthen its ability to bring enemy shipping under fire.

Cliffe fort was originally planned to be armed with thirty guns but this did not a materialize for, in common with many of the other forts, the size and number of guns was later moderated in order to save money. Cliffe, was of a similar construction to most of the other forts but it did have one particularly interesting feature which was not common to any of the other Thames and Medway forts. In the year 1886, Cliffe fort became an experimental station for the newly developed Brennan torpedo. These were wire guided torpedoes and were fitted with explosive warheads. They were launched into the water by means of a carriage which ran along a special mono-rail. Once the device entered the water the torpedo and carriage separated.

The motive power of the Bennan torpedo was provided by a steam winch which was housed on shore. This winch quickly unravelled two drums of piano wire stored in the torpedo itself. As the wire was unravelled it ran through a special gear mechanism which operated propellers at the rear of the torpedo. This provided sufficient thrust for a maximum speed of about twenty miles an hour.

These wires also allowed the direction of the torpedo to be controlled. When the device was launched it was clearly visible as it was fitted with a telescopic mast and flag. All the operator had to do was observe this and alternate the speed with which the port and starboard wires were released.

The fort at Cliffe had two launching rails for the Brennan torpedo, but they never really proved to be a great success and the idea was abandoned during the 1890s.

Only two other victorian fortifications need now be considered. These are batteries at Lower Hope Point and Church Beach, Grain. The original Lower Hope Point battery was abandoned sometime after the Napoleonic war but, in 1890, this site was chosen for a new gun emplacement, which was subsequently built in 1898. Fitted with a number of quick firing guns this battery remained operational until the end of World War One. The final battery to be considered, the one on Church Beach, Grain, was built in 1890 and was named Wing battery – presumably because it stands on the south wing of Grain fort. Again, armed with a number of quick firing guns it remained operational until the end of World War One.

All of the Victorian forts and batteries remained in service throughout the First World War – though Grain tower lost its smooth bored guns in 1910 and became, instead, a signal station. The forts of Grain and Cliffe were rearmed before the outbreak of hostilities and were also given Anti-Aircraft guns. Hoo and Darnet were disarmed before World War One but were not totally abandoned until 1919.

Today, all of these Victorian structures lie desolate and abandoned. Some remained in service until as late as 1956 – though, of course, by then they were hopelessly obsolete.

Cliffe fort now stands completely derelict, though any visitor can gain, at least, some idea of how it once used to be. Clearly visible, even today, are the rail platforms and the eastern launching bay of the long abandoned Brennan torpedo system. Of Grain fort, far less remains. All that can be seen is a massive crescent-shaped earth embankment which conceals the forts' massive granite walls. Beneath this, and completely inaccessible, lies the one time ammunition stores and lift shafts. Far more, though, remains of Grain battery which stands, rather like a medieval castle after a visit by Cromwell, on Smithfield marshes. Part way between Grain fort and battery the area once occupied by Wing battery can easily be identified due to the indentation of the ground. Slough fort also remains. During the inter-war period it was a zoo but, more recently, it has been incorporated into a riding stables.

Of all the forts, though, it is Hoo Ness and Darnet which are the best preserved. Standing out in the Medway they are the most difficult to reach and, as a result, nobody has an interest in either demolishing them or committing acts of vandalism. They are perfect examples of Victorian defences. Perhaps, one day, these two forts will be properly preserved. They are, after all, part of our heritage. Something, at least, should be kept of the millions of pounds that were once ploughed into defending the Medway from that same fate that befell it in the year 1667.

CHAPTER TWELVE

THE KING OF THE HUNDRED:
THE PENINSULA DURING THE
NINETEENTH CENTURY

'We are out of the stream here, and those who drift out
of the stream float into a backwater, and the
characteristic of a backwater is stagnation. Unfortunately, however, stagnation has its disadvantages and
we feel some of them at Cliffe.'

From the Cliffe Parish magazine 1881

At the beginning of the nineteenth century the Hoo Peninsula was
an area carefully avoided by all those who could. Its only
inhabitants, the poor, and a number of convicts in off-shore prison
hulks, were there by force of circumstances. Within both groups,
'marsh fever' took its deadly toll. The marshes were cold, dank,
inauspicious swamps used only for sheep and cattle grazing.
Nobody had a good word for them. All in all, the Peninsula was a
most inhospitable place, a place of hardship and wretchedness but,
above all else, a place where the dampness of the marshes pervaded
every corner of the district.

This aspect of the marshes is well described by Charles Dickens.
In his novel *Great Expectations*, the young Pip meets the escaped
convict Abel Magwitch. As the manacled convict departs across
the marshes, Pip adds to the account:

'I looked over my shoulder, and saw him going towards the
river ... picking his way among the great stepping stones
dropped into the marshes here and there, for stepping places
when the rains were heavy, or the tide was in.'

Later, Pip joins the soldiers who were looking for the escaped
prisoner and they head out for the marshes:

'We were joined by no stragglers from the village, for the
weather was cold and threatening, the way dreary, the footing
bad, darkness coming on ... the sheep stopped in their eating
and looked timidly at us, and the cattle, their heads turned from
the wind and sleet; stared angrily at us as if they held us
responsible for both annoyances; but, except these things, and the

shudder of the dying day in every blade of grass, there was no break in the bleak stillness of the marshes.'

Of the various marshland villages, Cooling is the one most usually associated with the events depicted in *Great Expectations;* this, for no other reason, than the passage where Pip makes reference to the gravestones in the churchyard:

'To five little stone lozenges, each about a foot and a half long, which were arranged in a neat row beside their grave, and were sacred to the memory of five little brothers of mine.'

Few dispute that the originals, for these small gravestones are to be found in the church graveyard at Cooling. In fact, the visitor will find thirteen lozenged shaped stones and they belong to various children of the Comport family. These children, none of whom exceeded the age of seventeen months, bear tragic witness to the unhealthiness of these marshland areas. Apart from these graves, however, Cooling little befits Pip's village which is so carefully described by the novelist.

Two other marshland villages have been put forward as the setting for the early part of *Great Expectations.* One is Lower Higham, and the other Hoo St. Werburgh. Dickens, himself, knew all three villages, as one of his favourite past times was tramping the marshes, and his favourite walk was from his home, at Gads Hill, to Cooling. It was doubtless during such a walk, that he decided to allow the Comport graves to become those of Pip's brothers. These walks, of course, also inspired him to write such vivid descriptions of the marshes and their inhabitants. As to which of the marshland villages most closely resembles Pip's the author gives us several clues, of which the following passage is perhaps the most important. Again, it comes from the opening scene of the book where Pip is talking to Magwitch:

'I pointed to where our village lay, on the flat inshore among the alder trees and pollards, a mile or more from the church.'

Clearly there could not be a better clue, as there is only one village in the whole area which has a church so far removed from the community which it serves. This is Lower Higham, whose church is just one mile from the village. Moreover, the church of Lower Higham fits one other aspect in Dickens' description. Pip's church is described as having a steeple; the church at Lower Higham does have a steeple, whilst that at Cooling does not.

The case for Pip's village being that of Hoo St. Werburgh is put by Edwin Harris, one time curator of Rochester museum, in his pamphlet 'The Hundred of Hoo and its Dickensian Associations'. Harris notes that Hoo has a number of features similar to Pip's village. Pip's village contained, apart from the church with a steeple, a sawpit, a general shop, a forge and a wheelwright's shop. All of these, Harris points out, were contained in the village of Hoo at the time of *Great Expectations.* Furthermore, anchored off Upnor were a number of prison hulks from which Magwitch could have escaped. Yet, this does not get us that much nearer to answering the question in hand, for we can probably assume that a number of marshland villages contained these self same features. Furthermore, on closer inspection the argument for Hoo St. Werburgh being Pip's village can be seen to be a rather weak one. A major flaw concerns the prison hulks for, at one point in the book, these are said to be more than an hour's walk from Pip's village. Hoo is never an hour's walk from Upnor. No, this is far more like the time it would take to walk from Lower Higham to Egypt Bay and the prison hulk moored there.

As regards the village itself:

'Of course there was a public house in the village, and of course Joe liked sometimes to smoke his pipe there.'

Pip refers to this as 'The Three Jolly Bargemen' and describes it as dark, with narrow passages and secluded rooms. Early photos of the now demolished 'Chequers Inn' at Lower Higham show a pronounced similarity. As well as the inn, the windmill (of which the base can still be seen), wheelwright's and saw pit of Lower Higham are more or less exactly where Dickens placed them. Only the forge presents any real difficulties:

'Joe's forge adjoined our house, which was a wooden house, as many of the dwellings in our country were – most of them, at that time.'

There was a forge at Lower Higham, but it does not fit this description. Instead, Dickens appears to have imported another forge with which he was familiar. This was the wooden forge at Chalk which can still be seen today.

The final point which, I feel, confirms Lower Higham as Pip's village, is the fact that whenever Pip went to Rochester, he would return via the turnpike road:

> 'It was a very dark night when it was all over, and when I set out with Mr. Wopsle on the walk home. Beyond town, we found a heavy mist out, and it fell wet and thick. The turnpike lamp was a blur quite out of the lamp's usual place apparently, and its rays looked solid substance on the fog. We were noticing this, and saying how that the mist rose with a change of wind from a certain quarter of our marshes, when we came upon a man, slouching under the lee of the turnpike house.'

There was in fact, only one turnpike road in this area. this was the Chalk road, with its gatehouse and lamp on the north side of Strood High Street, facing the Angel inn. It would be quite inconceivable to take this road, if one was heading anywhere else but Higham – or that particular area. This same road, incidentally, was the one that was carefully guarded by the riding officers during the time that smuggling was at its height.

Clearly then, Dickens, in providing a village for Pip, mostly based it on Lower Higham but chose to import a number of features. Hoo, on the other hand, does not really fit as a number of features are completely out of place. Cooling not only fails on the grounds of having a steepleless church but, at the time, it was a very small village and did not have a general shop, a windmill and a number of other important features.

That Abel Magwitch escaped from a prison hulk draws our attention to a totally different aspect of Peninsula life. During the early part of the nineteenth century there were a great number of these rotting hulks moored on both the Thames and Medway. The majority were on the Chatham/Sheerness side of the Medway but a number were moored between Hoo and Upnor as well as Egypt Bay on the Thames.

Not all the boats permanently anchored in the Medway were prison hulks. A number were warships in 'mothball' as it were. They had a small maintenance crew on board and were being kept until war was again declared. Samuel Ireland in his 'Picturesque Views of the River Medway' writes:

> 'The old ships of war stationed here are termed water breakers, from their breaking the violence of the tides. The hulks

are occupied by sixty or seventy families, and chimneys of brick are raised from the lower gun deck, which give them a wholesome appearance of a floating town.'

It was not until the Napoleonic war that the Medway became a permanent station for prison hulks. Then large numbers of prisoners of war were housed in overcrowded hulks. There are reports at this time of over a thousand French prisoners being housed in hulks not suitable for more than three hundred. In addition to this the food was inadequate, exercise was limited and consequently diseases were rife. The Peninsula's mosquito population found ideal conditions for spreading marsh fever whilst yellow fever, cholera and typhus (commonly referred to as 'gaol fever') were also common.

These hulks housing prisoners of war were, in turn, followed by civilian hulks which housed felons condemned by English magistrates. Some spent their entire sentence on board such hulks whilst others merely awaited transportation. Abel Magwitch was amongst the latter. In fact, the majority of civil prisoners much preferred transportation as it at least gave them a chance of a fresh start in life. If allowed to serve their entire sentence in a hulk – assuming they survived – upon release there was little chance of finding an employer and they would soon have to return to crime.

Prison hulks were finally abandoned in the latter part of the century and most of the prisoners held on the Medway were transferred to a new prison built on St. Mary's Island, Chatham.

The Hoo Peninsula, at the beginning of the nineteenth century, was still very much subject to marsh fever and sporadic flooding. Until something could be done about these two factors then there was little hope for the future of the Peninsula. Yet, in both fields, advances were to be made in the nineteenth century that, whilst not making the Peninsula completely immune from both, were to go a long way in easing both afflictions.

In the realms of sea defence the first move was made when the Commissioners of Sewers inaugurated the office of Surveyor. This office was to be given to men trained in the complexities of sea defence. The first surveyor for the Hoo Peninsula area was appointed in 1855, and he was soon advising on important changes which had to be made in order to counter the threat of flooding.

He immediately marked off two areas – the Isle of Grain and
Lower Hope Point – as the most likely to be flooded and, therefore,
the areas most in need of protection. For both places he advised the
future erection of concrete walls to replace the old earthen
embankments. As well as this, he stated that the stones being used
for the repair of sea walls, should no longer just be dumped in
position but carefully paved into the walls so that they stood the
best chance of fighting erosion.

Despite these advances being made in the realms of flood
protection, there was one serious flood in the year 1897. Even so,
the indications were that the Sewer Commissioners scientific
approach was having an effect. During the eighteenth century parts
of the Peninsula had seen regular flooding every twenty or thirty
years, but, prior to 1897, the only other recorded flood in the
second half of the nineteenth century was in February 1854.
Further, in the following century flooding came at much diminished intervals until, today, it is a most unlikely threat.

The flooding of November, 1897, coincided with severe gale
force winds which were recorded throughout the whole of South-
East England. According to the *Chatham Observer*, they were of
'unparalleled severity' and, even worse, they coincided with
extraordinary high tides. The winds started up some time on
Sunday, November 28th, and at 3 p.m., the following afternoon,
they were beginning to force the tide waters over the very tops of
the sea walls. At about the same time the first of the walls gave
way as a tremendous breach was created and tons of water began
cascading onto the low-lying lands. Other breaches soon followed.

The damage, of course, was tremendous. Low-lying houses
became completely submerged, parts of the Peninsula's railway
system was washed away, hundreds of sheep were drowned and the
Isle of Grain was completely cut off by floodwaters. Elsewhere in
North Kent Gravesend was flooded, the sea front at Margate was
wrecked and the piers at Broadstairs and Sheerness were severely
damaged.

On the Hoo Peninsula there were several lucky escapes, as
people tried desperately to escape from the rapidly rising flood
waters. Near Stoke, a railway signalman found himself cut off by
the flooding and soon found his own life in danger, as floodwaters
rose to shoulder height. Fortunately, being able to swim, he made
it to a tree and managed to cling to the branches for four hours.

An Oakum Island shepherd also had an unfortunate experience. He had to spend a good many hours on top of a post after his house was flooded. Both men were rescued by bargemen who had set out to see where they could be of assistance.

Some fifty per cent of the Peninsula was under water on this occasion. Practically the whole valley, between the Medway, just below Stoke, and the Thames, was submerged, as was the area from Coalmouth to Yantlet, and from Stoke through the flats to Hoo. This meant that Grain was once more an island and the only communication with Stoke was by boat – a situation which lasted for a week. Most of Stoke was also flooded, including the inn and the post office.

The floods, however, did bring one rather amusing incident. This was when the floodwaters floated two large hay stacks, and dumped one of them on the main Stoke–Grain road. Here, it remained for a number of weeks after the floodwaters subsided, and traffic had to carefully pick its way round the stack.

Towards the end of the nineteenth century, not only was the Peninsula less subject to frequent flooding, but its inhabitants – for reasons they could not really explain – were becoming less susceptible to the marsh fever. The basic reason for the existence of malaria was the large number of pools of stagnant water lying out on the marshes. These provided ideal breeding grounds for the malaria carrying mosquitoes. Medical advances prior to the turn of the century had not really established the mosquito connection with malaria, but instead, blamed the illness on bad air associated with these pools of water. Thus, the correct remedy was taken – that of draining the marshes – but for the wrong reasons.

Health improvements came to the area during the last quarter of the nineteenth century. In 1874, one of Her Majesty's inspectors for schools was still able to record the district as being 'low lying aguish, and unhealthy, where no one would live if they could help it'. Referring to the year 1876, C. B. Burnett was able to comment, in his *History of the Isle of Grain*, that as many as seventy-five per cent of Grain's population were subject to the attacks of marsh fever. Yet, in 1895, the same writer recalled that 'the enemy is subdued, for his victims are few, and there is not a more healthy place around the English coast, though what has induced the change is not easy to determine'. Nor was this a mere flash in the pan. From that time onwards, apart from a short period immediately following the First World War, malaria has ceased to be a serious problem either on the Isle of Grain, or anywhere else on the Peninsula.

Burnett, in the passage quoted above, was, as he says, quite unable to determine the cause of this dramatic change in the incidence of marsh fever. The answer, for which he was stumped, lies in the extensive drainage of both farm and marshlands during the second half of that century. Most of this drainage was carried out by local farmers, and in particular one Henry Pye, but the authorities also seem to have taken a hand following a cholera epidemic during this same period.

Henry Pye mastered the draining of the marshes and, as a result, gained the nickname, 'King of the Hundred'. Pye first came to the Peninsula in 1850, as tenant of St. Mary's Hall Farm, the property of the Dean and Chapter of Rochester Cathedral. When he moved to the Peninsula, the land was heavy and undrained. The ditches and dykes were choked up with the weeds and rubbish of bygone decades for there had been few previous attempts at draining the land either here, or anywhere else on the Peninsula. Pye was a go ahead and ambitious farmer who wanted to prove himself in Kentish farming circles. Doubtless he had been advised against renting land in such a god foresaken area – but nothing could put him off. He could see great possibilities for making a reputation – and a profit. Although the land was waterlogged, it was cheap and would help off set the initial costs of preparing the land for his crops. Investing large sums of money into the project, he directed his workers into clearing the dykes, cutting new ditches, laying much needed drainage pipes and chalking the land. Soon he had turned the wastelands, which were part of St. Mary's Hall farm, into some of the best farmland in Kent. From his first farm, he soon branched out. Leases were taken up on Swigshole, Ross Farm, Hopper's, Turkey Hall and New Barn Hall, whilst he purchased Clinch Street. This last-named farm was the only one he ever owned. All these farms received the same treatment as that at St. Mary's Hall. Other farmers followed in his footsteps and, it is said by 1880 that, every farm on the Peninsula had been drained according to the principles of Henry Pye.

Henry Pye was also one of the earliest farmers in Kent to exploit mechanical farming methods. He purchased three Aveling and Porter steam engines, complete with ploughing equipment and threshing tackle. These Aveling and Porter engines were made in Rochester, and the man behind this particular concern was Thomas Aveling. Aveling actually lived on the Peninsula, at Hoo St. Werburgh, and was a close friend of Henry Pye. Aveling started out in life as a farmer, but branched into the world of engineering when he made a straight forward conversion to a steam powered threshing machine. He found that, with the addition of a crankshaft, the steam engine could be used for not only powering the threshers, but also for making the machine mobile. Prior to that point in time, such machines were brought to the farm field, in which they were to be used, by a team of horses. Thomas Aveling is remembered at Hoo by a stained-glass window in the north aisle of St. Werburgh church.

The firm of Aveling and Porter also constructed road locomotives and steam rollers. Aveling rollers were, in fact, the best in the world and for these, their order books were for ever full. With their Invicta insignia, these became a familiar site on the Peninsula, as such machines eventually helped bring much needed improvements to the local road system.

Returning, briefly, to Henry Pye, we find that not only was he a leading local farmer but was also involved in local politics and commerce. During the 1890s, he was chairman of the Hoo Union, as well as being governor of St. Mary's Hoo School. His venture into the world of commerce also had far reaching effects on the Peninsula, as he was a leading light and director of the 'Hundred of Hoo Railway Company'.

In 1878, Pye, together with a number of other Peninsula farmers, formed themselves into a deputation and approached the South Eastern Railway, as regards that company building a railway line onto the Peninsula. This group of farmers had drawn up their own plans for such a line, and all agreed to sell the necessary land at agricultural prices. The South Eastern had their own plans for such a line, but had not pursued them very far. The deputation of farmers seems to have had some effect on the company for, shortly after this date, the South Eastern blew the dust off their own plans and set about getting parliamentary approval for such a line.

For purposes of building the Hoo railway line a separate company was formed, but controlled by the South Eastern. Known as The Hundred of Hoo Railway Company it immediately set about raising the necessary capital, and a loan of £10,000 was obtained from the South Eastern, whilst a share issue of £80,000, in £10 shares, was made. As a director of the new company Pye's main interest was in that of local traffic. It is unlikely that the South Eastern would have been interested in the line if this was the only source of profit: they were far more interested in the creation of a rail/ferry port complex on the Isle of Grain. Already, a similar venture was proving successful at Queenborough. Unfortunately, from the South Eastern's point of view, the Queenborough continental train/ferry terminus was owned by their bitter enemy – the London Chatham and Dover Railway Company. However, if the London–Chatham had a Continental ferry link, then so must the South Eastern.

The first section of the Hundred of Hoo Railway line was opened in March 1882. This was the Cliffe to Sharnal Street section, and it was opened with the due festivities accorded to the opening of every Victorian railway line. Cliffe and Sharnal Street were both bedecked with decorations, whilst free trips to Gravesend and back were given to all local children. One paper reporting the opening said that for many inhabitants of Cliffe it was the first time they had ever seen Gravesend – a town which was no more than five miles away! The final section of the line was completed in September 1882 when, this time, festivities were centred on the Isle of Grain.

For Henry Pye, and his ilk, the line was sufficient if it merely carried local traffic. Already he was supplying produce to markets in London and the arrival of the railway line would give him, and his fellow prospering farmers, a much more convenient and quicker access to the London markets. To the entrepreneurs of the South Eastern, the much bigger fish of a Continental rail head was the goal; This the *Chatham News* reported on September 16th, 1882:

'Sir Edward Watkins, chairman of the South Eastern, perceived in this spur line of railway from the South Eastern system to the deep water channel of the Medway great possibilities in the way of Atlantic and continental – mainly North German – traffic with this country, and more particularly London. He and his board, therefore, put themselves in touch with the Hundred of Hoo directors, and secured possession of the line on terms with which both parties were satisfied. The first business of the company is, so to speak, to create a traffic by building piers at which vessels of the deepest draught can load and unload their cargoes and passengers in any state of the tide, and then to construct docks for the accommodation of the largest ships afloat.'

In pursuit of these various plans the South Eastern which, as the newspaper account points out, had now fully taken over the Hundred of Hoo Railway, purchased some five hundred acres of land in the Grain area.

As built, the Hundred of Hoo railway line left the main London–Gravesend–Dover line at a point known as Hoo Junction. From there, the line crossed open country to Cliffe. From here the line continued to High Halstow Halt, Sharnal Street, Beluncle Halt, Middle Stoke Halt, Stoke Junction Halt and then on to the Isle of Grain, where it terminated on a wooden pier structure given the very regal name of Port Victoria. No other name could be considered when it is remembered that the London–Chatham's rail head was at Queenborough. Throughout most of its twelve and a half mile length, the line is single track and, when first opened, ran a service of six up trains and six down trains daily. In September 1882 they were time tabled, on weekdays, as follows:

Gravesend	depart	0800	1107	1400	1555	1812	1925
Cliffe	depart	0814	1121	1414	1609	1827	1939
Sharnal Street	depart	0822	1129	1422	1617	1834	1947
Port Victoria	arrive	0832	1139	1432	1627	1844	1957
Port Victoria	depart	0730	0900	1240	1500	1740	2055
Sharnal Street	depart	0745	0915	1255	1515	1755	2110
Cliffe	depart	0750	0920	1300	1520	1800	2115
Gravesend	arrive	0805	0935	1315	1535	1815	2130

Each of these trains connected with a ferry to Sheerness, and this added a further fifteen minutes to the journey. On sundays three up and three down trains were run.

Although the pier at Port Victoria was a wooden construction, it was planned that this should be replaced at a later date by a more permanent structure. Likewise, Port Victoria Hotel which, again constructed of wood, would be replaced when the whole complex was the flourishing Continental rail port of the South Eastern's dreams. To further this aim, the South Eastern started negotiations with the 'Zeeland Steamship Company', but this came to nothing. Over the years negotiations with other concerns also proved fruitless and it rapidly became clear that the South Eastern were in possession of a 'white elephant'. The 'London chatham' were triumphant and one of their directors felt justified in commenting that he doubted whether the Hundred of Hoo railway had 'earned enough to grease the wheels of the trains running over it'. Nor was this an unfair comment, as no railway line could possibly be making a profit when all it relied on was a few farmers sending produce to the London markets.

In 1890, the Port Victoria project did register one minor success when the Royal Corinthian Yacht Club was persuaded to move its headquarters to Port Victoria itself. Two factors were at influence in this decision. First, was the relatively quiet waters to be found at this point of the Medway and the other was the existence of a very convenient railway. The South Eastern went out of its way to be helpful and ran a special weekend train for the use of club members.

Fame also came to Port Victoria when its namesake – Queen Victoria – started using the pierhead for embarking and disembarking from the royal yacht *Victoria and Albert*. In the latter years of her reign Queen Victoria wanted peace and seclusion in her travels and at Port Victoria – in the midst of the North Kent marshes – this is exactly what she found. Anywhere else and she would have found herself surrounded by numerous loyal and faithful subjects. At Port Victoria her train, specially routed from Windsor, could travel right onto the pier and from where it stopped she had but a few yards to walk to the waiting yacht. On one occasion the Queen was actually hoisted onto the yacht by crane! This happened when the pier was out of action and to reach the yacht she was placed into a bath chair which was then fixed to a specially prepared hoist. It is not recorded whether the Queen was amused by the incident.

Queen Victoria was not the only personage to bestow a presence upon Port Victoria's facilities. Another was the Khedive of Egypt, who apparently was too ill to leave his yacht and as he was in Britain for important negotiations, these had to be conducted on the Isle of Grain itself. Another frequent visitor was the German Kaiser. His frequent visits to this country, via Port Victoria, explain why a brass plaque in Grain's otherwise insignificant church contains this message:

PLATE 31 Originally constructed during the nineteenth century, the Port Victoria Hotel shortly before its demolition. This photo was taken in 1951. (Photo courtesy BP.)

PLATE 32 The Pier at Port Victoria today. It consists of nothing more than a few stumps leading out into the Medway River. (Photo courtesy BP.)

PLATE 33   A prototype North Sea-type airship is tested at Kingsnorth.
(Photo courtesy Sir Victor Goddard.)

PLATE 34   The ill-fated attempt to match an aeroplane to an airship.
(Photo courtesy Sir Victor Goddard.)

PLATE 35   An Astra-Torres airship is brought out of its shed. There is a strong likelihood that this remarkable photo was taken at Kingsnorth. (Courtesy Fleet Air Arm Museum.)

PLATE 36   Pictured sometime between 1937 and 1940 the Kingsnorth site is occupied by Berry Wiggins. The two massive sheds are the buildings once occupied by airships. (Photo courtesy Mr. F. W. Pett.)

PLATE 37   Mr. Arthur Plewis, the High Halstow wheelwright, at about the time of his retirement. (Photo courtesy Mr. Arthur Plewis.)

PLATE 38   Hay making, Cooling, c. 1910. Note the farm cart which would have been the product of local wheelwrights. (Courtesy Mr. H. G. Fry, Lower Stoke.)

PLATE 39 H.M.S. *Bulwark*, the battleship which blew up in the River Medway. (Photo courtesy Min. of Defence, Navy Department.)

PLATE 40 The effects of a wartime bombing raid on Grain. Narrowly missing the Fort this unexploded bomb was later exploded by the army.

PLATES 41 and 42   Grain Fort. Shortly before its final demolition during the 1960s.

PLATE 43   Kentish weatherboarding on the Peninsula.
Longford House, Cliffe.

PLATE 44   Kentish weatherboarding on the Peninsula.
Whitehouse Farm, Grain.

PLATE 45   The Peninsula's Tudor-styled buildings.
The Manor House, Cliffe.

PLATE 46   The Peninsula's Tudor-styled buildings. The Hogarth, Grain.

PLATE 47   The Chequers, Hoo.

PLATE 48   Marshgate, Cooling.

Building types of the area—note the Dutch-styled roof.

PLATE 49   Dagnham, Allhallows.

PLATE 50   The Rectory, St. Mary's Hoo.

PLATE 51   Aerial view of the Isle of Grain (September 1977). In the foreground can be seen Grain Power Station under construction whilst **BP** oil tanks, Yantlet Creek and Grain village can also be seen. (Photo courtesy South-Eastern Region, Central Electricity Generating Board.)

PLATE 52   For a time the home of Henry Pye. This is St. Mary's Hall Farm showing the west wing.

PLATES 53 and 54   the Future? (*Above*) one of the many gravel pits on the Peninsula. (*Right*) the pylons and power station of Kingsnorth.

PLATE 54

PLATE 55   Kentish weatherboarding. Dalham Farmhouse, High Halstow.

'To the Glory of God. This church, over eight hundred years old, restored 1904. Among the contributors were King Edward VII and Queen Alexandria. The German Emperor and Duke of Connaught ...'

All were familiar with Grain because they used to visit Port Victoria.

Port Victoria had one, and only one, spell of prosperity. This came in 1900, when its rival pier at Queenborough was put out of use as the result of a fire. The important Flushing mail service operated from Queenborough and, during the time it took to repair the pier at Queenborough, this service operated from Grain. However, it was a short lived prosperity, and when it ceased to run from Grain in 1904, there is little else to record about Port Victoria, other than to catalogue its steady decline. In 1911, the last royal yacht tied up there, and then, in 1914, with war clouds looming, the Royal Corinthian Yacht Club looked for a safer area. Its grandiose club house was abandoned and eventually taken over by the Admiralty. During the war the pier at Port Victoria was badly damaged and part of it had to be blocked off.

The great changes that were coming to the Peninsula are, perhaps, best demonstrated by a glance at the population figures.* For many years the population of the Peninsula remained static and – due to the periodic attacks of marsh fever – even declined. Yet, from 1851 to 1901 the population of the Peninsula virtually doubled. This was partly due to the decreasing numbers of deaths from malaria, but was also due to an influx of people as the area grew in prosperity. In the wake of improved roads, better land drainage, and the railways, came industry. Cliffe, being the best situated of the villages, was the first to 'benefit' – if this is the correct term – gaining a rapidly expanding cement industry and a large gunpowder factory.

A survey of Cliffe, made for the Kelly's directory in 1887, showed the village to have eleven general shops, three bakers, a saddlers, carpenter, shoe maker, watch maker, dress maker and blacksmith. In size, it had quadrupled between 1821 and 1901. The rest of the villages on the Peninsula did not change quite so dramatically as Cliffe, and continued to be a little more cut off. St.

* See Appendix 1.

T.H.P.   K

Mary's Hoo and Cooling were both without shops whilst Allhallows, Grain and High Halstow had but one shop each. Stoke had several shops, as did Hoo St. Werburgh. In fact, in addition to three general shops Hoo also had a carpenter, wheelwright and a pottery works.

Despite the arrival of the railway, the carrier still remained important in the lives of the Peninsula dwellers. The carrier was a timeless servant of the people who, with his cart and horse, ran a regular service between village and town. He would take orders for the local shops, collect packages from the market and take an occasional passenger into town. As such, he was an indispensable member of the community. Towards the end of the nineteenth century there were five carriers on the Peninsula: three operating from Cliffe and one each from Grain and Stoke. The carriers from Grain and Stoke both passed through Hoo. Eventually the carrier was superseded by the motor bus. The first bus companies to operate on the Peninsula being the North Kent Motor Services and the more local firm of Messrs Sands. By then, of course, the Peninsula had entered well and truly into the twentieth century.

CHAPTER THIRTEEN

THE PENINSULA AND A WORLD AT WAR

'We don't want to fight,
But by jingo if we do,
We've got the ships,
We've got the men,
And got the money too.'

Old music hall refrain

Christmas is traditionally the time of peace and goodwill. But for the villagers of Cliffe, the first Christmas of the 1914–18 war fell rather short of these virtues. For it was on Christmas Day, 1914, that Cliffe had its first taste of war, and became, if only temporarily, the object of the German war machine.

The day did not start out particularly differently. There was a heavy mist rolling off the marshes which cleared as the morning wore on, being replaced by a thin mid-winter sun. The air was hardly broken by a breath of wind. As the day reached its zenith, families began to settle down to Christmas lunch. Many had attended that mornings church service and the parish encumbent, Canon Boyd, was slowly driving himself back to the old medieval rectory. Some villagers were returning from their pre-Christmas dinner walks, whilst others enjoyed the conviviality offered by the local pubs. The war, for most, was a million miles away.

At about ten minutes to one the first indication occurred that all was not to continue as peacefully as the day had begun. From the east came the first distant strains of an aero engine. The first head was turned skyward. This was no ordinary aeroplane though, and word quickly got round that the machine was a German bomber. The pubs began to empty. The enemy aircraft was a monoplane with a distinctive bird-like silhouette, which many immediately recognized as a 'Taube'. For those villagers who still did not recognize it as an enemy, they were soon put straight when a whole host of guns began to open fire. As the machine passed over the centre of Cliffe, heading towards London, it came under fire from guns at Chattenden, Upnor, Chatham, and Lower Hope Point at Cliffe, itself.

Several villagers came rushing out of their houses, only to find their lives endangered by falling shrapnel. Canon Boyd found himself in the thick of this as he drove away from the church and shouted to his parishioners to stay in their houses. In all, this state of affairs lasted a good few minutes as the rather slow aeroplane lumbered on to its destination. Eventually, it disappeared over Gravesend and the guns ceased firing.

Within half an hour the plane was back again and this time it was pursued by a British fighter. Nothing could keep the watching villagers off the streets. Now, once again, the surrounding guns brought the German aeroplane under fire and shrapnel once again fell on the village. This did not deter, however, the mesmerized observers of this the first aerial 'dog fight' ever to take place over Kent. For a later generation it was to become a familiar sight but in 1914 it was something new and unheard of. As the watching villagers heard the rata-tat-tat of the British aeroplane's machine-guns a cheer was raised. The British aeroplane, a Vickers Gunbus, had been despatched from Joyce Green, Dartford.

A few of the cheering villagers noticed a metallic object fall from the German plane but most failed to recognize it for what it was. Cliffe had become the first village in Kent to be bombed. The object, an eighteen-pound bomb, plummeted towards the earth and exploded on the main road into Cliffe, a little south of the railway station. Creating a hole some three feet in diameter the bomb caused no injury or any further damage. With its load suitably lightened the German hoped to make his escape from his faster opponent. Some minutes later both disappeared over the horizon and, although it has never been confirmed, there is some evidence to suggest that the German bomber was destroyed.

World War One was inevitable. The surprise was that it took so long in coming. As a result, Britain's defences, if not impregnable, were better prepared than at the outset of any previous war. The Peninsula's Victorian forts and batteries, built as a result of the 1860 Royal Commission, were all re-armed between 1890 and 1900. They received a number of large modern coastal guns designed to deal with the larger battleships then being launched. In addition, these same installations were also given new quick firing guns. Although not as powerful as the coastal guns, these were designed to deal with a new threat posed by the development of the destroyer. These were small heavily armed vessels and were capable of mounting a sudden torpedo attack upon shipping and other targets. Their considerable turn of speed meant that the standard coastal guns could not reload and fire with sufficient speed and precision in order to deter such attacks. It was as a result of this that the new quick firing gun was developed.

The outbreak of war saw the erection of a number of temporary batteries built around the country. These gun batteries were placed behind earth embankments, and one of these, Whitehall battery, was built at Grain in 1915. The pier at Port Victoria also had a temporary gun battery placed on it.

Another series of gun installations was constructed in 1914 as protection for the Admiralty oil tanks placed close to Port Victoria. These oil tanks date back to 1908, and were designed to refuel oil-fired battleships. To facilitate this operation, a jetty projected into the Medway. In all there were forty tanks each with a capacity of 5,000 tons. These particular tanks can still be seen at Grain, as they are the concrete affairs located within the present B.P. refinery. Because of these tanks B.P. must still give priority to naval needs should it be so required.

War, and the threat of war, brought considerable changes to the Peninsula. Not only was it covered with various batteries and forts, but the War Department also acquired large stretches of land for training and other purposes. This was very much the case at Grain. During the early part of the century the War Department took over land at Elphinstone Point for pistol firing practice. Elsewhere, in 1917, Lees Marshes were taken over – uder the Defence of the Realm Act – for future testing of huge guns. Earlier, in 1904, part of the Cooling marshes became a temporary artillery practice ground. A number of thirteen pounders and howitzers were placed in the woods between High Halstow village and Decoy farm and then fired upon a target some 3,500 yards nearer to the Thames.

At both Cliffe and Kingsnorth gunpowder factories were built prior to the 1914–18 war. By far the largest was the Curtis and Harvey works at Cliffe. The factory here was first proposed in 1901 and was developed over a sixty acre area. Numerous scattered buildings were constructed, together with two jetties. At its height the works here were employing in excess of 2,000 people. As regards the Curtis and Harvey works, the term factory tends to be a bit of a misnomer as the works were actually constructed for storage. To reduce any possible danger of damage from accidental explosions the storage areas were surrounded by earthen walls and the whole site by numerous planted trees. The works remained in operation until 1921, when it was closed and the main building has remained derelict ever since.

All this military activity on the Peninsula made the area a highly restricted one. In his book, *The Medway River and Valley*, W. Coles Finch described how he frequently travelled parts of the Peninsula. To do so, he was issued with a special pass, signed by the Assistant Provost Marshal, carrying his photo and such information as his nationality, his parents' nationality and details of relatives under arms.

The war also brought a certain prosperity to the area. There was an increase in employment in Grain, Cliffe and Hoo whilst the forts and batteries themselves generated employment in the servicing of these installations. Householders also found an additional income, as regards billeting troops stationed in the area. Rates for this were quite reasonable. It was often advisable to voluntarily take in a soldier as the billeting officer had certain powers of compulsion and would often billet several upon an unwilling householder.

The First World War was a total war. It required the commitment of every person in the land. Whereas previous national events had merely passed the Peninsula by without a glance, this could no longer be the case. The Peninsula was strategically very important and during those four years of war the area was directly affected. At the outbreak of war, Cliffe alone had sixty of its sons serving in the Royal Navy.

During these years the Peninsula witnessed a number of tragedies. Of these tragedies none could have been worse than the explosions which occurred on board the *Princes Irene* and *Bulwark*, two ships of the Royal Navy. Both were anchored in the Medway and both were completely destroyed as a result of internal explosions. The exact cause of the disasters has never been discovered and, as a result, the two separate incidents have been linked with the activities of enemy agents.

The success of the German army in capturing a number of Belgian channel ports during the early months of the war meant that Britain was once again faced with a very real possibility of invasion. It was for this reason, that November 1914 saw the Fifth Battle Fleet moved in to the Medway anchorage so that it would be more ready to combat any German moves in the Channel area. Amongst the ten ships of this battle fleet was the ageing *Bulwark*. Launched in 1899 she had once been an important flag ship but had long since been overshadowed by the later 'Dreadnoughts'. Nevertheless, she could still pack a powerful punch and was the equal of many a German ship.

On the morning of November 26th, the *Bulwark* was anchored at buoy number 17 in Kethole Reach. At a little after 7.30, the crew were called to breakfast while the ship's band provided some light entertainment. At Stoke a young school boy, Arthur Plewis, paused for a moment in his early morning chores and looked out across the Medway anchorage. From his house, just outside Stoke and on the Grain road, he could see the ships of the Battle Fleet. The next few minutes are ingrained for ever on his memory, for at a few minutes to eight he saw one of these vessels enveloped in a cloud of smoke. There was a tremendous explosion and, when the smoke cleared, where this ship had once been at anchor there was now absolutely nothing. The vessel, which he later discovered was the *Bulwark*, had just disappeared.

Another eyewitness was Charles Drage. He was a midshipman on board the *London*. This was a ship of similar design to the *Bulwark* and was lying at the next anchorage. The following account was written that evening in his diary. At the time Charles Drage was a midshipman on duty watch:

'When the catastrophe occurred I was reading a signal exercise on the port boat deck and had my back turned to the *Bulwark* who was our next astern.

'I experienced a slight shock, coupled with a blast of hot air and, on turning, saw a vast flame as high as the main truck, around which smoke was already beginning to form.

'Such debris as was in the air consisted of small objects and appeared to be largely composed of wood stored in the booms.

'There were two distinct explosions and then debris began to fall on our port quarter, a strong wind blowing it away from us. The place where the *Bulwark* had laid was entirely covered with smoke and it was impossible to ascertain the nature, extent or cause of the damage.'

The explosion, and the flash accompanying it, were recorded as

far away as Conyer Teynham, some fourteen miles distance. At
Sittingbourne, a man later described it to a *Chatham News*
reporter as being 'just like a wonderful sunset'. The flash of the
explosion was also seen at Leigh and Southend.

Once the immediate shock of the explosion had worn off, a
number of boats were sent out to search for survivors. Drage's
diary continues:

'I got away in my cutter with the Lieutenant T. and a scratch
crew and we were the first to reach the wreckage.

'By this time the smoke had entirely cleared away and the
situation was roughly as follows: Ahead of us, in a straight line
was the *Bulwark*'s buoy with her cable hanging from it, the
remains of her foremast protruding above water and the bows of
the *Prince of Wales*, the next ship in the line.

'From the *Bulwark*'s foremast, extending nearly to the bows of
the *Prince of Wales* lay a circle of floating debris, hammocks
etc., the centre of which was comparatively open and clear.

'Amongst this debris were about twenty men some of whom
were alive and calling for help. Three of these were picked up ...

'Besides these we only saw two corpses the rest having been
carried down stream by the very strong current. The bowman
very wisely did not attempt to pull these corpses inboard but let
them go as soon as they realised they were dead. Even so, one
horribly injured man sank before we could get to him.'

In all, of a crew comprising 741 officers and men, only twelve
survived.

At this point nobody could even surmise the cause of the
explosion. Rumours abounded. Some blamed it on to the action of
an enemy U-boat whilst others felt it must be the handiwork of an
enemy agent. Indeed, one national newspaper reported the story of
a foreign looking gentleman having been seen at Sheerness. He was
described as being dressed like a farmer and having a military
bearing – spy mania was shortly to reach its peak!

The following day Admiralty divers were ordered to examine the
wreckage to try to determine the cause of the explosion. Of course,
it was a hopeless job. All that the divers could do was report that
the entire upper deck had been blown completely away. The
damage was so complete that it was not even possible to discover
from where the explosion had come. The force of the explosion can
be partially gauged by the fact that large chunks of metal were

strewn over a one half mile radius, and an officer's wardrobe was found the following day on the Grain marshes. Elsewhere, a huge piece of metal, weighing, it is reckoned, some several hundredweight, went crashing through the cement barge *Dee*. At the time, the *Dee* was collecting mud from Dagnum Marsh and was over three-quarters of a mile from the battleship.

Following the disaster, an official enquiry was held. Although it interviewed numerous eyewitnesses and some of the survivors, the enquiry could do no more than conclude:

> 'It is unclear from the evidence which has been produced that the explosion which caused the loss of the ship was due to accidental ignition of ammunition on board.'

The failure of the enquiry to indicate a precise cause inevitably encouraged the sabotage theory. Later writers have attempted to suggest that an enemy agent successfully planted a bomb on board the battleship, but the evidence for this is extremely weak. Indeed, the official enquiry into the disaster examined the possibility and regarding this, they stated: 'There is no evidence to support a suggestion that the explosion was due either to treachery on board or an act of the enemy.'

The most likely explanation lies in the design of the ship. The *Bulwark* had a total of eleven magazines and each was connected by a passage running through the entire ship. At both the fore and aft ends there were further cross passages. At these passages were packed with shells and cordite at the time of the explosion they were as good as a powder trail leading round the entire ship. In his diary, Charles Drage considered this aspect as a possible cause:

> '... There seems no doubt that there was an abnormal quantity of cordite in the ammunition passages.
>
> 'The explosion may have been started in various ways, such as a wire fusing, a smouldering match dropped down an ammunition hoist from a casemate, or even a heavy object falling on the nose of a six inch lyddite, though the last is extremely unlikely.
>
> 'Once started it would have spread by the ammunition passages to the cross passages and twelve inch magazine and touched off every explosive in the ship.'

That this is the cause of the *Bulwark* explosion is partially supported by the fact that so many other British and allied ships met similar fates. All were of a rather similar design – a design in which little heed was paid to safeguarding against internal explosions. Two major British battleships blew up at anchor during that war, whilst another three sank at the Battle of Jutland as the result of internal explosions. Charles Drage, himself, also witnessed a similar explosion on board the Italian battleship *Leonardo Da Vinci* in 1916. On this occasion, the Italian ship, like the *Bulwark*, was lying peacefully at anchor in the harbour at Taranto.

As for the *Bulwark*, herself, she was to remain a menace to shipping for a good many years. At high tide much of the vessel's remaining structure was just below water level and at low tide huge pieces of ironwork protruded above the water's surface. Little could be done about this during the war years and the wreckage was simply buoyed and left. Even after the war, due to a slump in the value of scrap metal, the Admiralty could not find a salvage company prepared to undertake the costs of the *Bulwark*'s removal. It was only in 1935, when scrap metal began to rise in price, that a firm undertook salvage operations.

It was only nine months later that the Peninsula witnessed its second maritime disaster. In not dissimilar circumstances to those of the *Bulwark* another naval vessel, the *Princess Irene*, suffered a similar fate when she too sunk as the result of a major internal explosion. As a fast minelayer, the *Princess Irene* was carrying some five hundred mines at the time of the explosion.

The *Princess Irene* was a converted passenger liner. She had only been completed in 1914, and was due to enter service with the Canadian Pacific Line when she was commandeered for military services. On the morning of May 27th, 1915, she was anchored just a little off Port Victoria pier, in Salt Pan Reach. At eleven minutes past eleven there was a tremendous explosion which, according to one witness, hurled the ship into the air. The young Arthur Plewis, at that time attending lessons in Stoke school, also remembers the explosion. He recalls that the bang was so loud that he thought the windows of the school were about to come in. His brother, Ralph, a railwayman, had a narrow escape. On hearing the explosion, he threw himself under a railway truck. Upon emerging some minutes later, he found the entire top of the truck had been ripped off by a huge piece of iron.

A rather censored version of the *Chatham News* reported the main details of the explosion the following Friday:

'The force of the explosion was terrific. To many it seemed louder than the *Bulwark* explosion, and that shook many houses to their foundations. The spectacle, for a few moments was terrific in its grandeur – one who has seem Vesuvius in eruption, likened it to that spectacle for a moment, flames and smoke belched forth in great volume. Then the flames were no more, but over the spot where the *Princess Irene* had been moored hung a dense pall of white smoke ... Not a vestige of the majestic liner was visible when it dispersed – only wreckage'.

The *Princess Irene* was completely ripped asunder. Chunks of metal were thrown everywhere. A portion of the boiler fell on a passing coal vessel which at the time was about half a mile away while the nearby Port Victoria pier was partially wrecked, as metal fragments slammed into the massive wooden supports. In fact, the damage was so severe, that the seaward end of Port Victoria pier was sealed off and never used again as it was considered beyond repair. Flying metal also damaged the Admiralty oil tanks at Grain. Some of them were burst open and the whole area was covered by a pool of oil some three feet in depth.

On the Isle of Grain, one young resident was killed when playing in the garden of a bungalow. At about the time of the explosion a 9-year-old girl, Ida Barden, was struck on the head by a piece of metal plate, which a coroners court later identified as part of the minelayer. The plate had been fused on one side as a result of great heat. A witness at Ida Barden's inquest reported that gas and flames from the *Princess Irene* rose to a height of some two miles.

Of the crew of 273 officers and men, only one survived. For the medway towns the disaster was particularly acute as the death toll included seventy-six dockyard workers who were still working on the vessel. The one survivor, Stoker Willis, was rescued by the tug *Bruno*. The master of the tug, Mr. G. Pilcher later described the rescue and his account appeared in the *Chatham News*:

'I was fifty yards away abreast of the *Princess Irene*, with a loaded lighter in tow alongside, when the accident happened.

'After the smoke and falling fragments had cleared away one of my crew saw a man who proved to be Stoker Willis struggling in the water among the wreckage and oil about thirty yards away from my tug.

'I went to his assistance as quickly as possible, and as I got near him my Stoker, W. Rider, lay on his stomach on the deck of the lighter, and hung over her bow. He caught him by the hand the first time and dragged him from between the tug and the lighter. If he had missed him he would surely have drowned. He was covered in thick black oil.'

Naturally enough rumours again began to spread. It appears that most people held one of two opinions. Some felt a time bomb had been placed on board the ship whilst others put it down to an incorrectly primed mine. With so little evidence of German agents carrying out such activities in this country the most likely cause is the latter. Packed with such an explosive cargo it would only need the accidental detonation of one mine to cause the tragedy which has been described.

Two major centres of war time employment on the Peninsula have not so far been mentioned. One was the experimental seaplane station on the Isle of Grain and the other was the airship factory at Kingsnorth. Both were naval establishments and both were involved in a good deal of pioneering work during these infant days of military aviation. The air station at Grain employed about eight hundred workers, many of whom came from the ranks of local civilians. As the war progressed the air station undertook a number of different functions which ranged from repairing and converting seaplanes, to the construction of new machines. In fact, so large did the seaplane station become, that accommodation and service buildings formed themselves into a town much larger than the actual village of Grain to which they were appended. These buildings sited in the vicinity of the present day village hall, even included a cinema.

The airship factory at Kingsnorth also drew heavily upon civilian labour and a major task carried out at the factory was the assembly of partially completed airships. The various component parts, engines, fabric for the hydrogen filled envelope and numerous valves, all had to be assembled at Kingsnorth. In particular, large numbers of female labour were employed in the fabric shops. For both boys and girls just leaving school the airship factory provided opportunities previously unknown. Eric Smith – now a pensioner living in Hoo – recalls how, upon leaving school, he took his first job at Kingsnorth and received the grand weekly wage of sixteen shillings. He was employed in the experimental laboratories which were developing lighter alloys.

The Isle of Grain air station dates back to 1912 when the Admiralty decided to construct a number of coastal air stations for the defence of various ports. The Isle of Grain was an obvious choice for such a station as planes based here would be in a position to give aerial protection to Chatham and Sheerness docks, as well as to the Admiralty oil tanks on the Island itself. Grain was, in fact, the first of these coastal air stations to become operational, being commissioned in December 1912. A letter from the Admiralty to the Sewers Commissioners gives the following description of the station:

> 'The works consist of aeroplane sheds, landing pier, roadway from pier, an inclined way from Cockleshell Beach over the river bank into the marshes for use by hydroplanes &tc.'

The exact site of the air station is that area now occupied by the CEGB power station, with the inclined way situated near to the residential area. Today, the only remains of the air station are a series of concrete strips (to the west of the residential club) which once formed the base of various hangars and workshops. For accommodation, personnel of the air station took over the coastguard cottages – agreeing, in return, to carry out coastguard duties.

The Royal Navy had plans to make Grain the centre of naval flying activities. As such, the station rapidly increased in size. In June 1913, it was allocated £20,000 for buildings and sheds, whilst in January 1914, a Royal Naval Air Service document records that the station was allocated some thirty-seven aeroplanes – this was approximately one-quarter of all the Royal Naval aeroplanes at this time.

At the outbreak of war the seaplane station was given the task of patrolling the Thames estuary and part of the Channel. The first wartime patrol from Grain was on August 9th when the station's commander, Lieutenant Seddon, carried out a reconnaissance patrol over Belgium. By the end of November some 8,015 miles had been flown from Grain since the outbreak of hostilities. During those early months of the war, much time was taken up with the provision of regular two hourly patrols, giving the British Expeditionary Force air cover during its crossing to France.

From 1915 onwards, though, Grain tended to specialize in experimental work. Duties ranged from testing and handling all new seaplanes, converting landplanes for naval use, testing new guns and some experimentation into ground to air wireless communications.

One part of the station was the Experimental Construction Department. It was responsible for the design, and building, of nine different aircraft mostly to an Admiralty specification for a fast seaplane capable of destroying Zeppelins. None of the Grain designs were approved for mass production, however. Throughout the war, the main concentration of the station was upon converting various aircraft. One conversion was the Grain Griffin, which was a Sopwith Bomber fitted with hydrovanes and floatation bags, as well as folding wings.

Hydrovanes and flotation bags were more or less the brainchild of the air station at Grain. A hydrovane – usually called a hydrofoil these days – was fitted beneath the chassis and allowed a landplane to make an emergency landing at sea. Once the aeroplane hit the sea compressed air was forced into the flotation bags and this kept the plane afloat indefinitely.

Experimental and construction work was also carried out at Kingsnorth. Amongst the airships produced at Kingsnorth was the small Submarine Scout (or simply SS) type. This was a two seater and was used for patrolling the North sea and Channel. Later in the war the factory went over to the assembly of much larger air ships.

Kingsnorth also ran an advanced training course for airship pilots, a course which included navigation, seamanship and the principles of aerostatics.

Construction of the airship factory was started in July 1913 and it was commissioned in April 1914. Its major feature was two large sheds, which were used for the storage and construction of the airships. As an Admiralty establishment it kept the naval tradition of having a port and starboard side whilst leave was referred to as 'going ashore'. Kingsnorth was also an operational air station, with duties ranging from anti-submarine patrols to protection of troopships.

Included in the experimental work at Kingsnorth was an attempt to suspend an aeroplane to the envelope of an airship. This was for anti-Zepppelin operations, and the theory was that as soon as a Zeppelin was spotted, the aeroplane should be released from the envelope. Such an operation would allow Zeppelins to be engaged that much quicker. Once the aeroplane was released the airship envelope would be 'ripped' (i.e. the removal of a panel to allow air out) and the envelope would be returned to the ground ready for its re-use.

The first test flight of this new device was carried out on Monday, February 22nd, 1916. The two inventors of the idea, Wing Commander Neville Usborne and Squadron Commander De Courcey Ireland, were the pilots. Unfortunately things did not go according to plan. The plane was suspended by three cables and when the release lever was pulled, only the forward two disengaged. At the same time the envelope was 'ripped' and began to descend bringing the aeroplane down with it. It appears that Ireland tried to crawl along the tail of the aeroplane to disengage the cable but was thrown off in the process. His body was later recovered from the Medway near Strood. Usborne was no less lucky for the falling plane picked up speed and smashed into the ground at the railway depot in Strood. He was also killed.

This was by no means the only accident at Kingsnorth during these years. The airships were filled with highly inflammable hydrogen gas. Eric Smith remembers having seen one airship from Kingsnorth catching fire whilst in the sky. Experiments carried out at Kingsnorth into the nature of hydrogen were also a potential recipe for disaster. On one occasion a hangar was partially wrecked as the result of just such an explosion.

Both the Grain and Kingsnorth establishments survived the end of the war by only a few years. In 1918, Grain seaplane station was integrated into the newly formed R.A.F., and being honoured with the title 'Marine Aircraft Experimental Establishment' (M.A.E.E.) it was given the task of test flying all new seaplanes. During these years, the nearby Shorts aircraft company at Rochester also used the facilities at Grain. But with the amalgamation of the Army's Royal Flying Corp and the Navy's Royal Naval Air Service, there was an obvious duplication of facilities. Because of this, it was decided that Grain should be closed. In 1924, the wireless experiments were moved to the, then, new air field of Biggin Hill whilst the maritime work was transferred to Felixstowe. It was a similar attitude that led the Kingsnorth factory to be closed down in 1920. The experimental work being carried out at Kingsnorth was transferred to Cardington.

The inter-war period once again saw a run down of the Medway's defences. Hoo Ness, Darnet and Slough forts were totally abandoned at this time, as were the temporary batteries that had been built at the onset of hostilities, in 1914. Nevertheless, the Peninsula still remained an area of some military importance – although, for a good many years this importance tended to be restricted to the Isle of Grain.

Shortly after the Grain seaplane station was abandoned by the R.A.F. this same area was taken over by the Admiralty as their Armament's Depot (R.N.A.D.). This allowed ships entering Chatham dockyard, for refits, to unload their ammunition, and then rearm when leaving.

Grain also began its role as a gun testing station. Guns for such ships as the *Prince of Wales* were brought down from Woolwich and erected on the Lee's Marsh site (by now usually referred to as the Yantlet Range). One cannot easily imagine the noise that these massive naval guns must have made when fired. The residents of Grain were not particularly happy with this new Admiralty venture as becomes clear from this item which appeared in the *Daily Mail* and dated August 22nd, 1929:

'The 500 inhabitants of this little straggling village, which lies at the far end of the Medway mud-flats, have unofficially changed its name to the "Isle of Grin and bear it". And thereby hangs a tale.

'Six years ago the War Office constructed at Yantlet, a muddy creek just over a mile from the village, a testing station for the firing of big guns. Villagers declare that it cost round about a million pounds and that the justification for the huge expenditure was that it is the only place in the country where the War Office can fire their non-explosive shells in a definite direction and recover them at will from the sands of the east coast, 15, 20, 30, and even 40 miles away.

'Individual visitors protested to the War Office, but without result. The station was built and firing started. Very soon tiles began to fall from the village roofs, walls began to crack, and ceilings to fall in. Protests were again sent to the War Office, but merely brought the reply:

"The War Office cannot admit liability for damage by

concussion in connection with artillery practice carried out in the exigencies of the public service.

'And for five years the Isle of Grain has grinned and borne it.

'This year, however, the firing has increased to such an extent that steps are being taken to organise a stronger protest, in which Mr. I. J. Albery, M.P. for Gravesend, is taking a keen interest. During the last few months the village has been shaken to its mud and gravel foundations, many people fear their cottages may tumble down on top of them any day, and the older folk are complaining of "nerves".'

'The material damage already done is said to run into hundreds of pounds, and life in the village is becoming unbearable.

'After a heavy firing the village is strewn with broken tiles and pieces of glass from blown out windows, and in many of the houses which I visited I saw gaping holes in ceilings and roofs, cracked walls, and broken and cracked windows.'

Nor were the residents of Grain the only people to feel the effects of these bangs, as houses in Hoo St. Werburgh were frequently shaken to their very core.

The testing of these huge pieces of ordnance continued right on into the mid-fifties, with the largest guns being brought by barge and smaller guns often coming by road or rail. Once the guns arrived at the range they were transferred to special mountings prior to a series of test firings carried out by members of the Royal Artillery. The object of these tests was to establish both the range and velocity of each individual gun. To do this, the gun was fired on a number of different trajectories and the fall of the shell recorded. The velocity of each shell was measured electronically for, as it left the barrel, it passed between two metal towers, each carrying special recording equipment.

With the post-World War Two decline of the British navy the Yantlet range found itself being used less frequently, and so it was in 1963 that the entire area was handed over to the Royal Engineers. They are the current occupiers of the range and it serves, for them, the purpose of training military engineers in the handling of explosive material. It seems likely that the Royal Engineers will continue to use the range for a good many years. For them it has the advantage of being one of the few areas where they can use explosive of up to 40 lb (although it should be noted that such charges are always buried below ground in order to reduce shock waves) whilst recently the range was used to demonstrate, to both army and police personnel, the devastating effects of a car bomb. This latter was considered a most important exercise in view of the continuing problems associated with northern Ireland.

This short digression, though, has moved a long way from the particular theme of the present chapter. Returning to the inter-war period, it is only necessary to state that the various defence structures – apart from those already completely abandoned – were simply kept ticking over. However, in 1940, and the very real threat of a Nazi invasion, these defences were quickly strengthened with the addition of numerous pill boxes in the Cliffe and Hoo St. Werburgh areas. Elsewhere, Grain tower was armed with a six-pounder anti-aircraft gun; a searchlight battery was bestowed upon the remains of Port Victoria whilst a four-gun anti-aircraft battery was built at Fenn Corner.

Grain, during this period, was a highly restricted area with passes being checked by army personnel at a barrier sited close to the present filling station at the refinery. Grain housed not only the well armed fort and numerous batteries but also an engine for the anti-submarine boom. The boom stretched across the deep water channel of the Medway and was operated by an engine in a small concrete building standing next to the tall observation tower.

In 1940 both Home Guard and Auxiliary Fire Service units were formed on the Peninsula whilst Grain village – and perhaps others – had a secretly appointed triumvirate whose duties were to co-ordinate village affairs in the event of an enemy landing.

The Home Guard unit at Cliffe numbered more than thirty. It was based upon Cliffe fort and carried out regular nightly patrols along the Thames wall. Most members were armed with ancient rifles but they also had a device which was supposed to eliminate tanks through firing hand grenades.

An Auxiliary Fire Service unit was formed at Hoo St. Werburgh with a Bedford ETB lorry and auxiliary tender, whilst the ARP at Grain had a further lorry and pump. Eric Smith of Hoo was a member of the AFS and he recalls that the worst wartime fire on the Peninsula was at Church Farm, when the barn was ignited. On the whole, though, enemy raiders rarely bothered the Peninsula except for the occasional unloading of bombs on deserted fields. However, towards the end of the war considerable damage was done to Stoke church by a V2. At Hoo, Eric Smith felt a mighty thump as the rocket came down, with the thump being followed by a noise similar to a fast train going through a station. To people on the Peninsula, though, V2s were not unfamiliar, as frequently they could look up and count the vapour trails of thirty or more. Shortly afterwards there would be a vroomp sound as they came down somewhere in London.

The Peninsula's greatest contribution to the Second World War must undoubtedly be its connection with PLUTO. PLUTO was the code name for Pipe Line Under The Ocean, and was conceived in 1942 as a means by which large quantities of fuel oil could be transferred to the continent, during the invasion period. Basically, it consisted of a continuous thirty mile, three-inch diameter, reinforced pipe which ran under the English Channel. The main pumping station for PLUTO was at Dungeness and this drew petrol – via a system of inland pipes – from a number of locations, one of which was Grain. Inside the present Kent Oil Refinery are a number of mounds which once concealed the underground stores from which fuel was pumped to Dungeness and then across the Channel.

CHAPTER FOURTEEN

INDUSTRY ARRIVES

'Further commercial and industrial development in the
North Kent Marshes is not in general compatible with
the maintenance and exploitation of the area's scientific
and recreational potential.'
From a 1971 report by 'The Nature Conservancy'

The first large scale industrial enterprise on the Peninsula can be
dated to the mid-seventeenth century. Sometime during that
century, or perhaps even earlier, a fairly sizeable salt panning
works was established on a site now occupied by the Grain Oil
Refinery. A document, the original of which can be inspected at
the County Records Office, describes the works as they were in
1669 – the date the document was written. They are said to extend
over an area of sixty acres and to include ten boiling pans and
eighteen hundred brine pans. The boiling pans measured eight feet
by eighty feet and the brine pans were three foot square. At this
point in time salt was a highly important commodity, being mostly
used as a food preservative. However, large amounts of salt were
imported from abroad, and during the sixteenth century there was
a government campaign to increase home-produced salt, and it is
possible that salt panning at Grain was a direct result of this
governmental encouragement.

The works at Grain probably employed some forty men in the
salt extraction process. Quite simply, this consisted of flooding the
pans, and either letting the water evaporate naturally (this was the
purpose of the brine pans) or heating the water with a coal or wood
fire (this was the purpose of the boiling pans). Once the water
evaporated, the salt would be collected and taken to the storehouse
which, apparently, was large enough to house some two hundred
tons of salt. From time to time, we can assume that the finished
product was despatched, by river, directly to London.

On a number of local maps dating from the seventeenth century,
a windmill is shown to be associated with the site of the salt works.
It seems likely that this mill may have actually been used to draw
water from the Medway onto the pans. This was not an uncommon
process, and such mills were known to have existed at Southwold,
in Suffolk, and, somewhat further afield, in New England. These

same early maps also indicate a second salt works on the Isle of Grain. This time it is shown to be further north and adjacent to Yantlet Creek. A windmill is also shown to have existed on this site, but we know of few further details. The final reference to these two salt works is of a map dated 1810, and it seems likely that this was approximately the date in which they ceased operation, especially, as by that date, alternative and cheaper methods of obtaining salt had been discovered.

There are two other references relating to early commercial undertakings on the Isle of Grain. Burnett, in his *History of the Isle of Grain*, refers to the small-scale manufacture of leather, which he dates to the year 1579. In addition to this, he refers to the medieval practice of laying kiddles. A kiddle was a kind of stake net, with a very fine mesh, and these were staked out around the Yantlet. For reasons already explained, though, the Peninsula hardly had a magnetic attraction for industry and it was not until the latter half of the nineteenth century that this trend was reversed.

Kelly's commercial directory for 1887 gives the following information relating to industry on the Peninsula. The largest industrial enterprises mentioned are the cement works at Cliffe, with a pottery and tile works at Hoo. The directory also refers to a windmill at Hoo but, apart from farming, these, more or less, were the sum total of the Peninsula's industry at this time.

The windmill referred to was 'Ballard's' mill, which stood on Hoo Common. The first reference to a mill on this site was in 1769, when a smock mill occupied the site, but the following century saw its replacement by a post mill. In 1905, W. Coles Finch, who visited most of the mills in Kent, recorded that Ballard's mill was derelict and had been out of use for about a quarter of a century. Once owned by the Ballard family, the mill undoubtedly would have catered for the needs of most of the Peninsula farmers. The milling of corn before the twentieth century was very localized, due to the difficulties of transportation on the poor roads. These small mills had to rely on unpredictable winds, and with the later improvement of the roads, local millwrights were superseded by large scale millers.

The pottery and tile works at Hoo were owned by one Benjamin Baker, whose output included a wide range of products, from chimney pots and flower vases to a general selection of brown ware. The siting of a pottery and tile works at Hoo can be readily appreciated, when it is remembered that both are clay based industries and were able to use clay drawn directly from the banks of the Medway.

One nineteenth century industrial connection with the village of Hoo that has not so far been mentioned, is brickmaking. During the nineteenth and early twentieth century, Hoo was a local centre for the manufacture of bricks. This was in the days before the growth of the massive brick making companies. In Hoo, brick earth was dug from close to the modern day marina, whilst the finished product was exported out of Hoo by barge. In all, there were three brick making companies in Hoo, which were in the proximity of Hoo Creek. Hoo's association with brickmaking continued into the 1930s.

A further arm of the building industry also has a lengthy connection with the Peninsula. This is the cement industry, which with regard to the Peninsula, has always been centred around Cliffe. It was in 1853, that the first cement manufacturing works were established at Cliffe, when I. C. Johnson moved his factory from Frindsbury to Cliffe. Johnson was one of the pioneers of the cement industry, developing a hard setting mixture of clay and chalk in a 2:5 ratio respectively. At Cliffe he started the manufacture of cement under the name of Johnson and Poynter and the works here eventually came into the hands of Francis and Company. It appears that these works had a very low output which never arose above sixty tons per week. It was from the factory at Cliffe that cement was sent for the erection of the Eddystone, Lizard and Needles lighthouses. To commemorate this, three of the Thames sailing barges owned by Francis and Company were duly named after the three lighthouses.

The firm of Francis and Company first moved into Cliffe some years before they actually took over the Johnson site. In 1868 they established their own works and this became fully operational in 1871 when it was recorded as manufacturing Portland, Roman, Medina and Parian cements. This particular site was about one mile south-west of Cliffe village and close to the Thames. Here, there were two jetties for the despatch of finished cement. Close by were the chalk quarries and these, together with firing kilns and the jetties, were all linked by tramway upon which a number of Aveling railway locomotives operated. Earlier, in 1886, partners of

Francis and Company, Empson, Holcombe and Company, also started cement manufacturing at Cliffe. At the turn of the century, both of these works were absorbed into the 'Associated Portland Cement Manufacturers', and continued in operation until 1920, when the Francis works were eventually closed down.

It was one of the Francis cement kilns which became the subject of one of the earliest pollution controversies on the Peninsula. This was when the much famed General Gordon complained that fumes from the manufacture of cement were damaging the health of his soldiers stationed at Cliffe Fort. The matter was soon resolved, however, with the construction of a chimney, which carried the fumes over the fort.

The closure of the Francis works was not, by any means, the end of Cliffe's connection with the manufacture of cement. In 1910, a further company, the Thames Portland, opened their works at Cliffe. Situated close to the Francis works, it was taken over by the Alpha Cement Company in 1934. This particular works was fairly substantial, containing within the area of the works a number of kilns, quarries and wharves, together with a narrow gauge railway. This particular works continued in operation until 1969, when the chalk quarries were finally worked out. By that time, the site had been acquired by the Associated Portland Cement Company.

The attraction of cement manufacturers to the Peninsula lies in the area's ability to supply the needed amounts of clay and chalk. Chalk, of course, was obtained from local quarries, whilst clay could be obtained from two separate sources. For the cement manufacturers in the Cliffe area, clay was first dredged from the salt marshes along the Thames, though from 1934 onwards, the Alpha Company resorted to digging out the clay basins on the Cliffe marshes.

It was the abundant supply of clay on the Medway side of the Peninsula which was partially responsible for attracting a number of cement manufacturers to the Frindsbury area and other parts of the Medway valley. Indeed, there was a general belief that only Medway clay produced the best Portland cement. By digging out the various salt marshes, these companies acquired, at economic rates, all the clay they needed. The entire area from West Hoo Creek, to an area past the Isle of Grain, was extensively worked by the 'muddies'. A muddy was employed in digging out clay holes and loading the clay on to the waiting barges. They worked in gangs, and great numbers of them came from Hoo and Stoke. Often they lived close to the clay holes which they worked, occupying converted barges or lighters. The 'Muddies' had a great tradition. They were hard workers and as equally hard drinkers. Further, there was a great rivalry between the 'muddies' of Stoke and those of Hoo, and certainly the older residents of these villages remember the frequent fights that occurred between rival gangs.

Eventually, 'muddies' were replaced by grab cranes, of which the four owned by S. J. Brice replaced over one hundred 'muddies'. The firm of S. J. Brice was one of the largest firms in the area extracting clay from the Medway. Owning fifty barges, the firm held contracts to supply a number of cement factories with the clay they needed. Between 1881–1911, it is estimated that this one firm was responsible for digging out 1,356,000 tons of clay from East Hoo Creek alone. Brice was not the only contractor operating, his firm was just the largest. Other firms were taking clay from the Medway, and between them they are responsible for the present state of the saltings, which maps show to have diminished significantly over the last two centuries.

Today, it is the petrochemical industry with which the Peninsula seems to have its greatest associations. There are two refineries on the Peninsula, one on the Isle of Grain and the other at Kingsnorth, whilst at the time of writing the Burmah-Total Company are still pursuing plans for a third refinery to be sited at Cliffe. In addition to these, there are also the storage facilities at Cliffe for Jet petrol and on the Isle of Grain for Calor gas.

It was the Admiralty which first brought oil to the Peninsula when they established forty oil storage tanks in 1908, on the Isle of Grain, close to Elphinstone Point. At that time the Royal Navy was converting many of its major vessels from coal to oil, as the latter gave the advantage of greater range, the ability to re-fuel at sea and smoke elimination. Following the First World War, the Isle of Grain was chosen by an American, Charles Francis de Ganahl, as a centre for the storage, refining and marketing of a petrol product which was later marketed as 'Power Petrol'.

In 1923, de Ganahl had his refinery constructed upon a one hundred acre site purchased from the South-Eastern Railway Company. Situated at Elphinstone Point, the new company was named the Medway Oil and Storage Company (MOSCO). What attracted de Ganahl to the site was the deep water frontage he was able to acquire. This meant that the largest tankers of the day could anchor at the end of a short jetty, built for the purpose. In addition to a steel jetty, the Mosco site had two refining units, numerous storage tanks and loading points for both road and rail transit.

The first commercial oil tanker to tie up at the Isle of Grain was the 2,000-ton *Delmuir*, in the year 1923. From this point onwards a great deal of work was provided for those living on the Peninsula, especially as the company showed a great willingness to seek out and train local talent, instead of continuing to import American technicians. In 1928, de Ganahl sold out and the MOSCO works began to concentrate purely upon storage, marketing and blending of the Power Petrol product.

Close on the heels of the Medway Oil and Storage Company, came Berry Wiggins. In 1928, this firm started negotiations for the purchase of the 323 acre site once occupied by the Kingsnorth airship factory. Berry Wiggins were determined upon refining crude oil and, like de Ganahl, they chose the Peninsula because of the deep water facilities it could provide. The site was officially taken over in 1930, following which, refining units and numerous storage tanks were erected. To ease transport of products within the site, part of an old Admiralty tramway was utilised, and later Berry Wiggins, themselves, built a one and a half mile narrow gauge railway line from the jetty to their crude oil tanks. Oil refining at Kingsnorth started in 1931, and 39,803 tons of oil was refined during the first eighteen months of operation.

It was in 1947, that plans began to mature regarding the erection of a much larger oil refinery on the Isle of Grain. As planned, this was to be built by one of the BP group of companies (more specifically the Anglo-Iranian Oil Company) on a 2,000-acre site, which included some of the older MOSCO works. The government showed early anxieties over the vulnerability of the area to enemy action, but eventually granted permission for the development of the site in June 1950. An important aspect of the proposed refinery was its wide frontage onto the River Medway – a frontage which was eventually to be blanketed by nine jetties. Amongst these jetties, was the original MOSCO jetty which was taken over and lengthened. The, by now, very much dilapidated and long since disused Port Victoria pier was included in the area owned by BP, and this, together with the Port Victoria station and hotel, were all demolished. To satisfy the needs of local rail users, a small modern station named 'Grain' was built a little short of the original Port Victoria station.

A serious problem confronted by the engineers engaged in building the new refinery was that of drainage, as much of the refinery site was marshland. A report of July, 1949, stated that the land was incapable of bearing any heavy loads, without the addition of pile or raft foundations. Even so, pile foundations provided certain problems, as huge seventy foot piles sank into the marshy land up to a depth of twenty feet, before there was any need to strike them with hammers. However, despite these problems, the building of the refinery rarely slipped behind its construction time table and, in the spring of 1953, the refinery was ready to start production.

By modern standards the oil refinery at Grain is somewhat dated. Its sprawling ugliness is, amongst the other things, a sign of inefficient use of space. The writer of the Penguin Guide to Kent (Pevsner series) rightly states that it was Grain's remoteness which allowed the builders to forget their duties of producing a decent design. To partially offset the hideous appearance of the refinery, BP have done little more than lay out a few neatly grassed and flowered areas beside the main road as it passes through the midst of the refinery.

As a final point of interest relating to the BP Oil refinery, it should be mentioned that it was the reception area for Britain's first North Sea Oil when, in the summer of 1976, 15,000 barrels of crude oil were off-loaded and subsequently refined at Grain.

The arrival of the refinery at Grain has acted rather like a magnet, bringing, as it has, other concerns associated with the petro-chemical industry. In 1957 'Segas' set up a plant next to the refinery in order to produce gas from a feedstock of liquid petroleum products drawn directly from the oil refinery. More recently, however, this process has ceased and the site is now occupied by two containers which will be used for the storage of liquified North Sea Gas. Also, in the village of Grain there is a small concern owned by 'Calor Gas'.

The refinery at Grain was responsible for attracting the Central Electricity Generating Board to Grain. Their power station which is currently being constructed on the site of the old air station is designed to be oil fired and will take fuel direct from the refinery.

An outstanding feature of this power station is its eight hundred foot high chimney. The principle behind this is that all pollution issuing from the chimney will be carried well away from the Peninsula. Recently, though, this has become a debateable point. It is considered by some, that the main gas issuing from the chimney, sulphur dioxide, will be too heavy to be carried off into the atmosphere and, instead, will fall onto the area around Grain village and cause some unpleasantness.

The arrival of the BP refinery at Grain has somewhat over-shadowed the operations of Berry Wiggins at Kingsnorth, never-theless, the operations started by Berry Wiggins in 1931, have continued unabated to this day and have expanded when necessary. During the war years, gas oil and high octane petrol was stored there, as was the petrol used for re-fuelling of Royal Navy motor launches used for submarine searching, escort and hit and run duties. Since 1945, Berry Wiggins has launched out into products which include motor oils, mould oils, and bitumen emulsion. In 1964, Berry Wiggins, in conjunction with the Central Electricity Generating Board, built the new Oakham Ness jetty which extends into the Medway's deep water channel, and is one of the longest jetties in the world. A further chapter in the Berry Wiggins story came only a few years ago when BP purchased the Kingsnorth site, so that now these two refineries operate as one, with the Berry Wiggins site producing the BP 'Aquaseal' water repellant.

The other component of the Kingsnorth industrial complex, is the Peninsula's other CEGB power station. This dates from 1963, and has another one of those tall chimneys that can be seen from many miles around. The power station here has been on the receiving end of numerous complaints concerning both noise and air pollution. Frequent spates of holed tights are blamed on the chimney at Kingsnorth and, in 1977, a rather bizarre experiment was carried out in order to test such complaints. The CEGB procured the use of a helicopter and dangled a pair of tights over the chimney in order to examine the results!

Perhaps one of the most interesting commercial ventures on the Peninsula dates back to the inter-war period in the village of Allhallows. At that time, Allhallows was a tiny village with a population of just a little over three hundred. During the summer weekends, however, this small village found itself inundated by increasing numbers of day trippers, who made their way down to the pleasant sandy beach lying at Bell's Hard. That this should first occur during the 1920s was doubtless due to the increase of private transport and the proximity of the rapidly expanding London suburbs. Anyway, one enterprising farmer kept the ball rolling by offering parking space together with toilet and catering facilities. Before long, more ambitious plans were in the air and a small development company was formed to turn Allhallows into a worthy rival to Southend. The company, obviously not over enamoured with the name of the village, for its own purposes rechristened the village, Allhallows-on-Sea.

Not only did the company wish to further encourage day trippers to the area, but it also wished to encourage people to stay for the week, and even to purchase holiday homes. For the latter purpose, it began to advertise small plots of land ideal for housing. In order to facilitate all its objectives, the development company – by now calling itself Allhallows-on-Sea Estates – decided that the Bell's Hard area must have a suitable rail service. With this in view, the Southern Railway Company was approached and they agreed to build a branch line, leaving the Port Victoria line at a point just past Stoke Junction. The development company, for its part, agreed to donate all the land necessary for the construction of the line, together with a cash contribution of £20,000. In addition, the company also began work on a new road leading from the village of Allhallows down to the site of the new railway station.

The new rail service commenced operations in May of 1932. Most of the trains to Port Victoria were diverted to the new Allhallows-on-Sea station. In all, there were about three trains a day to Allhallows, with 2 of them having special London coaches which were detached at Gravesend. All of this, though, was of somewhat limited success as by the end of that first season Southern Railways decided that the through coaches from London were just not paying their way, and this side of things was terminated – though ordinary local trains continued to run.

Despite these set backs the development company still pursued its original aims. It was decided that more ambitious facilities must be built at Allhallows, in order to make it one of the grandest attractions in Kent. On February 13th, 1937, the *Gravesend Reporter* carried the following story:

'During the next month the Amusement Park will be started with a building of 60,000 square feet. When completed the park will be four times the size of the famous one at Blackpool. Other features proposed include: zoological gardens, yachting centre, physical training stadium, the largest swimming pool in the country with artificial waves, holiday camp and 5,000 houses, up to date hotels, restaurants, theatres and cinemas. The development, which will take some seven years to complete, is costing millions of pounds, and when finished, the town covering something like two and a half square miles of land, should prove to be of great convenience to millions of Londoners and others.'

Little of all this was actually built due, of course, to the outbreak of hostilities a few years later. Only an amusement park with a miniature railway line and a few houses and flats were built. Today, even less remains of this once grand scheme. The Allhallows-on-Sea branch line has been totally removed. The station, itself, is now a caravan store and only the 'British Pilot' and 'Albany Court' flats still remain as reminders of what once could have been. Day trippers, though, still visit Allhallows, for the beach area is now owned by Medway Council, who also own a large number of holiday chalets on the beach front.

Only one other major Peninsula industry has so far remained unmentioned. This is sand and gravel extraction, with which, at the present moment, there are numerous small companies involved, in various parts of the Peninsula. In the St. Mary's Hoo/Allhallows area there are three companies involved in the extraction of sand and gravel, whilst the north side of Grain village is dominated by the workings of one of these companies. At Cliffe there is the Brett (one time Marinex) Company, who dredge gravel from the Thames estuary and bring it to Cliffe for washing and grading, before it is transported away again by lorry. Probably the earliest company involved in the removal of gravel from the Peninsula, was the Aylesford Sand and Stone Quarry Company who were involved in the removal of gravel from the Yantlet area of Grain at about the turn of the century. It was this company that supplied gravel direct to the Admiralty during the time it was building its oil tanks close to Elphinstone Point. To facilitate this, they built a special tramway from Yantlet Creek to Perry's Farm.

The Peninsula has also been the object of a number of schemes which got no further than the planning stage. At Cliffe, there was the post-war Victory airport scheme. This was a plan for a third London airport which would specialize in the handling of large passenger seaplanes. Runways were also included for landplanes and these cut across the northern part of Cliffe marshes.

Another scheme which failed to get off the ground was a proposal, made round about the year 1929, to turn the marshes, near Lower Hope Point, into a yachting harbour. It was to be an eighty-acre site replete with boat houses, shops and bungalows. At about the same time, a similar scheme was proposed for the Yantlet Creek area. For this proposal there was also a plan to flood part of the marshes in order to create a yacht basin.

One final project was a scheme to store dynamite on a barge moored off Blythe Sands, Cooling. A planning application was made in 1890 but was successfully opposed by the Sewers Commission, who considered that the storage of dynamite there would be a constant hazard to the sea walls. Not that the idea of storing dynamite in barges was new to the Peninsula. During the Napoleonic wars a number of hulks around the Peninsula had been used for this purpose.

Looking to the future, the industrial potential of the Peninsula is very much in the balance. Already industry has gone along way in destroying the original bleakness that was so characteristic of the area in earlier years. However, if the terms of the Kent structure plan are adhered too, and no further industrial development is allowed outside of those areas where industry is already sited, then much could be achieved in preventing a further deterioration of the Peninsula's countryside.

CHAPTER FIFTEEN

THE TWENTIETH CENTURY:
A PERIOD OF RAPID CHANGE

Solicitor: Where do you live?
Witness: Hoo.
Solicitor: You.
Witness: Hoo, sir.
Solicitor: You, I mean; you yourself.
Witness: Hoo.
Solicitor: Oh! at Hoo?
Witness: Yes, sir.

Newspaper account of proceedings at Gravesend
magistrates court, March 13th, 1914.

Like any rural area, the Hoo Peninsula had its craftsmen, busily working away to supply the needs of the local village communities. The trade directories show blacksmiths, boot and shoemakers, carpenters, watchmakers and dressmakers to have existed in a number of the Peninsula villages. Yet, with the arrival of improved transport and cheap mass produced goods, these village trades rapidly disappeared – that is, with one exception. High Halstow was able to boast, up until 1971, the only wheelwright in the country still practicing.

The wheelwright, Arthur Plewis, now lives a life of retirement in Lower Stoke. It is easy to identify his house, as its hand-made front gate is carefully fashioned into the shape of a spoked wooden wheel. What else could you expect? The spoked wooden wheel is the emblem of the wheelwright, whose trade was the complete manufacture of those beautiful farm wagons that are so rarely seen today. For fifty years, Mr. Plewis had the highly satisfying task of constructing, repairing and converting various pieces of farm machinery. He was a craftsman in an age of bulk production and built-in obsolescence.

Having lived on the Peninsula all his life, Mr. Plewis has an unequalled knowledge of the area. He was born during the first decade of this century, and spent his earliest years in one of four cottages, collectively known as the 'Shant', lying half a mile outside of Stoke, and on the Grain road. After attending the Allhallows and Stoke Elementary school, Arthur Plewis took up an apprenticeship in wheelwrighting.

In the years immediately before World War One, neither electricity nor mains water had reached the Peninsula. Most houses had small oil lamps, and water had to be regularly collected from a communal pump situated in each of the villages. It was the job of the young Arthur Plewis to collect the family's drinking water. This was no easy task for a young lad, as the Stoke village pump was over half a mile away. Washing water, of course, was collected in barrels which were strategically placed under the various rain water pipes positioned around the cottages.

At this time, the road between Stoke and Grain was no more than a causeway made up of cockleshells collected from the local beaches. Where the Grain road intersected with the Yantlet it was always flooded at high tide. However, this was really of little consequence, for the daily traffic to Grain rarely exceeded two horse drawn vehicles. Motor cars were quite unknown. Of the first car seen at this end of the Peninsula, Mr. Plewis has an interesting story to tell. Around the year 1913, one local farmer, J. Mugeridge, purchased a Bellsize twin cylinder motor car. Upon Mr. Mugeridge taking delivery of the vehicle, he had it filled with petrol and tested it out by driving it round his horse meadow. All too keen on discovering how the car started, it had not occurred to the intrepid motorist to enquire as to how the machine stopped. Mr. Mugeridge appears to have spent a good deal of his afternoon driving around the horse meadow until his new car eventually ran out of petrol. As a postscript, it should be recorded that when Mr. Mugeridge bought a second new car, his first question of the man at Stoke garage concerned the exact use of the brakes.

It was because of the poor state of the roads, that most Peninsula farmers heavily relied upon water transport for a great deal of their needs. The old Thames sailing barge was certainly no stranger to the Peninsula's shores. Already referred to in the context of the cement trade, they were also used by the local farmers. All the local farms had access to at least one wharf cutting across the sea wall. From here, they would export their surplus crops to the ever open arms of the London markets.

Potatoes, corn and wheat were sent out of the Peninsula with monotonous regularity. Many Peninsula farmers had a regular trade going with the London bus companies. By supplying hay and straw they received, in return, a highly valued cargo of horse dung.

At the age of three, Mr. Plewis recalls that he entered the 'babies' class at Stoke school. Starting school at such an early age had one great advantage. It meant that by the time he entered the infants class, two years later, he was able to both read and write. As progress further up the school was regulated, not by age but by accumulated knowledge, it gave him a head start. At the end of each school year an exam was held and, if failed, the candidate would stay in the same class for the following year. Mr. Plewis recalls some pupils leaving at fourteen after having risen no higher than standard two – a class made up mostly of seven year olds.

Discipline, of course, was very strict. Misbehaviour in class was dealt with by a sharp caning upon the tips of the fingers; a punishment that would be repeated if the hand was moved even a fraction of an inch. The headmaster, Mr. Scales, in particular had a reputation for discipline. One of his early morning duties was to stand in the school porch just about the time the school bell was to stop ringing. He would be watching for loiterers and, if you were late, you had to have an exceptionally good excuse to avoid punishment. The school bell is something we rarely hear nowadays. In those years it would ring for three minutes at ten to nine, and then for the last five minutes. School would start at nine o'clock.

Classes at Stoke school were much larger than classes nowadays. Usually there was one teacher for two different classes and while the teacher took one class the other had to get on and work quietly. Work mostly consisted of copying and learning.

During these years at school, the young Arthur Plewis developed a life-long interest in the Peninsula's wildlife. It is probably in this area that the greatest changes to the district have occurred. Curlews, whimbrels, wild duck, skylarks, yellow hammers, buntings, partridge, pheasant, linnets, chaffinchs, gold finches, dunnocks and wrens all abounded in the upland areas. However, Mr. Plewis's more recent findings indicate a sad decline in the numbers of all these species of birds. he puts this down to changes in crops farmed, farm mechanization and the destruction of numerous hedgerows. The local council has not helped either for, with the introduction of mechanical hedging machines, there is now a

T.H.P.   M

patent disregard for nesting birds. Combined harvesters are a particular offender for Mr. Plewis frequently remembers that farm horses would never drag farm machinery over birds nests. They would always stop in front of the nest so that the machinery could be rearranged in order to by-pass the nest. it was not uncommon to see several clumps of uncleared vegetation in an otherwise empty field. Each clump marked a carefully avoided nest.

In one aspect of wildlife, though, some things have changed for the better. Before World War One, London sent, by river barge, household refuse to the Peninsula for dumping. A number of these sites were around Stoke, with one, in particular, being at Cold Harbour Creek and known as the Chalk Lump. A marked feature of such sites was their infestation with rats. On occasions, colonies of rats would leave these dumps, in search of less crowded homes. Sometime before World War One, Arthur Plewis saw one such fleeing column. At the time he did not realize what it was, and thought it not unlike a grey shadow passing over the land. Later, in the evening, his grandfather explained just what it was, and offered the excellent warning that if ever he should find himself in the path of such a column he should remain perfectly still and the rats would ignore him. Fortunately, Arthur Plewis never had to make use of this advice.

At the age of fourteen, Mr. Plewis left Stoke school and worked for a period of five months in a grocers' shop at Lower Stoke. This was shortly after World War One and, at the time, this area of Stoke was particularly well endowed with shops. In all, there were nine and these included two butchers, two grocers and two bakers. By all accounts, each was able to make a good living and most shopkeepers were able to retire early.

It was in 1921, that Arthur Plewis was apprenticed to David Harryman, the High Halstow wheelwright. It was an apprenticeship that was to last a total of ten years. The wheelwright is responsible for the complete construction of both farm waggons and carts. Each part is handmade and the finished product is a carefully fashioned work of art.

The 1920s, though, were a time in which traditional farm waggons were not in great demand. Most farmers were purchasing tractors and much of the work undertaken by the High Halstow wheelwright was that of converting farm waggons, so that they might be towed by tractor. This was not always a very happy marriage, as tractors moved considerably faster than the horse and caused overheating of the axles. Sometimes even the whole waggon caught fire as a result.

Wheelwrighting, like any craft, was extremely demanding. Everything had to be perfect. Wood, for one thing, often had to be seasoned for years. It was generally reckoned that one year of seasoning was needed for every inch of thickness. The wheelwright at High Halstow obtained his wood from Maidstone – it being sent down by train – and if it arrived green, it spent its first year chained down in a pond of water, which was maintained for this purpose. At the end of the year, it would be taken out and allowed to stand for a few more years. Often wood might be left for as long as twenty years and would be as hard as iron.

The actual wheelwright's shop at High Halstow was the old tithe barn which once occupied the site now covered by St. Margaret's Court. Close by was the Forge House belonging to the blacksmith who worked alongside the wheelwrights for a good many years. The blacksmith carried out the job of rimming the cart wheels. This was the only job the wheelwright did not do himself. However, during the 1920s the blacksmith at Forge House retired, and the High Halstow wheelwrights struck up a working relationship with a second blacksmith, whose forge lay at the end of Forge Lane.

With less demand for waggons and carts, Arthur Plewis extended his early apprenticeship so that it included instruction in most of the building trades. This was so that in future years building conversions could be undertaken in addition to wheelwrighting. In fact, this proved a very sound arrangement for, whenever there was insufficient call for buildiong or repairing of waggons, there was invariably somebody who desired some alteration to their house. One final trade was added, and this was the construction of coffins, a trade which was quite easy for a wheelright to carry out.

Shortly after finishing his apprenticeship, Arthur Plewis became general foreman of the wheelwright's shop. He continued as foreman for sixteen years before taking over the business in 1950, when David Harryman retired. In 1956, High Halstow's one remaining blacksmith retired, and with his own assistant doing National Service, Mr. Plewis had to undertake his own wheel rimming. This is a two or three man job, and many people have expressed great surprise that Arthur Plewis was able to do this. Nevertheless, he managed it, but was totally exhausted after carrying out a one man wheel rimming job. The year in which Mr. Plewis retired, 1971, marked his fiftieth anniversary of entering the trade and, at that time, he was the last practicing wheelwright in the country. A few years after his retirement, he donated his tools to the 'Historic Buildings Museum' at Singleton in Sussex. Here, a proper wheelwright's shop has been set up and, from time to time, they demonstrate just how each of the tools were used. For this alone, a visit to the museum is well worth while.

On the whole, the Peninsula still maintains a rural character. Within the area of the Peninsula, there are over twenty farms and they clearly occupy the greatest part of the land. Like everything else, farming, particularly during this century, has seen a great amount of change. At the beginning of the century the shire horse, together with large numbers of farm labourers, carried out all the necessary work. This is a far cry from today. Most of the Peninsula farms are new labour intensive and very highly mechanized.

During the first part of this century, every farmer would have at least two or three horses. They were used for pulling the plough, the harrow, and seeding the land. Corn, of course, would be cut by hand and, as was traditional in this area, the stooks left for 'three sundays' before being stacked. Often the stack had to stand for a considerable period of time, and so, these were thatched – a skill which has long since died out in this area.

The corn would usually be threshed during the winter, when a steam threshing machine could be hired. During this operation, a man would be on hand with a dog and a ready gun. He was on the look out for rats which always proved a problem on the farms, and great numbers would flee the stacks during threshing time. These machines were accompanied by a team of men and they would start work at about seven in the morning. A break would be taken about midday, when everyone would sit around eating sandwiches and 'brewing-up'. The engine driver and mate actually brought their own van with them, and would live in the field in which they were working. In summer, this same team would be employed on a different job, using alternative tackle.

Another employee on the farm would be a young boy, whose job would be to keep the birds off the crops. He did this by any means at his disposal, and usually this included clapping his hands and throwing stones.

The early part of the century saw a great diversification in crops. Crops such as potatoes, greens, kale, corn and wurzle were to be found on most farms. Nowadays, farms on the Peninsula specialize far more – this is partly due to lack of outlets. The Vidgens, of White House Farm, Hoo St. Werburgh, sent wool to Sittingbourne, fruit to London, whilst selling milk directly to the public. For milk, they kept a few cows and, every morning, Mr. and Mrs. Vidgen would take a seventeen gallon milk can loaded on to a small trap, around the village. The milk was siphoned into half-pint and one-pint sized jugs, and then sold. They, in fact, continued to do this until 1950, when the government insisted upon all milk being bottled and pasteurized. The Vidgens continued in small-scale milk production until October 1977, when EEC regulations came into force and demanded bulk production.

Little, so far, has been said about education on the Peninsula. This, undoubtedly, was the basis of all change, both in the country at large and on the Peninsula. The introduction, during the 1870s, of compulsory state education, literally catapulted Great Britain into the modern age. The provision of literacy meant that the greater part of the population would soon be in a position to undertake the more complex jobs, that the latter part of the industrial revolution was bringing. Fewer people would rest content as poorly paid farm labourers for the rest of their lives.

It was in 1870 that a law was passed giving every child, between the age of five and fourteen, the right to be educated. Before this date, large numbers of schools were provided on a voluntary basis. The majority of these were run by the National Society – a body strictly controlled by the Church of England. On the Peninsula, they furnished schools at Cooling (1864), Grain (1864), St. Mary Hoo (1868) and Cliffe (1854). The remainder of the villages had to await the passing of the 1870 Education Act before they received schools.

Following the passing of the Education Act two Board schools were built on the Peninsula and a further National Society School. The National Society School was at High Halstow (1876) and the Board Schools were at Hoo St. Werburgh (1876) and Stoke (1876). In each case, the nucleus of these schools was of a very similar style, being of red brick with large daunting interiors. A number of them can still be found in the area.

The smallest of these schools was the one at Cooling. It was originally built for thirty-five children and, in 1887, it was recorded as having an average attendance of thirty-five. However, as the population of Cooling was declining the number of children attending the school also fell. So much so, that, at about the turn of the century, the children attending the school at Cooling were sent to the schools at either Cliffe or High Halstow. At the other extreme, the largest school on the Peninsula was at Cliffe. In 1887 it had an average attendance of 288.

The standard of at least one of these schools was not considered to be very high. Writing of the school at Grain, C. B. Burnett, in 1905, states:

> 'The present teachers cannot be blamed for the results of the teaching, which the compiler of these notes regrets to state, appear to be very unsatisfactory, and to call for an inquiry. Under the present management the numbers have become so large that a staff, which formerly was sufficient, is now quite inadequate; and seeing that a number of the scholars are big boys, it is desirable that they should be under the control of a male teacher ...
>
> 'Coming, as one does, into daily intercourse with the scholars, it is only too evident that the boys, on reaching the age limit, leave school and start life with far less learning than do boys of similar age in other villages.'

Some of these comments were later backed by the County Inspectors Report for 1906. Mr. Emory, of Trenchard Cottages in Grain, said much the same when I interviewed him in September 1977. On the school, his comment was:

> 'If you learnt anything you were damned lucky.'

Most ex-scholars of the Peninsula's elementary schools remember, above all else, the discipline of these schools. Lateness, talking in class and failure to work were all dealt with by the cane. One of the headmasters of Hoo school – Mr. Richard Knight – always used to stand at the school house watching for anyone fooling around on their way to school. Playing pranks or failing to walk on the footpath were both dealt with by use of the cane. At Grain school, Mr. Emory re-calls how the headmistress would walk around her class and use a cane on anyone who was talking.

Education on the Peninsula, as described, remained substantially unchanged until 1947. The six Peninsula schools continued to provide education for pupils ranging from five until their time of leaving – although increasing opportunities existed for transferring to a grammar school in the Medway Towns.

The educational structure on the Peninsula dates primarily to the changes wrought by the 1944 Education Act. This act made it mandatory upon all education authorities to provide specialized teaching for all children between the ages of eleven and fifteen (the act had also raised the school leaving age). For the Peninsula this meant the establishment of a completely new school catering for these requirements.

It was in September 1947 that the doors of the Peninsula's only secondary modern school were first opened. Given the rather unusual name of 'Hundred of Hoo' the school was given no new buildings and, strictly speaking, it was not even on the Peninsula. Instead, it was at Wainscott and had to share the facilities that went to make up Wainscott County Primary school. These facilities – which consisted of the original Victorian school and additional huts – left a great deal to be desired. Nevertheless, this seemed about the best that could be offered in these times of post-war austerity.

During its first term the 'Hundred of Hoo' school had about one hundred and twenty pupils and four classrooms (two of these being for practical work only).

Parents of children at the Wainscott primary school were far from happy with these new arrangements. Even before the 'Hundred of Hoo' was set up they were writing letters of complaint to the education authorities. Nor is it likely that these parents felt any less aggrieved when they were told that the use of Wainscott was only a temporary measure.

It was genuinely hoped that the 'Hundred of Hoo' would only remain at Wainscott for but a few years. Yet this temporary arrangement lasted for some nine years. During those years the Wainscott site became ridiculously overcrowded with the secondary modern part of the school having to find room for an addititional one hundred pupils. However, in September 1956 the two schools parted company as the 'Hundred of Hoo' took over its new

building situated alongside Main Road in Hoo St. Werburgh.
Originally designed to accomodate 480 pupils, the Peninsula's
secondary school soon had to expand. So much so, that in 1976 the
school's population peaked at just on the one thousand mark and,
while this book is being written a whole new wing is being added to
the school.

With the introduction of a secondary modern school to the
Peninsula, the area's six original schools started to administer
primary education only. Although one of them, St. Mary's Hoo,
due to the loss of its senior classes, became far too small and was
closed down, with the remaining primary children being
transferred to High Halstow. Eventually, too, all the other old
school buildings – with the singular exception of Stoke – were
phased out and replaced by something a little more modern. In the
case of Allhallows, where no earlier school existed, a complete new
structure was erected.

Once again, though, education on the peninsula is undergoing
major changes with its various schools going comprehensive. The
particular scheme chosen for the Peninsula is a three tier idea and
incorporates a series of junior and middle schools together with one
upper school. The original village schools remain but have now lost
their nine year olds and above. This age group now transfer to one
of three middle schools (these are situated at Allhallows, Hoo St.
Werburgh and Cliffe), where they remain until the age of thirteen
when they finally transfer to the newly designated 'Hundred of
Hoo Upper Comprehensive'. Some of this, though, is for the future
as the 'Hundred of Hoo' will not be fully comprehensive untiil
1983.

Turning from education it is necessary to step backwards in
time so that we can take a further look at the Peninsula's two
reoccurring problems of malaria and flooding. During the
nineteenth century there was considerable progress in combating
these two evils and it was hoped, by many, that they had been
completely eliminated. Unfortunately, this was quite the case as
both menaces had one last final fling before their total eradication
in this present century.

Regarding the 1917 malaria outbreak one cannot but be
incredulous as to its cause. Grain, of all places, was chosen as a
rehabilitation centre for troops returning from Salonika. Many of
these troops had been invalid home as the result of a severe

malaria epidemic in that particular region. On arriving at Grain, many proceeded to suffer relapses. Anywhere else and this—would probably have been the worst aspect of the whole affair but Grain, with its anopheles mosquitoes, was the last place these men should have been sent. It was but a short while before these mosquitoes were once again transmitting the disease to the local villagers. By the end of 1918 some fifty per cent of Grain's population was recorded to be suffering from bouts of malaria. Fortunately, though, the outbreak did not spread to the rest of the Peninsula. This being due to the fact that anopheles mosquitoes tend to restrict themselves to the area from which they first get their taste of blood.

This was truly the last malaria outbreak on the Peninsula. During the 1920s and 1930s considerable strides were taken so that the problem might be eradicated for all time. The marshes were regularly sprayed and carefully surveyed in order to monitor the mosquito population. One final precaution was taken in the 1930s when the various east coast marshlands were designated according to whether they were a high or low malaria risk area. The areas of highest risk were designated by the letter A and those of only slight risk C. In fact, throughout the entire East Coast region only one area – the Hoo Peninsula – was rated A. Having been so designated it was further stated that, in the event of war, under no circumstances were troops, with a history of malaria, to be sent to Grain. It was as a result of this precaution, and the inter-war spraying of the marshes, that there was no reoccurrence of a malaria outbreak similar to that of 1917.

Precautions, of course, were continued after the war. With the arrival of 8,000 workers for the construction of the Kent Oil Refinery, a great many fears were expressed regarding a possible malaria outbreak but, in the end, such fears proved absolutely groundless. Finally, the story of malaria was brought to a conclusion in 1976 when Medway Borough Council commissioned a survey of the marshes which showed that the anopheles mosquito had been totally eliminated by the constant spraying of the marshes. What, of course, has not been eliminated are a wide variety of mosquitoes other than the anopheles. It is these which are responsible for many an uncomfortable summer's evening.

The second problem, that of flooding, was, by the middle of the century considered to be solved. Certainly the high tides of 1915 and 1934 had caused no problems but, had they occurred a century earlier, would almost definitely have done so. However, these experts who so confidently dismissed flooding as a danger reckoned without the extraordinary set of circumstances that led up to the 1953 floods. These, indeed, were a meteorologist's nightmare. A trough of low pressure out in the Atlantic brought a massive build up of water into the North Sea. Arriving in this area of strong northerly winds, this additional water was driven down into the narrow Channel straights. Hitting the channel bottleneck, a surge was created which had nowhere else to go, but up the Thames estuary. Coinciding as it did with a normal high tide cycle, it brought tides some seven or eight feet above those originally predicted.

It was on Saturday January 1st, that floods occured on the Peninsula. At approximately 12.45 a.m., the first of many breeches came about. As many of them were within the confines of the partially completed Grain oil refinery, this was soon awash and the village cut off from the mainland. Indeed, most of the breeches in the sea walls were on the Yantlet end of the Peninsula, with something like sixteen breeches on the Isle of Grain alone. Parts of Stoke were also flooded, and segments of the Allhallows and grain railway lines were washed away. Elsewhere on the Peninsula, damage was much more limited and was confined mostly to the flooding of a number of isolated cottages. In all, forty-six houses were flooded in the area, with four hundred sheep and thirty ponies being drowned.

Upon the arrival of daylight, troops were rushed into the striken zone in order to release the flood waters, and then repair the walls. This, in itself, was a lengthy process and the village of Grain was to remain cut off for a week. Bread, milk and other essential supplies all had to be brought into the village by boats rowed across the marshes from Stoke.

Of course, in 1953, the flooding was not, by any means, just restricted to the Peninsula. The entire North Kent marshes from Sheppey to Gravesend were flooded, whilst the dockyard town of Sheerness was also cut off. The Medway towns were also swamped.

Following World War Two, perhaps the greatest changes on the Peninsula were brought about as the result of the BP Oil Refinery at Grain. Not only did it bring considerable changes to the Isle of Grain's skyline, but it also brought the need for a considerable amount of new housing, which was needed to accommodate the refinery's massive work force. Many of the council houses built during the 1950s were a direct result of the arrival of the BP refinery. Prior to the arrival of BP, the Strood Rural District Council had decided upon the construction of a few council houses during the immediate post-war period. In the village of Grain, for instance, plans had been made for the erection of sixteen houses, but with the arrival of the oil refinery this number was dramatically raised to 120. In the villages of Hoo and High Halstow, very similar situations occurred. The refinery also necessitated the building of a better road on the Peninsula, whilst the villages directly benefited when many of them received monetary gifts from the oil refinery, so that they could build much needed Village Halls.

Another period of village expansion came in the 1960s. This was at a time when new houses were in great demand. Property developers, discovering that land was relatively cheap on the Peninsula, built large numbers of moderately priced houses. These two periods of development did present Parish Councils with one, if somewhat minor problem, that of naming all these new roads. In Grain, the current Councill policy is to name the roads after birds, but the first estates were given names referring to the old families of Grain: Fry, Levett and Pannell. Hoo has a policy of naming roads after local notables thus we have Knight's Road, which is named after a headmaster at the old Elementary School whilst there is also an Aveling Close. Stoke, as well, names its new roads after local birds, though Button Drive is named after a local councillor.

In between these two periods of development, the Peninsula saw the loss of its passenger rail service. The last passenger train ran on this line in December 1961. The authorities carried out this cut due to the falling off in passenger traffic. The only compensation that local people received, was the introduction of an Allhallows–Gravesend bus service which was operated by Maidstone and District.

Local inhabitants have never really been happy with the closure of their rail line. Indeed, as the line is still used by the oil refinery at Grain, there is an added frustration of still seeing the line in use. Because of this, a campaign was launched in 1974 to have the line reopened. Transport 2000, a national pressure group, has become involved in this campaign and believe that a convincing argument exists for the reopening of the line. One of their leaflets states their exact aims:

> 'Electric passenger trains could serve three stations at Cliffe Woods, Hoo and High Halstow, and Lower Stoke. The main station called Hoo and High Halstow and situated at Sharnal Street would be a manned park and ride station where cars could be left all day without risk of theft or vandalism. The other two stations would be of the kiss and ride type where housewives drive their husbands to trains and keep the car all day.
>
> 'The trains would take about 60 minutes to reach London from Hoo and High Halstow. Ultimately the timing could be only 50 minutes. Trains would take 5 minutes less from Cliffe Woods and 5 minutes longer from Lower Stoke. People living in Lower Stoke could reach Gravesend in 18 minutes or Chatham in 22 minutes. A new loop line would be constructed to provide the services to the Medway towns if the demand warrants it.'

The attempt to reopen the railway line is just one of the problems currently facing the Peninsula. Another serious difficulty is that of conservation, and this relates to the very quality of life in the area. If this particular subject is not solved satisfactorily then the Peninsula could become a most unpleasant place on which to live.

First, there is the problem of London's refuse. The Greater London Council actually has a plan to acquire 1300 acres of the Stoke Saltings in order to use it for the dumping of household refuse. For the Peninsula this would be a major disaster. it would attract rats, flies and give rise to an odious smell. In addition, it would destroy an area of great ecological importance. The Stoke Saltings are an integral part of the much wider North Kent marshes, and the destruction of the saltings would also seriously undermine the rest of these marshes. To indicate the importance of the North Kent marshes one need only consider the standing they have been given by various national and international bodies. The Nature Conservancy Council accords the marshes the status of special landscape area, area of high conservation value and a site of special scientific interest. The 'International Union for the Conservation of Nature and Natural Resources' includes the North Kent marshes as one of only sixteen wetland sites in Great Britain which it considers to be of international importance for migrating birds. As one further example it might be noted that, in 1971, an international conference held in Iran considered these marshes as being, again, of international importance.

A further problem for the Peninsula is the proposed oil refinery at Cliffe. Local conservationists have been fighting the Burmah-Total Company for a good many years and, in December 1975, Burmah-Total were granted outline planning permission. Once again, if built, this particular project would destroy an area of outstanding importance to the birdlife of the Peninsula.

Other industries already on the Peninsula frequently show an interest in expanding their activities. Berry Wiggins would doubtless approve of the GLC scheme to dump rubbish on the marshes. The Saltings would be reclaimed and could later be used for industrial expansion by them – or any other industry. The gravel companies are always searching for more areas to exploit and it is clear that several such companies have sites in mind where they would like to start working once their present sites have been worked out.

These, doubtless, are not the only plans that will emerge for the further industrialization and/or despoliation of the Peninsula. Yet, the obvious answer would be simply to maintain the existing level of industry, and firmly prevent its expansion outside of its present zones. In addition to this, great improvements to the present situation on the Peninsula could be made. The redundant cement works at Cliffe could be removed, whilst many parts of the Peninsula could be tidied up. Plans for a long distance coastal footpath around the Peninsula have been suggested, and could be implemented.

Another far seeing plan was put forward by the Nature Conservancy Council in 1971. They recommended the creation of a coastal regional park which would take in the entire marshland area, including the entire northern belt of the Peninsula together with the Stoke Saltings. The prototype for such an idea already exists around Chichester Harbour, where zones are carefully set aside for leisurely rambles, picnics and the more serious needs of the ornithologist.

These, of course, are ideas for the future. Yet they will only become the future if local residents approve of the ideas and work for them. Doubtless there are other conservation alternatives but certainly the dream of the conservationist is a better dream than that of the industrialist. For, if any of the industrializing projects became reality then the Hoo Peninsula would have a very bleak future. It would undermine all possible arguments for preventing any other industrialist developing further areas of the Peninsula. As a result, it would not be long before the entire coastline of the Peninsula became nothing more but one continuous mass of industrial estates, each generating its own pollutants into the atmosphere and rivers. Rapidly this unique area would have become a characterless extension of the Medway Towns.

APPENDIX 1

OFFICIAL CENSUS RETURNS
FOR THE HOO PENINSULA: 1801-1971

	1801	1811	1821	1831	1841	1851	1861
Allhallows	166	173	259	263	268	261	236
Cliffe	525	578	673	832	842	877	980
Cooling	97	90	124	131	144	128	121
Grain	191	196	254	240	337	260	255
High Halstow	227	295	350	351	373	354	363
Hoo St. Werburgh	550	710	960	910	930	1000	1065
St. Mary's Hoo	214	247	286	296	297	320	264
Stoke	263	315	350	432	445	522	557

	1871	1881	1891	1901	1911	1921	1931
Allhallows	285	313	388	295	250	314	329
Cliffe	1290	2245	2595	2537	2465	2581	965
Cooling	135	232	145	203	143	190	182
Grain	292	283	570	774	455	817	550
High Halstow	368	376	332	355	382	353	418
Hoo St. Werburgh	1260	1322	1400	1655	1789	2079	2120
St. Mary's Hoo	283	309	302	273	251	279	290
Stoke	520	570	675	705	682	686	640

	1951	1961	1971
Allhallows	369	584	1130
Cliffe	2279	2239	2640
Cooling	176	154	170
Grain	542	1403	1470
High Halstow	401	944	1025
Hoo St. Werburgh	2487	4343	7725
St. Mary's Hoo	242	206	155
Stoke	576	541	1065

A SHORT HISTORY OF THE YANTLET

The stretch of water that once separated the Isle of Grain from the Hoo Peninsula is known as the Yantlet. It has a fairly interesting history but one which does not necessarily fit into the main text of the book. For this reason the Yantlet has earned for itself a separate appendix.

The origin of the name Yantlet is debateable but it is probably a corruption of the Anglo Saxon 'genlade' which means the discharge of a river into the sea. Genlade later becoming Yenlade, Yenlet and finally Yantlet. At one time the Yantlet was well known to mariners as an open and unobstructed waterway, the use of which allowed them to avoid the more open Thames, with its treacherous currents. How long this remained the case we do not know. Certainly it was used as such during the Saxon period, and for a good many years after. In fact, the normal route to London, from Dover or Sandwich, was to carefully hug the Kentish coastline, using both the Swale and Yantlet. This route was not only much safer, but was also slightly shorter. In the *Anglo Saxon Chronicle*, there is a reference to the future King Harold using this exact route when he sailed to London in the year 1052.

At some point, possibly during the Saxon period of our history, the Yantlet was spanned by a bridge which connected the Isle of Grain with the mainland. The bridge seems to have been of a fair height as it allowed boats to sail underneath, although this undoubtedly necessitated the lowering of masts.

The Yantlet remained the normal passage for shipping well into the Middle Ages. During the reign of Edward III we have documentary evidence for this, as mention is made of the need for twelve armed men, with six hobelers (small horses from which we get the name 'hobby' horse), to watch and defend this particular stretch of water. The responsibility for their upkeep was placed in the hands of local landholders – one specifically mentioned was Sir Philip de Pimpe, of Allhallows Place House.

With the passing of the years the importance of the Yantlet diminished as slowly, but surely, it became silted up, and only vessels with the shallowest of draughts were able to make use of this shorter passage. The bridge, also, appears to have seen better days for at some point it collapsed into the Yantlet. Presumably the large stones of which the bridge was built now added to the earlier difficulties of silting. For the residents of Grain the collapse of the bridge does not appear to have been a serious problem. The Yantlet was, by now, so shallow that it was easily crossed by foot and, in fact, the users of the road went slightly further by building up a causeway during the following years. This meant that it was only during high tides that the Yantlet could still be used by vessels.

Shipping now used the Yantlet most infrequently – but use it they still did. One example of its use occurred in 1770 when a coastguard cutter, in pursuit of smugglers, was able to catch them by passing through the Yantlet and heading them off in the Thames. In 1797, it is further recorded that the Royal Navy made use of the Yantlet when despatching communications to London. The normal route was not available to them at this time, as the Thames was blockaded by naval mutineers under 'Admiral' Parker. This was the famous Nore mutiny which lasted several months and whose daily events were viewed by those living on the Isle of Grain.

As already mentioned, use of the Yantlet could only occur at high tide. At low tide the raised causeway allowed people to pass freely to and from the Isle of Grain. A piece of evidence for this is a legal document of 1782, when Grain parish was taken to court for failing to keep this road in repair. The court decided that the route over the Yantlet was an 'immemorial' road, and must be kept in good repair by the parishioners of Grain.

Even at the beginning of this century Grain was cut off twice a day by high tides. The infrequent traffic being consequently forced to carefully choose the time it left and re-entered the village. Occasionally, also, the very shallow bottomed Thames sailing barges used the Yantlet in order to gain for themselves valuable time in their journeyings.

During the last century, however, one body of persons showed themselves to be most unhappy with the on-going state of affairs. This was the Corporation of London whose duties included the conservation of the River Thames and its various tributaries. They discovered, somewhat belatedly, that not only was the Yantlet blocked by the already mentioned causeway but, in addition, it had once been a navigable passage open to all shipping. That the Yantlet had ceased to be a navigable waterway for something like three hundred years did not seem to bother the Corporation unduly.

On July 29th, 1823, the Lord Mayor of London presided over a meeting which discussed the Yantlet. The meeting concluded that the embankment should be cut, and the waterway dredged so that the Yantlet once again might be used by shipping.

On September 18th, 1823, workmen and officials of the Corporation arrived on the Hoo Peninsula and preceded, without any consultation with local residents, to remove the causeway and so cutting off the Isle of Grain from the mainland. In the process they also dug out many of the stones belonging to the original bridge and constructed – presumably for decoration – a Gothic arch with a span of seventeen feet six inches. According to the *Maidstone Gazette*:

'... the obstruction to the free passage of the waters between Stoke and Grain which had so long existed, was completely removed in the space of 24 hours, whereby the Tides from the respective Rivers were enabled to meet on Thursday last at 25 minutes before 11, and a Peter-boat which had entered at the Yantlet end of the creek, went through the opening with nine persons on board precisely at half past 11 o'clock, followed by the Water Bailiffs' skiff and a four oared boat ...'

The newspaper, which was dated September 23rd, was obviously in possession of a contemporary PR handout for it then went on to state the advantages of this particular move on the part of the City Corporation:

'... the circuitous and frequently dangerous course round the Nore for small craft, will be avoided and many valuable lives saved to their friends and families, as well as great facility afforded for the better supply of fish for the London Markets.'

The plight of those living on the Isle of Grain was completely ignored. That the residents of Grain had no obvious way on and off the island seems to have been of absolutely no importance.

Not surprisingly, those living on Grain were somewhat more concerned. Indeed, they were incensed by this high handed move. One can safely assume that the language of the regulars at Grain's 'Cock Inn' was as blue as its smoke filled room. Still, talking about the matter would hardly improved the situation. A number of local landholders – several of whom possessed land on both sides of the Yantlet – more constructively started legal proceedings.

It was one full year before the case was eventually heard. The court chosen being Guildford assizes where it was felt that a more neutral jury could be obtained.

The islanders rested their case on the simple point that the road in question was an 'immemorial' one and cited as evidence the earlier legal wrangle concerning Grain parish. As further proof of this contention, a number of elderly witnesses were produced who testified that, during their lifetime, the causeway had always existed. For their part, the City of London based the defence of their action upon ancient documents which gave them the right to maintain navigable passageways in all of the Thames tributaries – including the Yantlet.

The findings of the court, however, went against the City of London. Although it was recognized that the City had the rights it claimed it was felt that, in the case of the Yantlet, many years of neglect had led to their forfeiture. The landowners, on the other hand, by length and time of usage had acquired the right to fill, by degrees, the ancient channel.

Interestingly enough, there is an even earlier connection between the Mayor of London and the Yantlet. 'Magna Charta', from which so many of our earliest freedoms originate, outlawed, amongst other things, the use of kiddles – finely meshed stake nets. During the reign of King Henry III, it was brought to the attention of the Lord Mayor of London that such nets were being illegally used on the Yantlet. In his capacity of Conservator of the Thames he despatched a body of men to destroy the kiddles and arrest all those involved. The raid was carried out on January 6th, 1236, when fifteen master fishermen (from Rochester, Strood and Cliffe), together with nine servants, were arrested and taken to Newgate gaol. Some thirty kiddles were destroyed and the master fishermen were subsequently fined £10 each.

BUILDINGS OF ARCHITECTURAL, HISTORICAL OR GENERAL INTEREST

The following is a list (together with basic details) of most of the buildings on the Peninsula which can be considered to have some historic or architectural importance. In one or two cases buildings which have recently been demolished are included, though the fact of their demolition is, of course, noted. Also, where appropriate, buildings that are officially listed as being of architectural importance, is indicated. If a building is listed it simply means that it cannot be altered in any way without special approval of the local planning authority, or demolished without the approval of the Royal Commission on Historical Monuments.

ALLHALLOWS

At one time a clear delineation existed between the village of Allhallows and a separate community in the Bell's Hard/Slough area of the parish. The inter-war attempt at creating a seaside resort, together with the post-war building boom, has seen the complete integration of these two areas.

Parish Church of All Saints (listed)

Basically a Norman church, with late twelfth- and early thirteenth-century aisles. The clerestory dates to the fifteenth century whilst the porch and weatherboarded bell turret date to 1890. The chancel was restored in 1856 and the rest of the church in the period 1890–1.

Allhallows-on-Sea Station

This, together with the nearby 'British Pilot' and 'Albany Court' are surviving relics of the planned seaside resort. The station, dating from 1932, is now used for storage as the railway line which it once served is now closed, and the line completely removed. One other feature of the Allhallows line still exists, and this is the old water tower which can be found in the caravan park.

Bay Tree

A fairly large two-storey red-brick house with a tiled roof. Bay Tree lies back from the Stoke road and is nearly opposite the church. According to the Rev. Hammond (1927) it dates to the reign of George III.

Brick House Farm (listed)

A very pleasant eighteenth-century farmhouse in an isolated setting, on the very outskirts of the Allhallows parish. Constructed of red brick, it has a hipped tiled roof and is not dissimilar in style, and date, to nearby Newlands.

Dagnham

Only a short distance from Brickhouse, Dagnham is a red brick building also dating from the eighteenth century. The front is patched in places with modern brickwork, whilst there are nineteenth-century additions to the rear. All in all, it is much plainer than Brickhouse, but has a definite character of its own.

New Hall

The present house occupying this site is a modern structure which replaced an earlier building demolished in the 1960s. Hammond (1927) described the earlier New Hall farm house as having signs of age. He also indicates that the remains of a moat were once visible and suggests that an even earlier, and moated manor house, once occupied this area of the parish.

Rose and Crown

Possibly sixteenth century in origin the 'Rose and Crown' has an eighteenth-century façade. Early references are made to it in the poor rate account books when, in an entry of 1715, it is called 'ye alehouse'. Later, it was known as 'The Ship', 'Tower of London' and, eventually, in about 1841, 'The Rose and Crown'.

CLIFFE-AT-HOO

The relatively early industrialization of Cliffe, when compared with the rest of the Peninsula, explains why the dominating architectural feature of the village are the numerous terraced houses built in the decade or two immediately prior to the outbreak of World War One. Some of these, of course, are gradually being removed in order to make way for newer residential accommodation. Such was recently the case with Turner Street and Millcroft Road whose terraced houses were removed in the early part of 1977. Considerable new housing development has taken place in the Cliffe Woods area of the parish.

St. Helen's Church (listed)

The church appears to have a late Norman nave but with considerable rebuilding carried out above the year 1260. Then the nave was remodelled, with the transepts and lower part of the tower being added. More rebuilding followed in 1350 when further alterations were made to the nave and chancel. A two-storey porch was added at this time. The upper stages of the tower were built in the fifteenth century. Limited restoration took place during the nineteenth century, when a new east window was added and some work was carried out on the nave and transepts. Of special note are the medieval wall paintings.

Methodist Chapel

The first reference to Methodism in Cliffe can be traced to June 1861 when it was recorded that there were seven practicing methodists in the village. The first chapel was built in the early part of the nineteenth century and, in 1901, work started on a larger chapel immediately adjoining the earlier building. The Sunday school was added in 1909. The chapel is no longer in use.

School

A national school was first built in the village in 1854 to which enlargements were added in 1874, 1884, 1889 and 1894. Even these numerous additions and extensions were inadequate to accommodate the rapidly increasing village population and so a further building was constructed in 1910. The original buildings still stand but have been replaced by a modern school.

Church Street/High Street Area

A number of interesting buildings are to be found in this area, including a number of weatherboarded houses, mostly dating to the early nineteenth century. Amongst these is Longford (listed) which is timber framed and has a distinctive overhanging west front. It seems likely that Longford has an earlier date than the other weatherboarded houses in this immediate area. Two other listed buildings are Courtsole and Quickrills, both of which are red brick, tiled, and dating to the eighteenth century.

Gattons Farmhouse (listed)

Built at the beginning of the nineteenth century, Gattons stands to the south-west of the village and about a mile out from the centre. It is a brick building with a hipped slate roof.

Manor Farmhouse (listed)

Rarely does this house fail to surprise as it is quite unique to the Peninsula. It is a fine example of Tudor architecture, replete with ornate chimneys, timber framework, leaded windows and overhanging first floor. The doorway is eighteenth century.

The Rectory (listed)

Originally a medieval manor house much altered during the nineteenth century. Only the original walls remain. It is supposedly haunted, with furniture being mysteriously removed.

Red House

Situated in Reed Street this is an eighteenth-century, two-storied red-brick house, with a hipped tiled roof.

Rye Street

The former farmhouse occupying this site was a large brick house of some age. It was badly damaged during World War Two when a Short Stirling bomber, returning from a raid on Italy, crashed into the house whilst trying to execute an emergency landing. A woman living in the house was killed. After the war Rye Street farmhouse was demolished and replaced by the present Stirling House.

Walnut Tree Cottage

Situated in Wharf Lane this is a late eighteenth-century timber-framed building with a plastered front. It has a steeply pitched hipped tiled roof.

Wharf Farm

The farmhouse is sited at the end of Wharf Lane and is a pleasant eighteenth-century house. Constructed of brick it has a Kent peg tiled roof.

COOLING

One of the smallest of the Peninsula's villages, Cooling has considerable historical interest centring, for the most part, around its medieval castle. Surrounded by farm and marshland, the village is virtually unspoilt by twentieth-century development.

St. James Church (listed)

A slow growth medieval church with a late thirteenth-century chancel, fourteenth-century nave and a fifteenth-century tower. When visiting Cooling church the fine medieval stone canopied stalls, situated in the chancel, should not be missed. Outside the church the lozenged gravestones – which are featured in *Great*

Expectations – should also be viewed. The church is no longer used for services and is invariably locked.

Cooling Street Methodist Chapel

About a mile outside of Cooling village the Methodist chapel was originally sited at Cooling Street because here was the only land that the Methodist community could acquire at the time. The chapel, with an accompanying schoolroom, was erected in 1889 and, because of its remote situation was known as the 'chapel in the orchard'. It is still in use.

Cooling Castle (listed)

The design of this castle is most unusual for, as originally designed, it had two wards which were connected by a drawbridge over a moat. The moat is now mostly dry but the fine gatehouse together with fairly lengthy parts of the curtain wall remain. Building of this castle started in 1381 with a licence to crenellate was granted. The house, just inside the outer ward, was built about 1670, but it is much modernized.

Cooling Castle Barn

Situated just to the north-east of the castle gatehouse, this red-brick and weatherboarded barn is thought to date to the seventeenth century. It has a hipped tiled roof and a queen post interior roof support.

Cooling Court (listed)

Within site of Cooling castle, and set behind a willow tree and small pond, this is a red-brick house which carries the following inscription on the south wall: 'This is Cooling Court built by Eliza Clay Widdon 1700'. The east wall also carries a plaque which simply states: 'E.C. 1700'.

Lodge Hill

A large red-brick building which stands on the crest of Lodge Hill amidst land used by the army for the training of engineers. It is in a state of dereliction and likely to be totally demolished within a few years. The house dates to the year 1760 when one Samuel Clay Harvey commissioned its erection, though it was not completed until some years later.

Marshgate (listed)

Eighteenth-century, two-storeyed (with additional attic) red-brick house with hipped tiled roof. Situated on the outskirts of the village, Marshgate, as the name implies, commands an excellent view of the marshes.

HIGH HALSTOW

It is only in more recent years that the village of High Halstow has approached anything of size. Formerly, the population of the parish was divided between the several small communities of Clinches Street, Sharnal Street, Fenn Street (part of which lies within High Halstow) and Halstow Street (the village itself) together with a number of outlying farms. The village started to expand during the late nineteenth and early twentieth centuries but any real growth did not come until the last few decades.

Parish Church of St. Margaret (listed)

Primarily St. Margaret's is a thirteenth-century church which was remodelled in the Perpendicular style during the fifteenth century. A tower was also added at this time but it was subsequently rebuilt during the eighteenth century and given brick buttresses and a pyramidal slate roof.

Village School

The original village school stood just opposite the church and was built in 1876. It remained in use until the completion of the present school in 1956. Subsequently the Victorian building was sold and demolished in 1973.

Buckhole Farm (listed)

This is an eighteenth-century red-brick Georgian farmhouse and is fairly typical of the area. It is to be found in a pleasant orchard setting just outside the village and along the Cooling Road. It is two-storeys high, with an additional attic, and has a tiled roof.

Dalham Farm House

Not far from Buckhole Farm, this, again, is in an extremely pleasant situation commanding some fine views of the surrounding area. The house is an eighteenth-century building faced with weatherboarding. It is of two storeys with a hipped tiled roof.

Decoy Farm

Demolished in the early 1960s the original farmhouse dated to 1694 but was heavily altered during the late eighteenth or early nineteenth century. It was of red brick with a hipped tiled roof and carried the stone inscription: '1694 B.
T. E.'
The name of the farm originates from the trapping and shooting of ducks which once took place in the vicinity of the farm. Decoys were once placed on the local ponds and the ducks were trapped as soon as they alighted.

Great Dalham

An eighteenth-century two storey weatherboarded house to be found on the Cooling Road. It has a hipped tiled roof and a gabled porch.

Red Dog

The village 'pub'. This is supposedly of Tudor origin being a one-time pig farm (tradition holds that pigs were kept in the present saloon bar). The building has undergone much modernization.

Shade House

Far out on the marshes this house has smuggling connections, as well as once being used by the coastguards.

Wybornes

A two-storey (with additional attic) red-brick building dating to the early nineteenth century. It has a mansarded tiled roof and a nineteenth-century gabled porch.

HOO ST. WERBURGH

Usually referred to simply as Hoo, this is now the largest village on the Peninsula. It has seen a constant growth throughout the last eighty years, or so, and this can best be observed by examining the differing periods of building construction that have taken place. First, there are a number of cottages such as Bakers Terrace (1884) and Roseberry Cottages (1914) which were built during the late nineteenth and early twentieth centuries. Also during this period the Institute (1894) was erected. The next period of growth was immediately after World War One when the firm of Bryce was contracted to build a number of council houses including Kingsnorth Terrace (on the east side of Bell's Lane), Haig and Armitage Cottages. The 1950s brought one very large council estate, built as the result of the influence of BP, and the 1970s a number of private estates.

The majority of buildings mentioned below are to be found in the old part of the village which is that area immediately clustered around the church and the village crossroads.

Parish Church of St. Werburgh (listed)

The nave and aisles of the present church dates to the thirteenth century but the remainder of the church mostly dates to a later period. The aisles were widened in the fourteenth century and again in the fifteenth. The tower, originally Norman, received considerable fifteenth-century alterations at which time, the present chancel was also built.

Methodist Chapel

The original, and now much dilapidated, chapel is situated in Stoke Road and was replaced in 1968 by a new Chapel in Bell's Lane. The old chapel was built in 1831 and was later lengthened by some ten feet in order to accommodate a number of new members. As early as 1912 this building was considered inadequate and a building fund was started. Land was donated in Bell's Lane by Mr. G. A. Batchelor but a drop in the chapel's attendance meant that it was not for some years that this land was utilized. Demolished 1979.

School

The Stoke Road school was orginally opened in 1876 when the building was constructed to accommodate 170 pupils. As the village expanded a separate infants building (Church Street) was added in 1894. Neither building is currently used as a school, having been replaced by modern Junior, Middle and Upper school complexes.

The Chequers

Midway along Church Street this is a two-storeyed red-brick Georgian building with a tiled mansarded roof. As one of the village pubs it provides 'regulars' with an extremely narrow front bar and, because of its easily overcrowded character, it was nicknamed the 'Altmark' during the Second World War.

Hoo Lodge

A two-storeyed Victorian brickhouse which was once the home of the marine artist, W. H. Wyllie. He lived here from 1885 until about the turn of the century. Perched on one of the highest points in Hoo it is not hard to see why the artist chose this house. It has the artist's studio constructed on top of the house and this commands some wonderful views of the Thames and Medway rivers.

Ivy House (listed)

Also in Church Street, this house resembles in many ways the previously described 'Chequers'. It is also Georgian, being two storeyed, of red brick and having a tiled mansarded roof.

Meadow House

To be found in Main Road, Meadow House, again, is Georgian, two storeyed, red brick, tiled with a mansarded roof.

Mill House

This lies outside of the village and on the Ratcliffe Highway. On its north face it has a stone inscription which states: 'B 1799 R.S.' One can assume that 1799 is its date of completion. It is a red-brick building with a hipped tiled roof. Once owned by the Ballard family.

North Street

This area of Hoo parish is mentioned in Hogarth's peregrination and is described as a small village (this description should be read carefully as the same source credits Stoke with being a town). Amongst the buildings in the North Street area, there is one dating to 1690. It is a two-storyed building, with an additional attic, and faced with plaster.

White House

An eighteenth-century farm house situated along the Stoke road. It has a plastered front, a tiled roof and some additional nineteenth-century brickwork at the north-east end.

ST. JAMES VILLAGE, ISLE OF GRAIN

Dominating the entire Isle of Grain there is, of course, the extensive oil refinery owned and operated by BP. With its numerous chimneys, stoarge tanks and huge boiler house it occupies about a third of the total land area of Grain, but is, itself, partly overshadowed by the adjacent power station with its eight hundred foot high chimney. The village of Grain is fairly compact, though this compactness has never really been a feature of the village in previous centuries. Instead, clusters of buildings were to be found throughout the parish and some of these such as Perry's and Whitehouse still remain. Today, the village dates mostly from the twentieth century and has seen extensive building during the early fifties and again in the early seventies.

Parish Church of St. James (listed)

The present church dates extensively from the late twelfth and early thirteenth century when the present nave and chancel were built. At this time the church also had side aisles but these were removed in 1815 when the church was heavily restored. The porch, as its date stone indicates, is also of this period. The tower, although it looks to be a solid Norman affair, is in fact part of a rebuilding and restoration programme of 1904–5.

Bethel Chapel

Opened on October 15th, 1895, Bethel Chapel was built by the nonconformists of Grain at a cost of £421. The history of nonconformity on Grain dates back to 1822 when Thomas Castle, a coastguard, started preaching here. In 1823 he rented a room and later, in 1827, was able to have a small chapel built. This chapel was later replaced by the present one which stands on land donated by Mr. J. R. Dickens.

Coastguard Cottages

During the nineteenth century coastguards were stationed in watch vessels anchored off Colemouth Creek and Yantlet. However, both of these were damaged during the floods of 1897 and, as a result, the present coastguard cottages (the quarters) were built. Construction of these was finished in 1900. In 1913 the Royal Navy took them over for accommodating officers stationed at Grain seaplane station and they, in turn, were followed by members of the Royal Artillery stationed at the Yantlet range. The cottages are now privately owned.

The Hogarth (listed)

Other than the church, this is the oldest building in the village and was visited by Hogarth during his 'Peregrination'. Originally the 'Chequer' and later the 'Cock Inn' this is a Tudor building which, after becoming the post office and general shop has reverted to its original use. Timber framed, it has a hipped tiled roof and red chimney breast in the south-west wall. Immediately next to the 'Hogath' is the 'Cat and Cracker' which was built in 1900.

White House Farm

Rather out of the way, and in a quiet part of Grain village, this is an eighteenth-century house faced with Kentish weatherboarding. A former farmhouse it is two storeys, has a hipped tiled roof and is rather in need of some external repair work.

ST. MARY'S HOO

St. Mary's Hoo divides into three separate communities. There is the group of post-war council houses midway along the road to Allhallows, the main village situated about a quarter of a mile to the north of this road and, finally, Fenn Street. The actual village is well worth a visit as it remains virtually untouched since Victorian times for, apart from the buildings specifically mentioned below, there are one or two other interesting Georgian and Victorian buildings (notably Red House and Moat Farm). The other two communities, for the most part, are much more modern.

Parish Church of St. Mary (listed)

The nave and tower of this church both date to the thirteenth century, as did an original chancel. The present chancel, however, was rebuilt during a period of heavy restoration which took place around the year 1881. It was also at this time that the church porch was added. Like Cooling parish church, St. Mary's church has also been made redundant and is rarely open.

School Building

The village's original National school still stands, but now does service as a private house. It ceased to function as a school in 1947. Erected in 1868, in order to accommodate some seventy children, it consisted, at the time, of one partitioned classroom and a schoolmaster's house. The nearby commemoration stone indicates that the school was opened by Mrs. Burt, the daughter-in-law of the Rev. Robert Burt.

Fenn Farm

Located in the Fenn Street area of the parish, this former farm house is now a private dwelling. It is L-shaped, being timber framed and re-faced, in part, with weatherboarding (though some of the south front is red brick).

Newlands Farm House (listed)

Dating to the year 1746 this is a red-brick farm house with a tiled roof. Inside, it has an excellent oak staircase. Newlands Farm is about half a mile south-west of the main village and was, at the time Hasted was writing, held by the treasurers of the Chatham Chest.

The Rectory (listed)

Known as the old rectory, this building is two storeyed of red brick with a hipped tiled roof. It has, in addition, a weatherboarded extension attached to the north-east side of the house. The rectory was possibly built by the Rev. Robert Burt who acquired the living in 1786 and died in 1791. The Rev. Burt was the parson who secretly married the Prince of Wales (later George IV) to Mrs. Fitzherbert. As Mrs. Fitzherbert was a Roman Catholic the marriage should automatically have excluded the prince from succeeding to the throne. It was, for this reason, the marriage was kept secret and, as a result, the Rev. Burt was well rewarded. Rewards which included the livings of St. Mary's Hoo and High Halstow. His son, the Rev. Robert Gascoyne Burt, also held these two parishes.

Rose Cottages

Situated close to the boundary with Allhallows these are a series of late Victorian farm cottages. As this was a period of prosperity on the Peninsula a number of such cottages were built throughout the Peninsula in order to accommodate farm labourers. This particular series of cottages are, of course, heavily modernized.

St. Mary's Hall

Actually in the village of St. Mary's Hoo, this is the one-time home of Henry Pye. It is a house which has had many additions built onto it. The original building dates to the eighteenth century, the east wing to about 1830 and the south-west wing to the late nineteenth century. This last addition was made during the time of Henry Pye's occupation of the house.

STOKE

As with much of the rest of the Peninsula, Stoke has undergone a good many changes during the last few decades. Modern housing estates have brought an entirely new character to this once isolated parish. The village, itself, is divided into three separate hamlets of Upper, Middle and Lower Stoke. Of these, Lower Stoke is the larger. Much of the rest of the parish consists of marshland.

Parish Church of St. Peter and St. Paul (listed)

The nave, chancel and aisles of the present church date mostly from the late twelfth and early thirteenth centuries, though an earlier church is known to have existed here. The peculiar stump like tower, built between 1470 and 1541, was designed to have a steeple on its summit but sufficient finances were never raised. The porch dates to the nineteenth century. The east wall was extensively damaged during World War Two when a V2 exploded close by.

Methodist Chapel

Methodism was first established in Stoke sometime about the year

1821 and came about as a result of visits made by Bible Christian missioners who had established themselves at Brompton. It was they who were responsible for building, during the year 1843, the now demolished Providence Chapel. The present chapel dates to 1889 when it was erected at a cost of £614. The Sunday School was added in 1913. During the First World War the chapel was damaged as a result of the Princess Irene explosion and again, in World War Two, by the same V2 that extensively damaged the parish church.

Village School

This is the only Victorian school building on the Peninsula still being used for its original purpose. It was opened in 1876 in order to accommodate two hundred children drawn both from Stoke and Allhallows.

Court Lodge (formerly Parsonage Farm)

Situated in Upper Stoke this is a late eighteenth-century farm house and similar in design to several other buildings on the Peninsula. It is constructed of red brick and is a two-storey house (with attic) with a tiled mansarded roof. There are nineteenth-century additions to the rear.

Forge House

Situated in Lower Stoke, and next to the general store, the front part of this two-storey house is red-brick and Georgian. The rear is of timber frame construction with wattle and daub filling. Neglected for a good many years and badly vandalized during a recent period of non-occupation, it is in much need of attention.

Mackay's Court (listed)

This is a sixteenth-century building with an eighteenth-century exterior. A two-storey affair, it has a tiled roof which is hipped at the south end. The house has recently been reconditioned.

Malmaynes Hall

The former site of a medieval manor, Malmaynes took its name from the Malmaine family who obtained the land during the twelfth or early thirteenth century. The manor is recorded as having been sold on a number of occasions and, by the time Hasted was writing, was owned by the Duppa family of Hollingbourne Hill. It was possibly the Duppas who erected, around the turn of the eighteenth century, a red-brick house that was demolished during the 1960s. This was a three-storey building which stood midway between Fenn Street and Middle Stoke. A number of the windows were blocked, following upon its completion, as a result of the window tax. In its time, it was an admirable house with box frame windows, a fine staircase reaching to the top of the house and a period brick porch with modillion cornice, parapet and a four-centured archway. By 1960 the house had become dilapidated with all the windows being filled with corrugated iron. Its demolition, nevertheless, was a sad loss.

Mill House

Sometime during the mid-1920s Stoke mill was pulled down (although the base still exists) and the mill house became the local maternity home. The building, to be found along the Allhallows Road in Lower Stoke, is a red-brick Georgian house faced with rough cast pebble dash (this was added during the 1940s whilst a new top-floor window was added when it became a maternity home). Now a private house the owners received a reminder that it was once the mill house when they suffered an infestation of Grain weevil. This insect had apparently been dormant for a good many years, but had been disturbed by structural alterations then being undertaken.

South View

A weatherboarded cottage standing adjacent to Stoke garage. It probably dates from the sixteenth century – and is, therefore, one of the oldest buildings on the Peninsula – for the interior woodwork is rather crude, and the low door cases are typical of this period. Much of the wood used for the interior is secondhand and consists of ship timbers and an old cabin door. South View was formerly two cottages which, due to the removal of a partition wall, has been converted into one. A second weatherboarded building, of very similar design (but not necessarily age), stood on the ground now occupied by the Stoke garage car park but was demolished about 1965.

Walnut Tree Farm

A former farmhouse and now a private residence this is a red-brick Georgian house typical of the area. The Georgian 'two-up two-down' part of the house is augmented by nineteenth-century additions to the rear. It is situated in Lower Stoke and close to the Grain Road.

APPENDIX 4

BIBLIOGRAPHY WITH A DISCUSSION
OF SOURCES

SOME GENERAL BOOKS

Arnold, R., *The Hundred of Hoo* (1947)

Burnett, C. B., *A History of the Isle of Grain* (1906)

Cracknell, B. E., 'Alluvial Marshlands of the Lower Thames' (unpublished London University thesis – 1950)

Finch, W. C., *Medway River and Valley* (1929)

Hammond, Rev. F. J., *The Story of an Outpost Parish* (1928)

Hasted, E., *History and Topographical Survey of the County of Kent* Volumes III and IV (first published 1797 and 1798 re-pub. 1972)

Ireland, S., *Picturesque Views of the River Medway*

Ireland, W. H., *England's topographer, or a new and complete history of the County of Kent* (1828)

Jessup, F. W., *A History of Kent* (1958)

Matthews, B., *A History of Strood Rural District* (1971)

Mee, A., *Kent* (1961)

Smetham, H., *Rambles Round Churches* (1925–9)

Smith, J. J., *The Story of Cliffe-at-Hoo* (undated)

CHAPTER 1   Impressions

The quoted accounts of early visits to the Peninsula can be found in the following list. The most extensively used was Hasted's *History and Topography* and it is from this book that I also drew the quotes of Johnson and Holinshed.

An Account of what seem'd most Remarkable in the Five Days Peregrination of the Five Following Persons Viz'. Messieurs Tothall, Scott, Hogarth, Thornhill and Forrest (1732)

Holinshed, R., *A Short Tour of England*

Johnson, Dr., *Iter Plantarum Investigationis Ergo Susceptum* (1629)

The information concerning Charles Dickens' liking for the area was taken from his biographer and friend who wrote *The Life of Charles Dickens* and it was published shortly after the novelist's death in 1870.

References to smuggling in this chapter are partly based on local tradition – the smugglers, themselves, not having a vested interest in recording their doings.

One final source was: *Birds of North Kent Marshes* (1950) by R. C. Holmes.

CHAPTER 2   *Early Days*

Undoubtedly, the single most useful piece of published research concerning this period of the Peninsula's history is J. H. Evans 'Archaeological Horizons of the North Kent Marshes' which appeared in Volume 66 of *Archæologia Cantiana*. Evans was an amateur archaeologist who did a great deal of work on the Peninsula and the article is based on his findings. In addition, numerous other volumes of *Archæologia Cantiana* contain references to this period of the Peninsula's history. References to pottery finds, salterns, burials and so forth will be found in volumes: 11, 46, 62, 64, 68, 76, 80, 82 and 88. Special note should be made of volumes 11 and 88 as they record the important Bronze Age hoards found at Hoo and Allhallows. Concerning this topic there is the much dated *Archaeology of Kent* (1930) by R. F. Jessup.

With regard to early settlements at Cliffe I had a very useful conversation with Mr. R. Hutchins (who has studied the area for a number of years) and he put me straight on a number of points. For those wishing to find more about the Roman allotments at Cliffe reference should be made to *Archæologia Cantiana* 76.

For general background to the Saxon period I found *Anglo-Saxon England* (1947) by Sir Frank Stenton useful. It makes a number of reference to the Peninsula and places them in the light of national events. Specifically, though, *Archæologia Cantiana* 47 has an article on Hoo St. Werburgh's Saxon nunnery whilst Bede's *A History of the English Church and People* carries references to the Cloveshoo Council.

CHAPTER 3   The Middle Ages

Without any doubt the most important source material for this chapter was the 'Domesday Book' and the *Domesday Monachorum*. Translations of parts of these can be found in Hasted and the Victoria County History whilst the complete version of the 'Domesday Book' can be found in Larking, L. B. (ed.) *The Domesday Book of Kent* with translations, notes and appendix (1869). For all of this a very useful back-up book is *The Domesday Geography of South-east England* (1962) by Darbey and Campbell.

Reference to the stake nets comes from Burnett's *History of Grain* whilst the official documents regarding the Cade uprising are *Letters Patent* which can be found in the Public Records Office.

CHAPTER 4   The Medieval Church

Apart from those books already mentioned in the general section the following are the most useful sources:

Archæologia Cantiana Volumes 11 and 78

Glynne, S. R., *Churches of Kent* (1877)

Hussey, A., *Notes on the Churches in the Counties of Kent, Sussex and Surrey* (1852)

Newman, J., *West Kent and the Weald* (1969)

In addition, the church guides for Allhallows and Hoo St. Werburgh provided useful additional information, whilst fuller details concerning the dispute between the encumbents of High Halstow and St. Mary's Hoo can be found in *Hasted* Volume 4.

CHAPTER 5   Cooling Castle

There are several accounts of the Cobham family in existence but the most complete is probably *The Lords of Cobham Hall* (1959) by E. Wingfield-Stratford. This is a general history of the family with information about Cooling castle. Hasted adds some useful information about Cooling castle, and the Cobhams, as does *Archæologia Cantiana* Volume 11, which contains the best account, so far written, of the castle itself.

The Lollardy uprising is well documented by *Wycliffe and English nonconformity* (1972) by K. B. MacFarlane. This book also contains references to the preacher that Sir John Oldcastle introduced to the Peninsula.

Another useful book is M. J. Becker's *Rochester Bridge 1387–1856* (1930)

It has many references to land owned by the Bridge Wardens. In addition the Bridge Wardens' archives contain numerous documents relating to their land, including Rose Court Farm. *Archæologia Cantiana* Volume 66 containsan article by J. H. Evans entitled 'The Rochester Bridge Lands in Grain'.

The documentary material relating to the building of Cooling castle are all contained amongst the Harlian collection of manuscripts held in the British Library. Further, the Harlian collection contains manorial deeds and charters relating to Cooling.

CHAPTER 6   *Cliffe: A Small Medieval Town*

For this chapter I must firstly acknowledge my debt to Mr. R. Hutchings who indicated a number of sources that I later used for the writing of this chapter.

Fuller details concerning the ships that are mentioned as operating from Cliffe will be found in an article entitled 'Maritime History of Kent' and published in the *Victoria County History.*

Both Hasted and Lambarde's *A Perambulation of Kent* make references to the fire of 1520 though it is obvious that Hasted is merely quoting Lambarde, without acknowledging the face.

For information of Cliffe Manor two references are well worth following up:

Smith, R. A. L., *Canterbury Cathedral Priory* (1943)
Smith, A., 'Regional Differences in Crop Production in Medieval Kent' in *Archæologia Cantiana.*

CHAPTER 7   *The Reformation*

The most useful material regarding the effects of the reformation are to be found in the preserved Allhallows churchwarden's accounts. Extensive portions of these accounts are reproduced in Hammond's *Story of an Outpost Parish.*

Wyatt's siege of Cooling castle is well documented in an article written by Major Brian Cope, and appearing in *Archæologia Cantiana* Volume 39. For more general background information refer to both Anthony Fletcher's *Tudor Rebellions* (1968) and *Before the Armada* (1966) by R. B. Wernham.

With regard to roods and rood screens there is some excellent material in *Medieval Rood Lofts and Screens in Kent* by Aylmer Vallance and published in *Memorials of Old Kent* (1907) which is edited by Ditchfield and Clinch.

CHAPTER 8   The Dutch in the Medway

The material used in this chapter was as follows:

The diaries of Samuel Pepys
Upnor Castle, Department of the Environment guidebook.
Burnett, C. B., *A History of the Isle of Grain* (1906)
Daly, A. A., *History of the Isle of Sheppey* (1904)
Finch, W. C., *Medway River and Valley (1929)*
Hogg, I. V., *Coast Defence of England and Wales* (1975)
Jones, M., *History of Coast Artillery in the British Army* (1959)
Knight, C., *The Dutch in the Medway*
MacFarlane, C., *The Dutch in the Medway*
Rogers, P. G., *The Dutch in the Medway* (1970)

CHAPTER 9   The Passing Years

The most indispensable source for this chapter is Hasted's *History and Topography* – it is, of course, contemporary to the period. In addition, estimates of the area's population can be made from the Compton census of 1676 and the Hearth tax returns – both held in the County Records Office. Defoe's *A Tour Through the Whole Island of Great Britain*, whilst not mentioning the Peninsula, is very good on the effects of 'ague' during the period. Another primary source are the records of the Gravesend to Sheppey levels of the Sewers Commission. These contain minutes and correspondence relating to flooding and the erection and repair of sea walls. The parish records of births, deaths and marriages – some of which are held by the encumbents and others by the County Records Office – are, of course, quite invaluable. An excellent map of this period is that of Andrews, Drury and Herbert of which a copy is held at the Records Office at Maidstone.

My information concerning smuggling on the Peninsula is drawn almost entirely from the papers of John Collier, surveyor general of the riding officers during the eighteenth century. These are held in the archives room of H.M. Customs and Excise, London.

Of the secondary source C. W. Chalkin's *Seventeenth Century Kent: A Social and Economic History* (1965) proved indispensable.

CHAPTER 10   The Poor

The primary sources for this chapter were the Allhallows overseer's accounts and the minutes and other remaining records of the Hoo Union. The bulk of the material will be found at the County Records Office.

Hammond's *Story of an Outpost Parish* was also used whilst volume 3 of Hasted's history contains considerable detail about the running of the 'New College of Cobham'.

CHAPTER 11   Preparing for War

The sources for this chapter were as follows:

The Royal Commission reports for 1860 and 1869 (held at the R.E. library, Brompton Barracks and the Royal Artillery Inst., Woolwich)

Various newspaper reports: *Chatham News, Sheerness Guardian* and *Illustrated London News*

Survey of the English Coast 1779–1793 by T. Blomefield and Maj. A. E. Macrae

Gulvin, K. R., *The Medway Forts – A short guide* (1976)

Smith, V. T., 'A Brennan Torpedo Station at Cliffe Fort', published in *Kent Archæological Review*, vol. 24.

Wilson, J. D., 'Late nineteenth century defences of the Thames including Grain fort' published in the *Journal for the Society of Army Historical Research* (1962) vol. XLI

CHAPTER 12   The King of the Hundred

The most useful document dealing with the problem of malaria is an unpublished report commissioned by BP in 1955 and entitled 'Malaria and the Thames'. It was written by W. D. L. Smith who, at the time, was medical officer to the Kent Oil Refinery. In addition, the Sewers Commission minutes together with the local newspapers supplied useful information about flooding.

Apart from Arnold's *Hundred of Hoo* the following books contain discussion on the interesting topic of Pip's village:

Allbut, *Rambles in Dickens' Land*
Dexter, W., *The Kent of Dickens* (1924)
Gadd, W. L., *The Great Expectations Country* (1929)
Harris, E., *The Hundred of Hoo and its Dickensian Association* (1921)
Hughes, W. R., *A Week's Tramp in Dickens Land* (1897)
Matz, B. W., *Dickensian Inns and Taverns*

Also used for this chapter were Kelly's commercial directory (various years) and other nineteenth-century trade directories. A pariculary useful booklet was the mistitled *Isle of Grain Railways* by Adrian Gray.

CHAPTER 13　The Peninsula and a World at War

A major part of this chapter was written using documentary material held at the Imperial War Museum and the Public Records Office. At the Imperial War Museum there were recordings of personnel who served at Kingsnorth airship station and the diaries of various midshipmen who witnessed the *Bulwark* explosion. At the Public Records Office, Kew, there is much material relating to Grain air station and it includes flight reports, technical reports and an official station history.

Published material used was as follows:

Jane's All the World's Aircraft 1920
Barnes, H., *Short's Aircraft since 1900* (1967)
Hampshire, A. C., *They Called it Accident* (1961)
Moore, W. G., *Early Bird* (1963)
Orthostyle Ltd., 'Petrol Pipe Lines Under the English Channel' in *The Engineer* (1945)

CHAPTER 14   Industry Arrives

The bulk of the material for this chapter was drawn from the following:

The Kingsnorth and Isle of Grain files held at Rochester Library.

Sewers Commission correspondence at CRO

Francis, A. J., *The Cement Industry 1796–1914: A History* (1977)

Longhurst, H., *Adventure in Oil. The B.P. Story* (1959)

Preston, J. M., *Industrial Medway an Historical Survey* (1977)

Willmott, F. G., *Cement: Mud and muddies* (1977)

CHAPTER 15   The Twentieth Century

The information about education on the Peninsula was drawn from four sources: Kelly's commercial directories; the annual inspectors reports; the minutes of the Stoke and Allhallows Board (all held at the County Records Office) and the minutes of the Divisional Education Committee (held at Fort Pitt).

Fundamentally, though, this chapter is based on interviews with the people mentioned either in the chapter or in the acknowledgements.

Mr. Arthur Plewis was also kind enough to let me read his unpublished manuscript concerning his early years on the Peninsula.

Certain material published by the 'Dickens' Country Protection Society' together with the Kent Structure Plan was also very useful.

INDEX